TIM SAWTELLE

LIFE
UNVEILED

Life Skills for Today
Wisdom for Tomorrow
Faith for the Journey

PART OF THE UNVEILED SERIES

Life Unveiled
Life Skills for Today, Wisdom for Tomorrow, Faith for the Journey
By Tim Sawtelle

Copyright © 2025 by Tim Sawtelle

ISBN: 979-8-9987097-0-8 (paperback)
ISBN: 979-8-9987097-2-2 (hardback)
ISBN: 979-8-9987097-1-5 (ebook)

Library of Congress Control Number: 2025908102

Printed in the United States of America
Green Mountain Journey Publishing

Cover Design: KeithLocke.com
Edited by Sherri Sawtelle

Visit our websites at: TimSawtelle.com and GreenMountainJourney.com

Disclaimer:
This book is here to help you think through real-life challenges from a Christian perspective, with plenty of honesty, faith, and practical wisdom. You'll find stories, ideas, and lessons from my own journey—things I've learned (sometimes the hard way) and hope will help you too.

Remember, your life is a unique adventure! While I hope this book sparks fresh perspective and helpful "aha" moments, be sure to do your own digging and seek advice from trusted professionals in areas like finances, health, and career decisions.

This isn't a one-size-fits-all manual—it's an invitation to walk more intentionally with God. May it help you dream bigger, think deeper, and follow Him with confidence and joy.

Dedication

I dedicate this book to my grandchildren and to all who read it, that they may find insight and wisdom to navigate life's journey with success and joy.

Ian, Corbin, Oliver, Tristan, Brinley, Nevan and Austin

Throughout my life's journey, I have encountered many Bible verses that have profoundly impacted me. Among them, three stand out as my life verses—foundational truths that guide my heart and mind as I navigate this path we call life.

> This is what the Lord says: "Don't let the wise boast in their wisdom, or the powerful boast in their power, or the rich boast in their riches. But those who wish to boast should boast in this alone: that they truly know me and understand that I am the Lord who demonstrates unfailing love and who brings justice and righteousness to the earth, and that I delight in these things. I, the Lord, have spoken!"
>
> —Jeremiah 9:23-24 NLT

The Lord says, "I will guide you along the best pathway for your life. I will advise you and watch over you."

—Psalms 32:8 NLT

"Taste and see that the Lord is good. Oh, the joys of those who take refuge in him!"

—Psalm 34:8 NLT

Contents

RELATIONSHIPS

"So be careful how you live.
Don't live like fools, but like those who are wise.
Don't act thoughtlessly, but understand
what the Lord wants you to do."
—Ephesians 5:15,17 NLT

"Then the way you live will always honor and please the
Lord, and your lives will produce every kind of good fruit.
All the while, you will grow as you learn to
know God better and better."
—Colossians 1:10 NLT

"I will be your God throughout your lifetime
until your hair is white with age.
I made you, and I will care for you.
I will carry you along and save you."
—Isaiah 46:4 NLT

Foreword

I wrote this book because it's the book I wish I had when I was just starting out in life. My desire is that it will give you a greater vision for how to do life as a Christian—how to live with purpose, walk with wisdom, and grow in faith. I hope it helps you avoid some of the challenges and mistakes I made along the way. I also did many things the right way, by God's grace, and through my journey I've gained wisdom and understanding from His Word and His guidance. That's what I want to pass on to you.

I don't claim to have all the answers—life is a journey, and we're all learning as we go. But one thing I do know is this: you were created for a purpose. God has a plan for your life, and stepping into that purpose requires wisdom, faith, and intentional action.

This book focuses on some of the most important things in life—your walk with God, freedom, finances, budgets and banking, credit, insurance, retirement, relationships, communication, loving people, dating, marriage, and children. We'll also cover practical day-to-day skills like grocery planning and meals, renting and purchasing a home and a car, jobs, college, trade or tech school, working, rest, and planning—just to name a few.

These aren't just life skills—they're heart skills. They reflect the kind of maturity that grows out of love for God and others. My hope is that through these pages, you'll find both practical wisdom and spiritual encouragement to help you move forward with clarity and confidence.

Let's take this step forward together.

Introduction

Imagine being dropped into the middle of a vast, unfamiliar forest. You have no idea where you are or how to survive. No map, no guide—just you and the unknown.

For many of you, stepping into this next season of life feels exactly like that. You're out on your own, unsure of what to do next, feeling lost, unprepared, and maybe even afraid to move forward.

It is my hope that within the pages of this book, you will find clarity, wisdom, and knowledge to guide you on the journey ahead—through every season of your life. Like many who have lived a significant portion of their lives, we often reflect on our journey, reexamining the choices we made—some we might have done differently, and others we wouldn't change for anything.

If you are reading this book, it means your heart and mind are open to the path God has set before you. I truly believe there are golden nuggets of truth within these pages that have the potential to transform your life and help you step into all that God has for you. My deepest desire is that you discover each of these pieces and walk in the abundance of life He has designed for you—fully embracing who He created you to be and the purpose He has called you to fulfill.

I have no doubt that if you embrace and apply the principles in this book, you will experience great success. Some of these lessons I learned early in life and have seen their benefits firsthand. Others have taken me a lifetime to understand and apply.

My hope is that your life will be transformed in the best way possible—that you walk in wisdom, knowledge, and understanding as you navigate your journey. No longer will you feel trapped in uncertainty, unsure of the next step. Instead, you will move forward with confidence, direction, and clear goals, equipped with the steps needed to achieve them.

Most importantly, always walk with God and follow where He leads, for with Him, you will never fail.

THE FOUNDATION

Through the Wilderness

Have you ever noticed how God designed birds to grow up? Some bird parents literally give their kids a little push out of the nest! It might seem a bit harsh, but it's really just their way of saying, "You've got this!" It's how the young birds learn to fly and start doing life on their own. Honestly, God does the same with us sometimes—giving us a little nudge when it's time to grow, try something new, or take a leap of faith. Scary? Yep. But also kind of amazing!

In the introduction of this book, I painted a scenario: imagine being dropped into the middle of a vast, unfamiliar forest. You have no idea where you are or how to survive. No map, no guide—just you and the unknown.

Now, pause for a moment. Close your eyes and picture yourself in that situation. You're standing in the middle of this forest, surrounded by towering trees, unfamiliar sounds, and the weight of uncertainty pressing in. You have no clue where you are or how to find your way out.

What are your thoughts?

Are you frozen in fear, unsure of what to do? Do you immediately spring into action, instinctively knowing the next step? Or do you fall somewhere in between—uncertain but determined to figure it out?

I grew up in the state of Vermont—its name meaning "Green Mountain"—a place of breathtaking beauty. If you've never been, I hope you get the chance to visit someday. As a child, my days were spent outdoors, playing with friends, exploring the fields, climbing trees, and venturing up the mountain behind our house. It was a wonderful way to experience the beauty of God's creation.

My love for the outdoors only grew when I joined the Cub Scouts and later the Boy Scouts. There, I learned essential survival skills—how to read nature, build shelter, find water, and adapt to the environment. Each new skill came with an achievement badge, which my mom would proudly sew onto my uniform. These experiences shaped me, teaching discipline, endurance, and the importance of preparation.

One of the passions that emerged from my time in the Scouts was hiking. While I loved the adventure, trekking alongside 30 or 40 other scouts often felt chaotic. So, a few close friends and I began exploring on our own. By the time I was 14 or 15, my parents would drop me and a couple of friends at the base of Vermont's tallest peak—Mount Mansfield—on a Friday evening. We'd spend the weekend hiking, exploring, and surviving in the wilderness, only to be picked up again on Sunday afternoon.

Mount Mansfield stands at around 4,400 feet, and our hikes were no small feat. Most of the time, we trekked in the dark, often in the dead of winter. We carried snowshoes, ski poles, and sometimes even plastic sleds to navigate the terrain. Temperatures often dropped to 20 degrees below zero, with winds howling at 50 to 60 miles per hour.

One night, I sat at the very peak of the mountain—at a place called "the Chin," the highest point in Vermont. Looking out under the midnight sky, I could see several states and even into Canada. It was breathtaking—a reminder of how small we are in the grand scheme of things, yet how capable we can be when we prepare and persevere.

Through those years of hiking, I learned critical survival skills. The foundation of survival was simple: first, find shelter. Then, secure water. Finally, obtain food. If you had those three things, you could endure.

Life works the same way. Just like in the wilderness, there are foundational things in life that we must focus on—what I call "the big rocks," the things that truly matter. If you establish these on a solid foundation, everything else can be built upon them.

When life feels overwhelming, when you feel lost, fearful or uncertain, the key to moving forward is identifying what truly matters. Once you do that, everything else begins to fall into place.

"Building on the big rocks first will help lead you safely and successfully through the wilderness of life!"

Your Journey Starts Here

B efore moving forward, let's take a moment to assess where you are in life. A little honest self-evaluation can go a long way. Have you ever heard the saying, "You don't know what you don't know"?

Often, we want to make a change or take action, but we don't even know where to start or what questions to ask. This lack of clarity can keep us stuck, preventing progress.

So, let's walk through a self-evaluation process. Make sure to invest the time in this section—it will provide valuable insights that will enrich your journey through the rest of this book.

This is just for you—so be open and honest with yourself. The goal is to understand your current position in life. Rather than thinking about being right or wrong in your selection, your answers serve as a map, showing where you stand and how to move forward on your journey.

Think of it like the example I used earlier with you being dropped in the middle of a forest. Before you can find your way out, you first need to figure out where you are.

Let's start there!

Carefully reflect on the following statements and rate yourself using the scale below:

Rating Scale:

1 – Never

2 – Rarely

3 – Sometimes

4 – Often

5 – Always

Be honest with yourself—this exercise is for your personal growth. Your answers will help you gain a clearer picture of where you are and where you want to go.

Section 1 Statements: Section Score = _____

1 – Never 2 – Rarely 3 - Sometimes 4 - Often 5 - Always

_____ I hesitate to take action because of fear of failure or making mistakes.

_____ I feel uncertain about what steps to take next in my personal or professional growth.

_____ I have allowed negative words from others influenced my confidence in pursuing goals.

_____ I struggle to see a clear vision or direction for my future.

_____ I avoid opportunities for learning or growth because they feel overwhelming or out of reach.

_____ I feel like I'm not capable of achieving success or making a meaningful impact.

_____ I compare myself to others in a way that makes me feel stuck or unworthy.

_____ I struggle with motivation or feeling like I have no direction in life.

_____ I avoid trying new things because I fear judgment or rejection from others.

_____ Distractions (such as social media, entertainment, or peer pressure) keep me from focusing on my personal growth and future.

Section 2 Statements: Section Score = _____

1 – Never   2 – Rarely   3 - Sometimes   4 - Often   5 - Always

_____ I have specific habits, distractions, or mindsets that slow down my progress.

_____ I have people in my life who discourage or drain my energy, making it harder to stay focused.

_____ I am usually waiting for the "perfect moment" instead of taking action with what I have now.

_____ I tend to overthink decisions, causing delays in taking the next step.

_____ I struggle with time management or prioritizing what truly matters for my goals.

_____ I hold on to past failures or mistakes that make me hesitant to try again.

_____ I have financial, emotional, or physical limitations that I need to address before moving forward.

_____ I usually don't know what I need to change right now, and have been avoiding doing anything about it.

_____ I try to handle everything alone instead of seeking guidance or support from others when I feel stuck moving forward in life.

_____ I get overwhelmed by the big picture instead of focusing on small, actionable steps.

Section 3 Statements: Section Score = _____

1 – Never 2 – Rarely 3 - Sometimes 4 - Often 5 - Always

_____ I believe I have the ability to overcome challenges and achieve my next big goal in life

_____ I remind myself of past successes when facing new obstacles.

_____ I actively seek new opportunities for growth, even when they seem uncertain.

_____ I feel excited about my future, even if I'm unsure of the exact path.

_____ I make time for self-reflection to gain clarity on my next steps in life.

_____ I surround myself with people with a positive influences on my life and who encourage my success.

_____ I take intentional steps to manage stress and maintain mental well-being in a fast-paced world.

_____ I embrace technology and innovation as tools to help me move forward in life.

_____ I believe that setbacks are temporary and use them as learning experiences for my future success in life.

_____ I am open to adapting to change and learning new skills for the every changing world around me.

Section 4 Statements: Section Score = _____

1 – Never   2 – Rarely   3 - Sometimes   4 - Often   5 - Always

_____ I believe that I am capable of achieving even greater things than I have in the past.

_____ I take time to celebrate my progress, even if it feels small thing.

_____ I look for mentors or role models who inspire me to take my next step.

_____ I challenge myself to step outside my comfort zone to create new opportunities for my future.

_____ I stay informed about new trends, skills, or industries that align with my future goals and desires.

_____ I take advantage of online learning, networking, or remote op-portunities to expand my knowledge and connections.

_____ I actively work on developing a growth mindset instead of dwelling on my past limitations.

_____ I believe that my future is not limited by my past but shaped by the actions I take today.

_____ I make time to invest in relationships that motivate and challenge me to move forward.

_____ I regularly set short-term goals that help me gain momentum toward bigger achievements in my life.

Go back and total the scores for each section, then enter them in the designated areas in that section.

The next page provides a summary of each previous section, explaining its focus, what it measures, and why it matters.

Your scores will highlight areas of strength and reveal opportunities for growth. Use this as a tool for reflection, celebrating progress, and identifying your next steps.

Write your final scores in the spaces provided and review the summaries—each section may have unique scoring criteria.

Section 1 – Stuck in Place: Self-Evaluation

This section of 10 statements was designed to help you identify any feelings of being stuck, fear, or obstacles that may be holding you back. It guides you in uncovering emotional, mental, and external barriers that could be preventing you from moving forward on your journey.

Section 1 score _____

Score Interpretation:

- **15 or lower** – You're doing well in this area with little to no major obstacles.

- **15 to 30** – There are some areas that need attention and growth.

- **30 to 50** – These are red flags indicating a need for focused effort to build a stronger foundation in this area.

NOTES: (write below 3 things from this section that seemed to standout to you)

Section 2 – Obstacles: Self-Evaluation

This section included 10 self-evaluation statements designed for you if you have a clear vision for your future and the determination to pursue it but feel stuck due to various obstacles. These statements help you identify and assess the emotional, mental, and external barriers that may be holding you back. By recognizing these challenges, you can begin to develop a strategy to overcome them and take intentional steps toward making meaningful progress in your life.

Section 2 score _____

Score Interpretation:

- **15 or lower** – You're doing well in this area with little to no major obstacles.

- **15 to 30** – There are some areas that need attention and growth.

- **30 to 50** – These are red flags indicating a need for focused effort to build a stronger foundation in this area.

NOTES: (write below 3 things from this section that seemed to standout to you)

Section 3 – Unlocking Progress: Self-Evaluation

This section was designed for you if you've experienced success in the past but now feel stuck, especially in the face of life's challenges. Through 10 positive-focused statements, it encourages you to reflect on your strengths, resilience, and mindset shifts. It empowers you to recognize your potential and see the importance of using this book to take intentional steps forward in your life.

Section 3 score _____

Score Interpretation:

- **20 or lower** – These are red flags indicating a need for focused effort to build a stronger foundation in this area.

- **20 to 35** – There are some areas that need attention and growth.

- **35 to 50** – You're doing well in this area with little to no major obstacles.

NOTES: (write below 3 things from this section that seemed to standout to you)

Section 4 – Moving Forward: Self-Evaluation

This section provides 10 positive-focused statements to help you if you've achieved success but feel stuck, especially amid today's evolving challenges. These statements guide you in recognizing and identifying barriers while promoting self-awareness, resilience, and a forward-thinking mindset. They address modern obstacles such as technology shifts, online learning, and career uncertainty, helping you gain clarity and motivation to move forward.

Section 4 score _____

Score Interpretation:

- **20 or lower** – These are red flags indicating a need for focused effort to build a stronger foundation in this area.

- **20 to 35** – There are some areas that need attention and growth.

- **35 to 50** – You're doing well in this area with little to no major obstacles.

NOTES: (write below 3 things from this section that seemed to standout to you)

Now that you've completed this self-evaluation, you should have a clearer understanding of where you are on your life journey. It may have sparked new thoughts and insights about areas where you can grow.

In the chapters ahead, we'll explore key topics that will bring deeper clarity and understanding to these areas. You'll gain valuable knowledge and practical skills to help you move forward with greater confidence, knowing you are on the right path for your life.

Your Life, Your Responsibility

You might be just beginning life on your own, standing at the edge of a long road ahead. Right now, all you can probably see is your future here on Earth—but there's a much bigger picture. It's vital to step back and view your life from God's perspective.

God has entrusted you with a set number of years—your lifetime. On average, men live around 70 to 73 years, and women around 75 to 78. That means you've got the next breath... and, Lord willing, several decades more. That time is yours to steward.

You can waste it. You can spend it all chasing your own desires. Or—you can seek God, follow His lead, and walk in His ways. Only then will you discover true peace, lasting joy, deep contentment, and real blessing.

Jesus said,

> "And what do you benefit if you gain the whole world but lose your own soul?"
>
> —Mark 8:36 NLT

That's the lens you need as you look toward the years ahead—however many God gives you. Time is a gift. Use it well.

Shalom

When you walk with God, align your heart with His, and follow where He leads, you begin to live in His shalom. That's more than just peace—it's wholeness, harmony, purpose, and flourishing. It's knowing you're exactly where you're meant to be—living each day with the One who made you, sustained by His love, and grounded in His goodness. That's the life God longs to give you.

There comes a moment in life when responsibility shifts entirely onto our shoulders. For some, it happens gradually. For others, it comes as a harsh wake-up call— I knew someone that told me their father handed them a plate on their 18th birthday and said, "It's time to leave. Have a nice life." Suddenly, they were on their own, expected to navigate adulthood without a roadmap.

Maybe your transition wasn't as dramatic, but here's the deal: your life is now your responsibility. Whether your parents gave you a full playbook or just handed you the remote and said "good luck," you're the one in the driver's seat now. You're steering your own course—and yeah, that can feel a little exciting, a little scary, and a whole lot real.

There are things in life beyond your control—your circumstances, your upbringing, the world around you. But there are also things within your control—your choices, actions, and decisions.

The question is: What will you do with what you've been given? Will you give up? Or will you seek wisdom, make a plan, and walk in it?

The world bombards us with influences—social media, family, friends, teachers, news, entertainment. Many people shape their lives based on these voices without ever considering what God says yet He has the answers.

The problem is, most are looking for guidance in all the wrong places and that's why so many feel stuck in depression and fear with a deep sense of being lost. Rejection, failure, guilt, the feeling of worthlessness—these are all lies that hold people captive.

Most people don't realize that life is shaped by the choices they make and the actions they take. Some decisions will be difficult and come at a cost, but these are often the ones that yield the greatest growth and impact. The hardest choices—those that require sacrifice, discipline, or stepping out in faith—are usually the ones that bear the most fruit in a person's life.

Choices

In life, every choice falls into one of two categories: wise or foolish. There is no neutral ground.

Wise choices are rooted in truth, guided by discernment, and lead to growth and lasting fruit.

Foolish choices, on the other hand, are impulsive, short-sighted, and often driven by emotions or influenced by the wrong voices.

A wise person seeks counsel from God, studies His Word, and listens to those who have walked the path before them. They weigh the long-term consequences of their choices, understanding that every decision plants a seed for the future.

In contrast, a foolish person ignores wisdom, acts on impulse, and follows the crowd without questioning where they are going.

> "There is a path before each person that seems right, but it ends in death."
>
> —Proverbs 14:12 NLT

The difference between wisdom and foolishness isn't just about intelligence—it's about seeking the right foundation, making choices with eternity in mind, and walking in obedience to God's guidance.

Every decision we make—big or small—either moves us closer to God's purpose or further away from it. The question is, which path will you choose?

Truth

So, where do you start? With God's truth.

The "Shema" in the Old Testament, along with its fulfillment in the New Testament, serves as a foundational truth. Jewish people recite this prayer twice a day—once in the morning and once in the evening—as a daily reminder to love God with all their heart, soul, and strength. It is a declaration of devotion, anchoring their lives in the command to put God first in everything.

"Listen, O Israel! The Lord is our God, the Lord alone. And you must love the Lord your God with all your heart, all your soul, and all your strength."

—Deuteronomy 6:4-5 NLT

From there, we base our lives on His commands—living in obedience, sowing seeds, and making disciples. There is good and evil in the world, and God is the plumb line. His truth is the standard.

This book contains Truths that will help you grow. Growth is essential, but many don't ask themselves: Why do I want to grow? What's holding me back?

The parable of the sower speaks to this—the different types of soil, the different responses to truth.

Let's review those scriptures:

He told many stories in the form of parables, such as this one:

"Listen! A farmer went out to plant some seeds. As he scattered them across his field, some seeds fell on a footpath, and the birds came and ate them.

Other seeds fell on shallow soil with underlying rock. The seeds sprouted quickly because the soil was shallow. But the plants soon wilted under the hot sun, and since they didn't have deep roots, they died.

Other seeds fell among thorns that grew up and choked out the tender plants.

Still other seeds fell on fertile soil, and they produced a crop that was thirty, sixty, and even a hundred times as much as had been planted!

Anyone with ears to hear should listen and understand."
—Matthew 13:3-9 NLT

What kind of soil is your heart? The condition of your heart determines how well you receive and grow in truth. This book is here to help you cultivate your heart into good soil—ready to absorb wisdom, take root in God's truth, and produce a harvest that lasts. As you read, plant the seeds you gain from this book deep into your life. With God's guidance and a foundation built on His truth, your life will bear lasting fruit for His purpose.

What are you passionate about? What are you naturally good at?

I remember diving into programming in seventh grade, connecting through university dial-up, working on clunky old terminals, and printing on noisy line printers. Punch cards were a hassle, but they were part of the process. Then came the IBM personal computer and the DOS manual—dry reading for most, but I found it fascinating. I read it cover to cover, not because I had to, but because I wanted to understand, learn, and grow. I would stay after work, studying it on my own time, driven by curiosity and a desire to master what others overlooked. Few were willing to put in that extra effort, but I knew that real growth comes from the willingness to go beyond what is required.

And that's the real point—growth requires both curiosity and effort. Whether it's in faith, skills, or life decisions, we must plant ourselves in the right soil and be intentional about the seeds we sow.

This chapter is about the big rocks—the foundational things that will shape your life. What you prioritize will determine the kind of future you build. The question is, what will you choose?

Let's get started!

The Rocks!

I heard a story one time about a teacher that was standing before a class with a large empty jar on the table. Without saying a word, they begin placing big rocks into the jar, one by one, until no more can fit. Then they ask the class, "Is the jar full?"

The students look at the jar, packed with large stones, and nod. "Yes," they answer.

The teacher smiles, then picks up a container of small pebbles and begins pouring them into the jar. The pebbles trickle down, filling the spaces between the big rocks. Again, the teacher asks, "Is the jar full now?"

The class hesitates but still agrees, "Yes, now it's full."

Without a word, the teacher grabs a bag of sand and slowly pours it in. The fine grains slip into the tiny gaps, settling between the rocks and pebbles. He gently taps it on the table and adding more sand up to the brim of the jar. Once more, they ask, "Is it full?"

The students laugh, catching on, but some still say yes.

Finally, the teacher takes a pitcher of water and pours it over the contents of the jar. The water seeps through every remaining crevice, completely saturating the jar.

Then, the teacher looks at the class and asks, "What's the point of this?"

One student eagerly responds, "No matter how full your life is, you can always fit more in."

The teacher shakes their head. "No, that's not the lesson. The point is this—if you don't put the big rocks in first, you'll never fit them in at all."

Applying This to Your Life

The big rocks represent the most important things in life—God, faith, purpose, wisdom, family, and the things that truly matter. If you make these a priority first, everything else—daily responsibilities, work, hobbies, social activities—can fit around them.

The pebbles are the necessary but secondary things—job, school, friendships, and tasks that support your bigger purpose. They matter, but they shouldn't replace your big rocks.

The sand represents smaller, time-consuming distractions—entertainment, social media, endless scrolling, and things that eat away at your time without adding real value. If you prioritize these first, they'll take up so much space that there's no room for what truly matters.

The water represents the smallest, often unnoticed details of life—the things that fill in the gaps naturally when the bigger priorities are already in place.

Your Thoughts?

If you start with sand and water—meaningless distractions and minor concerns—your life will feel full, but there won't be room for the things that matter most. But if you prioritize the big rocks first, everything else will fall into place in its proper order.

So ask yourself:

What are the big rocks in your life?

Are you making room for them first?

The Big Rocks
Building a Life That Lasts

L ife is full of choices, responsibilities, and distractions—each one competing for your time, energy, and focus. Imagine your life as a jar, and everything you do, every commitment you make, has to fit inside it. Some things are small, like grains of sand or drops of water. Others are larger, like pebbles. And then there are the big rocks—the things that matter most.

If you don't put the big rocks in first, the smaller things will quickly fill the jar, leaving no space for what truly matters. That's why it's essential to prioritize the big rocks first.

At the core, the three biggest rocks in your life should be God, family, and work. These foundational priorities shape your life's course and provide stability in every season. Beyond these, other meaningful "big rocks"—such as personal growth, ministry, relationships, and health—will also find their place in your journey.

However, the order in which these priorities fit into your life will change over time. Seasons of life bring transitions—singlehood, marriage, parenthood, career shifts, ministry callings—and with each transition, the focus may adjust. But no matter how life evolves, keeping God, family, and meaningful work at the center will ensure that everything else falls into place.

This book is structured around these three big rocks, weaving in and out of them in each chapter. They are not isolated concepts but deeply connected parts of a whole. How you prioritize and balance these areas will determine the kind of life you build.

Before we dive into the journey ahead, let's take a step back and look at these big rocks up close. Understanding them at a deeper level will help you see how they form the foundation of your life and how, when placed in the right order, they create a life built on wisdom, purpose, and God's truth.

Let's take a closer look.

God: The First and Greatest Rock

When it comes to the Big Rocks in our life journey, God is the first and most important. In fact, compared to Him, nothing else even comes close—no other rock holds weight in comparison. He is not just a part of life; He is the foundation upon which everything else must be built.

As we navigate the three big rocks—God, Family, and Work— we must start with the One that matters most: God. Without Him at the center, everything else eventually crumbles. A successful career, a strong family, and even personal growth mean little if they are not rooted in the unshakable foundation of His truth.

Jesus made this clear when He said:

> "Anyone who listens to my teaching and follows it is wise, like a person who builds a house on solid rock. Though the rain comes in torrents and the floodwaters rise and the winds beat against that house, it won't collapse because it is built on bedrock."
>
> —Matthew 7:24-25 NLT

Your relationship with God is the cornerstone of your life. It's what gives meaning to everything else. Before you focus on your family, before you chase success in your work, God must come first. When He is your foundation, everything else will find its rightful place.

Born Again: The Only Way to Know God

The only way to have a true relationship with God is to be born again. Without this, everything else in this book—building your life on the right foundations, seeking wisdom, growing in faith—will never fully make sense.

Jesus made it clear in the book of John:

> "I tell you the truth, unless you are born again, you cannot see the Kingdom of God."
>
> —John 3:3 NLT

This is the first and most important step in your journey of life.

Are you born again? If you're unsure, or if you want to be, then the good news—the Gospel—is that Jesus has made the way for you.

When Jesus walked the earth, He told people to repent from their sins, turn to God, and believe in the One He sent—Jesus Himself. This means making a decision to stop living in sin, to turn to God, and to receive new life through Him. Salvation is not automatic—it is a choice that we make, and we receive it through faith and prayer, trusting in what God has said.

> "Jesus told him, 'I am the way, the truth, and the life. No one can come to the Father except through me.'"
>
> —John 14:6 NLT

This verse is one of the most powerful statements Jesus made about salvation and the only way to have a relationship with God. Jesus makes it clear that there are not many paths to God—He is the only way. No amount of good works, religious efforts, or personal achievements can bring us to the Father. Only through Jesus—by believing in Him, repenting of our sins, and being born again—can we enter into a real, eternal relationship with God.

This is why being born again is not just an option; it is a necessity. Without Jesus, there is no access to the Father. If we want to build our lives on the big rocks—God, family, and work—the first step is making sure we have come to God through Jesus.

Being born again isn't about trying harder or being a better person. It is a spiritual transformation that happens when we put our faith in Jesus Christ, trusting in His death and resurrection for the forgiveness of our sins. When we do this, the Holy Spirit comes to live inside us, making us new creations (2 Corinthians 5:17) and bringing us into a real, personal relationship with God.

If you have never made this decision, now is the time. Pray and ask God to forgive your sins, surrender your life to Jesus, and receive His gift of salvation by faith. This is where your journey truly begins—because without being born again, there is no relationship with God.

Keeping God First: A Daily Commitment

Keeping God first isn't just a nice idea—it's a way of life. It means staying connected to Him throughout your day, not just squeezing Him into a quiet time and moving on. It's about talking to Him like a friend, listening for His voice, and making choices with Him in mind. When He's first, everything else lines up better.

So what does that look like in everyday life? Let's break it down.

1. Start Your Day with Him

> "Seek the Kingdom of God above all else, and live right-eously, and he will give you everything you need."
> —Matthew 6:33 NLT

Instead of waking up and reaching for your phone, what if your first thought was, *"I get to meet with God!"*

Imagine starting your day with that kind of anticipation—the Creator of the universe, your Abba Father, is waiting to spend time with you. Not out of obligation, but out of love. He delights in you. He's not too busy. He's not distracted. He's already leaning in, ready to hear your voice and speak to your heart.

There's something powerful about waking up and realizing you're deeply loved by the One who holds all things together. You're not just checking a box—you're entering a conversation with the God who knows you, cares for you, and longs to walk with you through every moment of your day.

Spend time reading His Word—just 15 minutes a day, and in a year, you'll have read the entire Bible! Go for it. Open your heart and let Him speak to you through His love letter to you—the Bible. The Holy Spirit will bring the living Word of God to life in your heart, applying it to your life in real, powerful ways today.

2. Anchor Your Decisions in His Word

> "Your word is a lamp to guide my feet and a light for my path."
>
> —Psalm 119:105 NLT

Every decision you make—whether it's who to date, what job to take, or how to spend your money—works best when you run it through the filter of God's truth. Life throws a lot of noise your way, and it's easy to get pulled off track by emotions, opinions, or what's trending. But God's Word? It doesn't change. It's solid, reliable, and always points you in the right direction.

Culture might say "follow your heart," but let's be real—your heart can be all over the place. That's why you need something stronger, something steady. God's truth is like GPS for your soul—it helps you avoid the detours and dead ends. So before you make a move, check in with Him. His Word is the ultimate guide, and it's packed with wisdom that actually works in real life.

3. Stay in Constant Conversation with Him

> "Never stop praying."
>
> —1 Thessalonians 5:17 NLT

Prayer isn't just for emergencies or big life decisions—it's for *everything*. God isn't looking for perfect words or fancy prayers; He just wants to hear from you. Whether you're brushing your teeth, stuck in traffic, or walking into a tough meeting, you can talk to Him. He's always listening, and He actually cares about what's going on in your heart—even the little stuff.

Think of prayer like texting your best friend throughout the day. Got a win? Share it with Him! Feeling stressed or overwhelmed? Tell Him about it. Need wisdom or peace? Ask for it. God doesn't clock out or put you on hold—He's with you in every moment. The more you include Him in your day-to-day life, the more you'll realize He's not just part of your story—He's right there writing it with you.

4. Surround Yourself with Godly Influence

"Walk with the wise and become wise; associate with fools and get in trouble."

—Proverbs 13:20 NLT

The people you hang out with have a way of rubbing off on you—kind of like glitter. Whether you mean to or not, you start picking up their habits, their values, even their vocabulary (yes, even those weird catch-phrases). That's why it's so important to surround yourself with people who encourage your faith and cheer you on as you grow in your walk with God.

When you spend time with others who love Jesus, you'll start to notice your own priorities shifting. Suddenly, things like kindness, truth, integrity, and prayer matter more. You'll be reminded of who you are and Whose you are. These kinds of friendships don't just keep you grounded—they help you grow. And bonus: you'll laugh more, pray more, and probably eat more snacks together. Win-win-win.

Of course, that doesn't mean you avoid everyone who's not walking with God. In fact, God may use you to be a light in their life. But your closest circle—the people who have your ear and your heart—should be the ones who lift your eyes to Jesus, not pull them away. Choose wisely. The right friends can help you become the person God created you to be.

5. Worship and Serve Him Daily

> "And whatever you do or say, do it as a representative of the Lord Jesus, giving thanks through him to God the Father."
> —Colossians 3:17 NLT

Worship isn't just singing with your hands raised on a Sunday morning (though that's awesome too). It's so much bigger than a song—it's a way of life. Every moment is a chance to say, "God, You're worth it." Whether you're doing laundry, helping a friend move, or studying for a test, it can all be worship when your heart is focused on Him.

Think of worship as living your life like a thank-you note to God. When you use your gifts, serve others, and choose to live with kindness, generosity, and love—that's worship! It's not about perfection; it's about pointing your life in His direction. Even the little things, like showing patience when someone's testing your last nerve, can be an act of worship when done with a heart that says, "I'm doing this for You, God."

So don't box worship into one hour on a Sunday. Worship when you drive. Worship when you clean your room (yes, even that). Worship when you show up for a friend or stay late to help someone out. It's all worship when it flows from a heart that loves God. He sees it. He loves it. And He's worthy of every bit of it.

6. Trust Him Above All Else

"Trust in the Lord with all your heart; do not depend on your own understanding. Seek his will in all you do, and he will show you which path to take."

—Proverbs 3:5-6 NLT

Keeping God first isn't just about reading your Bible or praying before meals—it's about handing Him the steering wheel, even when you really want to drive. Surrendering control can feel scary, especially when life is throwing curveballs faster than you can catch. But here's the good news: God isn't surprised by anything. He sees the whole picture, and He's way better at leading than we are at stressing.

So when things feel overwhelming and out of your hands... good! That's the perfect time to let go and trust the One who holds it all together. Your future isn't some random mess—it's in the hands of a loving Father who already has a plan. Take a deep breath, unclench your fists, and say,

"God, I trust You." Because honestly? There's no better place for your life to be than in His hands.

The Heart of It All: A Relationship with Our Abba

It's easy to turn faith into a checklist—prayer, Bible reading, church attendance, serving. While these are all important, they are not the ultimate goal. The goal of our faith, the entire purpose of putting God first, is to have a deep, personal, loving relationship with Him.

God is not a distant figure or a set of religious rituals to follow. He is our Creator, our Father—our Abba.

In Jewish culture, the word "Abba" is not just a formal title; it's an intimate, personal way to say "Daddy." It speaks of a relationship built on love, trust, and closeness.

Walking with God Like Adam and Eve

To truly understand what God desires, we need to go back to the very beginning—to the Garden of Eden God tells us:

> "When the cool evening breezes were blowing, the man and
> his wife heard the Lord God walking about in the garden."
> —Genesis 3:8 NLT

Before sin entered the world, Adam and Eve walked side by side with God. They talked with Him, lived in His presence, and experienced His love without barriers.

Imagine the scene—the greatest Father ever, walking with His children, speaking to them with love and delight. Perhaps He told them how much He loved them, how proud He was, and how He had provided everything they needed.

They weren't just His creation; they were His family.

And this is still what God desires with us today. Sin may have separated us, but through Jesus, our relationship has been restored. We can still walk with God, know Him personally, and experience His love as Abba—our Daddy.

More Than Religion—A Relationship

Putting God first isn't about following rules or fulfilling religious obligations. It's about living in constant, daily relationship with Him. It's about talking to Him through joys, struggles, questions, and victories.

Paul describes this beautifully in the book of Romans:

> "So you have not received a spirit that makes you fearful slaves. Instead, you received God's Spirit when he adopted you as his own children. Now we call him, 'Abba, Father.' For his Spirit joins with our spirit to affirm that we are God's children."
>
> —Romans 8:15-16 NLT

God doesn't just want your obedience—He wants your heart. He longs to be the One you turn to first, not out of duty, but out of love. He is not a distant king watching from afar; He is Abba, your Daddy, walking beside you every step of the way.

We Don't Have to—We Get To—We Want To

A friend once told me, "Dead religion says we have to, but a loving relationship with Abba means we no longer have to—we get to—we want to." That simple truth changes everything.

When we view God through a religious mindset, faith becomes a set of rules and obligations. Prayer feels like a chore. Reading the Bible is just another task. Serving becomes duty-bound instead of an act of love.

But when we truly know God as our Father, our whole perspective shifts:

- We don't have to pray—we get to talk to our Father.

- We don't have to read Scripture—we get to hear His heart.

- We don't have to serve—we get to be part of His kingdom work.

This kind of relationship is built on love, not obligation.

> "We love each other because he loved us first."
> —1 John 4:19 NLT

We don't love God because we have to. We love Him because He first loved us.

And when we understand that, putting Him first isn't a burden—it's the greatest joy of our lives.

So keeping God first is not just a principle—it is the very heartbeat of a life well-lived. When He is our foundation, everything else finds its rightful place. This isn't about striving harder or following a rigid set of rules; it's about walking daily in relationship with Abba, our loving Father. He is not a distant God watching from afar—He is close, speaking, guiding, and longing for us to know Him as deeply as He knows us.

The choice is yours:

Will you build your lives on the solid rock of His presence, or will you let the shifting sands of this world dictate your priorities? True joy, peace, and purpose are found in walking with Him, not just working for Him. When you seek Him first, you don't just experience a better life—you experience life as He meant it to be.

Family: The Second Big Rock

After God, family is the second big rock in our lives. No matter where we go or what we do, the relationships we have with our family shape us deeply. Family was God's design from the very beginning. Before churches, governments, or businesses existed, God established family as the foundation of human relationships. It is meant to be a source of love, strength, and belonging—a place where we grow, learn, and experience the love of God in tangible ways.

Whether you are married or single, family is a crucial part of your life. It looks different depending on the season you are in, but the heart of it remains the same: God created us to live in relationship, not isolation. Family is where we learn how to love, forgive, serve, and grow. It is a gift, but it also comes with responsibility. In a world that often devalues family, we must choose to prioritize it, nurture it, and honor it as God intended.

Marriage: Building a Christ-Centered Family

For those who are married, family starts with the covenant of marriage. A strong, godly marriage is not just about companionship; it is about reflecting Christ's love for the Church (Ephesians 5:25-27). Marriage is a sacred commitment between a husband and a wife with God at the center.

A healthy marriage requires intentionality. Just like our relationship with God, a strong marriage doesn't grow automatically—it must be cultivated. Love is not just a feeling; it is a daily choice to serve, respect, and honor each other.

"Love is patient and kind. Love is not jealous or boastful or proud or rude. It does not demand its own way. It is not irritable, and it keeps no record of being wronged."

—1 Corinthians 13:4-5 NLT

In a world that often encourages self-focus and independence, biblical marriage calls us to selflessness, humility, and unity. A husband and wife are meant to build each other up, encourage spiritual growth, and create a home where God's presence dwells.

Family in marriage doesn't just stop with husband and wife—it extends to children, in-laws, and the generations that follow. If children are part of your family, they are not just an addition to your life; they are a sacred responsibility. God calls parents to raise their children in His truth, leading by example and teaching them to love Him.

"Direct your children onto the right path, and when they are older, they will not leave it."

—Proverbs 22:6 NLT

Even if children are not in the picture, marriage is still a powerful ministry. A Christ-centered marriage is a testimony to the world, showing what it looks like to love, forgive, and walk in unity with another person. When we prioritize our marriages and invest in them, we strengthen the foundation of our families and glorify God.

Family as a Single Person: Walk in Love & Commitment

For those who are single, family is still an essential part of life. Being unmarried does not mean you are without family—it simply means your family relationships take a different form.

First, you have the family you were born into. Whether it's parents, siblings, or extended relatives, God calls us to honor and love them. Even if our family relationships are complicated or strained, we are still called to reflect Christ in how we treat them.

> "Honor your father and mother. Then you will live a long, full life in the land the Lord your God is giving you."
> —Exodus 20:12 NLT

Second, as a believer, you have a spiritual family—the body of Christ. The Church is not just a building or a weekly service; it is a family of believers walking together in faith. As a single person, your spiritual family can provide encouragement, accountability, and support.

> "So now you Gentiles are no longer strangers and foreigners. You are citizens along with all of God's holy people. You are members of God's family."
> —Ephesians 2:19 NLT

Singleness is not a waiting period—it is a season of purpose. Whether you are single for a time or for life, God has called you to live in community, love others, and serve within His family. You are not alone, and your role in God's family is just as significant as that of a married person.

Honoring Family in Every Season of Life

Regardless of our marital status, we are all called to honor and invest in family relationships. This means:

- Prioritizing time with those we love, not letting busyness take over.

- Practicing forgiveness when conflicts arise, choosing grace over bitterness.

- Serving one another selflessly, just as Christ served us.

- Encouraging spiritual growth within our families, pointing each other toward Christ.

In every season—whether married or single—family is a gift from God. It is a place of belonging, a source of strength, and a reflection of His love. When we make family a priority and cultivate relationships with intentionality, we honor God and build a legacy that lasts for generations.

Work: The Third Big Rock

The third big rock in life is work—the job or career that provides for us and allows us to contribute to the world around us. From the very beginning, God designed work to be a part of life. Even before sin entered the world, He gave Adam the responsibility of tending the Garden of Eden (Genesis 2:15). Work is not just a means of survival—it is a God-given opportunity to steward resources, develop skills, and serve others.

A job is more than just a paycheck. It shapes how we spend a significant portion of our lives. It provides for our needs, allows us to support our families, and positions us to be a blessing to others. Through our work, we have opportunities to reflect integrity, diligence, and excellence—qualities that honor God:

> "Work willingly at whatever you do, as though you were working for the Lord rather than for people."
> —Colossians 3:23 NLT

There are many types of jobs in life—some are careers that require years of preparation, while others are stepping stones along the way. Some may feel like callings, while others may be seasons of provision. Regardless of what job we have at any given time, it is important to remember that God is our ultimate provider (Philippians 4:19). Our job is simply the means through which He provides for our needs.

As we move through life, we will make decisions about what kind of work to pursue, how to manage what we earn, and how to balance work with the other priorities in life. These are important conversations that we will explore in later chapters. For now, it's important to understand that our jobs are a foundational part of life, but they are not our identity. Who we are in Christ comes first, and the work we do should always align with His purpose and calling for our lives.

When we keep work in its proper place—under God and in balance with family—it becomes a tool for provision, growth, and service rather than an all-consuming pursuit. Work is a gift, but it is not meant to be our master. When we approach our jobs with the right mindset, we can build a life that honors God, blesses others, and provides for the journey ahead.

Stewardship

Stewardship is the responsible management, care, and oversight of something that has been entrusted to a person, typically on behalf of another.

—Definition of Stewardship

In the Bible, stewardship isn't just about money—it's about everything. God has entrusted you with some pretty incredible stuff: your time, your talents, your relationships, your resources, and even this beautiful planet we live on. None of it really belongs to us; it's all His. We're just managing it for a little while. Think of yourself as God's trusted manager, not the owner—kind of like being handed the keys to your dad's car with the understanding that you better not trash it.

So what does that look like in real life? It means using your time wisely, not just binging shows all weekend (though rest is good too!). It means discovering and developing your talents—not to show off, but to serve others. It means handling your money with purpose, being generous, and making choices that reflect God's heart. And yes, it even means being thoughtful about how we treat the environment—because He made it, and it's awesome.

At its core, stewardship is a lifestyle that says, "God, everything I have is from You and for You." It's living with open hands, a grateful heart, and the desire to honor Him with every part of your life.

Biblical Perspective of Stewardship

From a biblical standpoint, stewardship is recognizing that everything belongs to God, and we are His managers, not owners. Our role is to faithfully oversee what He has entrusted to us.

The Parable of the Faithful and Wise Servant

"A faithful, sensible servant is one to whom the master can give the responsibility of managing his other household servants and feeding them. If the master returns and finds that the servant has done a good job, there will be a reward. I tell you the truth, the master will put that servant in charge of all he owns.

But what if the servant is evil and thinks, 'My master won't be back for a while,' and he begins beating the other servants, partying, and getting drunk?

The master will return unannounced and unexpected, and he will cut the servant to pieces and assign him a place with the hypocrites. In that place there will be weeping and gnashing of teeth."

—Matthew 24:45-51 NLT

The Parable of the Talents

"Again, the Kingdom of Heaven can be illustrated by the story of a man going on a long trip. He called together his servants and entrusted his money to them while he was gone. He gave five bags of silver to one, two bags of silver to another, and one bag of silver to the last—dividing it in proportion to their abilities. He then left on his trip.

The servant who received the five bags of silver began to invest the money and earned five more. The servant with two bags of silver also went to work and earned two more. But the servant who received the one bag of silver dug a hole in the ground and hid the master's money.

After a long time, their master returned from his trip and called them to give an account of how they had used his money. The servant to whom he had entrusted the five bags of silver came forward with five more and said, 'Master, you gave me five bags of silver to invest, and I have earned five more.'

The master was full of praise. 'Well done, my good and faithful servant. You have been faithful in handling this small amount, so now I will give you many more responsibilities. Let's celebrate together!'

The servant who had received the two bags of silver came forward and said, 'Master, you gave me two bags of silver to invest, and I have earned two more.'

The master said, 'Well done, my good and faithful servant. You have been faithful in handling this small amount, so now I will give you many more responsibilities. Let's celebrate together!'

Then the servant with the one bag of silver came and said, 'Master, I knew you were a harsh man, harvesting crops you didn't plant and gathering crops you didn't cultivate. I was afraid I would lose your money, so I hid it in the earth. Look, here is your money back.'

But the master replied, 'You wicked and lazy servant! If you knew I harvested crops I didn't plant and gathered crops I didn't cultivate, why didn't you deposit my money in the bank? At least I could have gotten some interest on it.'

Then he ordered, 'Take the money from this servant and give it to the one with the ten bags of silver. To those who use well what they are given, even more will be given, and they will have an abundance. But from those who do nothing, even what little they have will be taken away. Now throw this useless servant into outer darkness, where there will be weeping and gnashing of teeth.'"

—Matthew 25:14-30 NLT

Stewarding your journey is knowing that your life is a gift, entrusted to you by God. You were fearfully and wonderfully made, created with purpose and intention, not by accident. The very breath in your lungs, the opportunities before you, and the days ahead are all part of His divine design.

> "You made all the delicate, inner parts of my body and knit me together in my mother's womb. Thank you for making me so wonderfully complex! Your workmanship is marvelous—how well I know it. You watched me as I was being formed in utter seclusion, as I was woven together in the dark of the womb. You saw me before I was born. Every day of my life was recorded in your book. Every moment was laid out before a single day had passed."
>
> —Psalm 139:13-16 NLT

God knew you before you even took your first breath, and He has entrusted you with this life, giving you the freedom to choose how you will walk it out.

You can choose to drift through life, taking things as they come without direction, or you can seek God, gain wisdom, and walk in the path He has set before you.

> "Trust in the Lord with all your heart; do not depend on your own understanding. Seek his will in all you do, and he will show you which path to take."
>
> —Proverbs 3:5-6 NLT

Walking with God doesn't mean life will always be easy, but it does mean that every step will have purpose. You will experience victories, but also failures. There will be seasons of joy and times of challenge. But through it all, God's greatest desire is not for you to accumulate wealth, success, or recognition—the true purpose of your life is to know Him deeply and intimately.

Life is not about your job, how much money you make, the friends you have, or the possessions you own. It's not about the kind of car you drive or the clothes you wear.

The greatest journey you will ever take is walking through life with God. He desires to teach, lead, and shape you, just as He walked with Adam and Eve in the cool of the day.

> "This is what the Lord says: 'Don't let the wise boast in their wisdom, or the powerful boast in their power, or the rich boast in their riches. But those who wish to boast should boast in this alone: that they truly know me and understand that I am the Lord who demonstrates unfailing love and who brings justice and righteousness to the earth, and that I delight in these things.'"
>
> —Jeremiah 9:23-24 NLT

The more you walk with God, the more you will realize that life is not about what you have, but about who you know—it's about really knowing Him.

The choice before you is clear. You can choose to fall madly and passionately in love with God, giving your life fully to Him and following Him all your days, or you can live for yourself—chasing after temporary pleasures, pursuing success for its own sake, and trying to get all you can out of life. But in the end, only one path leads to real fulfillment.

> "And what do you benefit if you gain the whole world but lose your own soul? Is anything worth more than your soul?"
>
> —Matthew 16:26 NLT

God is not against you having good things in life, but the key is that those things should never have you—God should. When you put Him first, everything else finds its rightful place.

> "Seek the Kingdom of God above all else, and live righteously, and he will give you everything you need."
>
> —Matthew 6:33 NLT

The rest of your life begins now. From this moment forward, how will you choose to live?

Will you be the faithful steward, walking with God, growing in wisdom, and living in His purpose? Or will you live for yourself, chasing things that will never fully satisfy?

"Today I have given you the choice between life and death, between blessings and curses. Now I call on heaven and earth to witness the choice you make. Oh, that you would choose life, so that you and your descendants might live! You can make this choice by loving the Lord your God, obeying him, and committing yourself firmly to him. This is the key to your life."

—Deuteronomy 30:19-20 NLT

The choice is in your hands. Will you choose life with Him?

Following God doesn't mean you won't have good things in this life, but the right heart in all of this is that those things won't have you—God will! So choose to steward your life well and walk closely and intimately with God.

Can you imagine entering the gates of Heaven and hearing God say over you,

"The master was full of praise. 'Well done, my good and faithful servant. You have been faithful in handling this small amount, so now I will give you many more responsibilities. Let's celebrate together!'"

—Matthew 25:21 NLT

What greater reward could there be than to know you lived your life fully for Him?

Freedom

When Life Doesn't Go as Planned: Hope in the Middle of Mistakes

This book is filled with wisdom from scripture and practical steps to help you process through the many seasons of life.

But as you read, here's something important to remember:

No matter where you are—don't let your past keep you from walking in the truths and wisdom God has for you. The words in this book are not just information; they are an invitation. An invitation to grow, to heal, and to step into all that God has for you. Push forward, knowing that there is a great journey ahead with God—no matter your past. Don't let yesterday's mistakes keep you from receiving God's best for your life today.

Right here, right now God is inviting you to let Him heal the broken places of your heart and bring you to the place of complete freedom. You don't have to have it all figured out. You don't have to clean yourself up first. There's a seat at His table just for you. We all need Jesus!

When we truly begin to understand the depth of what God has done through Jesus, everything changes.

"When you were slaves to sin, you were free from the obligation to do right."

—Romans 6:20 NLT

And here's even more good news:

"So now there is no condemnation for those who belong to
Christ Jesus."

—Romans 8:1 NLT

Everyone in the world needs salvation—not just to live a better life, but
to be rescued from eternal separation from God. Hell was never made
for mankind; it was created for Satan and his fallen angels. But without
Jesus, people are headed there. That's the truth.

No matter what you've done or where you've been, the blood of Jesus
was shed for you. When He died, He made forgiveness available. And
when God raised Him back to life, He offered us a brand new way to
live.

Salvation is a free gift. All you have to do is say yes. Receive it. Walk in it.

But know this—you have an enemy. He name is Satan. He is called the
father of lies.

"The thief's purpose is to steal and kill and destroy. My
purpose is to give them a rich and satisfying life."

—John 10:10 NLT

Whether you realize it or not, you're in a spiritual battle. The enemy wants to destroy your life and everything God created you to do for His Kingdom. But don't get stuck looking at your past. Look at what God has given you in Jesus.

If our God isn't powerful enough to redeem us and set us free from our junk and sins, then why are we even serving Him?

But the truth is—He is able. He is willing. And He is the only one who can set us free.

The enemy uses events in our lives—maybe from years ago, maybe from this week—and twists them to cause pain, suffering, depression, defeat, and hopelessness. That's exactly where he wants you: stuck, ashamed, and full of regret.

And how does he do it? He gets us to believe a lie as if it's truth. That's deception: believing a lie and not realizing it's a lie.

The Cycles and the Power of Strongholds

Once we begin to believe a lie as truth, it starts to shape how we see the world. And here's what happens next:

When something happens in life that's even *similar* to the original event that caused us pain, our minds and hearts kick into defense mode. We don't want to go through that hurt again. So we develop automatic reactions—things that are designed to keep the pain away.

For some people, that reaction might be yelling or screaming.

For others, it could be shutting down completely—sinking into depression, hiding, or withdrawing from people.

Some might cry, lash out, fight, or simmer in anger.

Whatever it looks like on the outside, the pattern is the same: it's a reaction built to protect a wound. And over time, these reactions start to affect the way we relate to other people, the way we see ourselves, and even the way we respond to God.

This becomes an endless cycle. One that many people stay trapped in for life. The pain might dull over time—but the trap remains, and the stronghold gets even stronger.

What Is a Stronghold?

In biblical times, a *stronghold* was a fortified structure—a high-walled tower or fortress built to protect people from outside attacks. Think of castles, stone walls, and hiding places dug into the mountains. They were built for safety.

But spiritually speaking, a stronghold is a *mental or emotional fortress* built on a lie—something we've trusted in to protect us, but it ends up keeping us locked in fear, shame, and pain. What begins as a defense becomes a prison. We hide behind anger, control, perfectionism, addiction, or isolation—whatever we believe will protect us from being hurt again. But instead of finding safety, we get stuck.

And the only way to break free is to let God tear it down and rebuild our minds with truth.

So how does God set us free?

"We use God's mighty weapons, not worldly weapons, to knock down the strongholds of human reasoning and to destroy false arguments. We destroy every proud obstacle that keeps people from knowing God. We capture their rebellious thoughts and teach them to obey Christ."

—2 Corinthians 10:4–5 NLT

That's where the war is—in our thoughts.

Romans 12 shows us how transformation begins:

"Don't copy the behavior and customs of this world, but let God transform you into a new person by changing the way you think. Then you will learn to know God's will for you, which is good and pleasing and perfect."

—Romans 12:2 NLT

Tearing Down Strongholds

Sometimes the most important thing you can do is to simply get away with the Lord. Don't hurry. Find a quiet place, somewhere outside of your normal routine—because being at home often brings distractions or reminders of unfinished tasks.

Personally, I've found that sitting by a quiet lake on a picnic bench, away from people, is a beautiful place to meet with God.

Find your place. A place you enjoy. A place where you can be alone with Him.

Don't rush. Sit with your Abba Father. Talk to Him.

Tell Him that you realize there may be strongholds in your life—areas of bondage or emotional patterns—and you probably don't even see them yet, because they are lies you've accepted as truth.

Ask Him:

- "Lord, is there an area of my life where I'm stuck?"

- "Would You show me where this stronghold first began?"

- "Holy Spirit, would You take me to the very first moment this lie was planted in my heart?"

Be willing to wait.

Sometimes it might take 20 or 30 minutes just to quiet your heart and mind enough to really hear Him.

But don't give up. He's faithful. I've seen God do this over and over again in people's lives. Many have been reminded of the exact moment they believed a lie—and that was the beginning of a stronghold.

Once He reveals the moment, ask Him to show you the lie you believed.

Then, ask Him to show you His truth from His Word that replaces the lie. When He does, pray something like this:

- "Father, I reject the lie I believed. I now declare Your truth over my life."

Ask Him for victory going forward. If the enemy tries to bring that lie back up, do what Jesus did when He was tempted in the wilderness—use the Word.

> "But I say, walk by the Spirit, and you won't be doing what your sinful nature craves."
>
> —Galatians 5:16 NLT

If you're ever struggling or feel like you've failed, come back to this place with Him. God is always ready and willing to set you free.
Believe Him and believe His Word.

You were not just saved *from* something—you were saved *for* something.

> "For we are God's masterpiece. He has created us anew in Christ Jesus, so we can do the good things he planned for us long ago."
>
> —Ephesians 2:10 NLT

But for those who have been born again—those who are now His—we are no longer slaves to sin.

> "So Christ has truly set us free. Now make sure that you stay free, and don't get tied up again in slavery to the law."
>
> —Galatians 5:1 NLT

That's who our Abba is. That's what He does for every one of His children. And that's what the world desperately needs to hear.

They're looking for Him—but they don't know who He is. You get to tell them.

You get to scatter the seed of God's Word every single day—into the hearts of people around you. Then, walk alongside those who choose Him. Read scripture together. Do life together. Make disciples.

FINANCES

Financial Foundations

L et's start with this truth: money isn't just about math—it's about wisdom.

Out of all the adult responsibilities that show up when we grow up, money is one of the most visible—and one of the trickiest. It affects our choices, our stress levels, and even how freely we're able to love, give, and serve. And yet, so many young adults head into independence without much of a clue on how to handle it wisely.

Without wisdom, it's easy to fall into the trap of debt, worry, or living paycheck to paycheck. Doors that could've opened might stay shut. Stress takes over. And money, instead of being a helpful tool, becomes a heavy burden.

The Bible doesn't say money is evil—but it does say that *"the love of money is the root of all kinds of evil"* (1 Timothy 6:10, NLT) and that *"you cannot serve both God and money"* (Matthew 6:24, NLT). So what's the deal? Money isn't the enemy. It's just a tool—one that we've been entrusted with by God. *"The earth is the Lord's, and everything in it"* (Psalm 24:1, NLT). That includes our bank accounts, side hustles, and even the coins in the couch cushions.

God calls us to be wise, generous, and self-controlled with what we have—not to hoard it, stress over it, or chase it like it's the goal of life. True financial freedom isn't about stacking up cash—it's about using our money in ways that honor God and bless the people around us.

This chapter is about laying that foundation. Not just tips and tricks for budgeting (though those will come later!), but a whole new mindset: seeing money through God's eyes. When we understand what He says about stewardship, generosity, and trust, we can walk into any financial situation with confidence and clarity.

So let's dive in and build a solid foundation of biblical wisdom—because when we get this part right, everything else starts to click.

Let's Start with Giving!

Quick question... How did you feel when you just read that statement—"Let's start with giving"?

You probably had one of two responses. One may have been: "Yes! I love to give, and I want to learn more about what God says about generosity." The other might have been: "Oh no—here it comes. I can barely afford to live, and now I'm expected to give?"

If you had the first response, you already understand the joy of giving and are eager to deepen your knowledge. If you had the second, you're not alone. Many people struggle with the idea of giving when finances are tight. It can feel like an impossible expectation, especially when just getting by is a challenge.

But here's the key: giving isn't about what we have—it's about trusting God with what He's given us. Whether we feel excited or uneasy about it, understanding God's heart for giving is essential to financial stewardship. So before we jump into numbers, budgets, or savings, let's explore what the Bible really says about giving—why it matters, what it looks like, and how it changes our hearts and lives.

I remember when I was a young Christian, I knew that every time we gathered at church, there would be an offering. I understood that this was a time to give, an opportunity to support the work of God. But I also felt the financial pressure of my own life. There were moments when I truly wanted to give, but my financial situation made it difficult.

I wrestled with questions like: How can I give when I barely have enough for myself? Does God really expect me to give when I'm struggling? What if I give and don't have enough left to pay my bills?

These thoughts are real, and many people experience them. But over time, I learned that giving isn't about what's left over—it's about trusting God first. Giving and generosity are not about the size of the gift, but about the posture of the heart. When we give, even in times of uncertainty, we acknowledge that God is our provider, and He is faithful to meet our needs.

If you've ever felt the tension between wanting to give and feeling financial strain, you're not alone. But God's principles for giving are not meant to burden us—they are meant to set us free.

What is Tithing?

Tithing is the biblical principle of giving the <u>first 10%</u> of your in-crease—your gross income and any other financial blessings—back to God as an act of worship, trust, and obedience. The word "tithe" literally means "tenth," and throughout Scripture, God commands His people to set aside a portion of their increase for His purposes.

Old Testament View on Giving

The principle of tithing as 10% comes from several key scriptures in the Old Testament.

1. The Tithe Belongs to the Lord

> "One-tenth of the produce of the land, whether grain from the fields or fruit from the trees, belongs to the Lord and must be set apart to him as holy."
>
> —Leviticus 27:30 NLT

This verse establishes the principle of tithing, indicating that a tenth of all agricultural produce is to be dedicated to the Lord, recognizing it as holy and <u>belonging to Him</u>.

2. Abraham Gave a Tenth as an Act of Worship

"Melchizedek blessed Abram with this blessing: 'Blessed be
Abram by God Most High, Creator of heaven and earth.
And blessed be God Most High, who has defeated your
enemies for you.' Then Abram gave Melchizedek a tenth of
all the goods he had recovered."

—Genesis 14:19-20 NLT

This passage highlights Abram's act of giving a tenth of his recovered
goods to Melchizedek, acknowledging God's provision and blessing.

3. Tithing Supports God's Work

"As for the tribe of Levi, your relatives, I will compensate
them for their service in the Tabernacle. Instead of an al-
lotment of land, I will give them the tithes from the entire
land of Israel."

—Numbers 18:21 NLT

This verse explains that the Levites, who served in the Tabernacle, were to
receive the tithes from the Israelites as their inheritance, since they were
not allotted land like the other tribes.

4. God's Promise for the Faithful Tither

> "Bring all the tithes into the storehouse so there will be enough food in my Temple. If you do," says the Lord of Heaven's Armies, "I will open the windows of heaven for you. I will pour out a blessing so great you won't have enough room to take it in! Try it! Put me to the test!"
>
> —Malachi 3:10 NLT

In this verse, God challenges His people to bring their full tithes into the storehouse, promising abundant blessings in return.

New Testament View on Giving

While the New Testament does not command a specific percentage for giving, it reinforces generosity, faithfulness, and cheerful giving:

> "You must each decide in your heart how much to give. And don't give reluctantly or in response to pressure. 'For God loves a person who gives cheerfully.' "
>
> —2 Corinthians 9:7 NLT

This verse emphasizes that giving should be a personal decision made willingly and joyfully, not out of obligation or reluctance.

"What sorrow awaits you teachers of religious law and you Pharisees. Hypocrites! For you are careful to tithe even the tiniest income from your herb gardens, but you ignore the more important aspects of the law—justice, mercy, and faith. You should tithe, yes, but do not neglect the more important things."

—Matthew 23:23 NLT

In this verse from the New Testament, Jesus emphasizes that tithing is important and still for Christians today.

The 10% tithe is a biblical principle that teaches stewardship, trust, and faithfulness to God. Jesus even taught about the heart of tithing—putting God first and giving with joy—remains a foundational principle of biblical finance.

What is an Offering?

Offerings are any giving beyond the 10% tithe, given freely and voluntarily as an expression of gratitude, generosity, and love for God and others. While not required, they are encouraged as an act of cheerful and sacrificial giving, demonstrating trust in God's provision and a desire to bless others. Unlike the tithe, which is a set portion, offerings come from the overflow of a willing heart and can take many forms, such as giving to family, supporting missions, funding church projects, aiding charities, or helping those in need.

Giving an offering allows us to participate in God's work, reflect His generosity, and cultivate a heart that prioritizes His kingdom over material possessions. It is an opportunity to move beyond the obedience of tithing and embrace extravagant generosity, expressing love and faith in action.

Returning the Tithe and the Joy of Giving

Over the years, my wife Sherri and I have learned a foundational truth about finances: we bring the firstfruits back to God before we spend anything else. Not out of religious obligation, but out of love for God with all our heart, mind, and soul

> "You must love the Lord your God with all your heart, all your soul, and all your mind." .
>
> —Matthew 22:37 NLT

We don't give the tithe to God—we return it because it already belongs to Him

> "One-tenth of the produce of the land, whether grain from the fields or fruit from the trees, belongs to the Lord and must be set apart to him as holy." .
>
> —Leviticus 27:30 NLT

But beyond the tithe is where our giving truly begins—whether it's to missions, church projects, family, or people in need.

This is an amazing truth that God reveals in His Word – let's look at it again. It comes with a blessing, and He even challenges us to test Him in this:

"Bring all the tithes into the storehouse so there will be enough food in my Temple. If you do," says the Lord of Heaven's Armies, "I will open the windows of heaven for you. I will pour out a blessing so great you won't have enough room to take it in! Try it! Put me to the test!"

—Malachi 3:10 NLT

We tithe and give out of love and obedience, not to get a blessing—but God is so faithful to His Word. Time after time, we have seen His provision and blessing in our lives.

The Journey of Generosity

Once you understand this foundational principle, it transforms your mindset about money. It starts with returning the tithe to God, but it goes so much deeper.

I've met people who give away 90% of their income and live on 10%—but they didn't start that way! They began with tithing, then gave more and more as God blessed their finances, until they were able to live well on 10% and give generously with the rest.

There's something incredibly special about giving in moments when only you and God know what you did. Those quiet, unseen acts of generosity bring some of the greatest joy in giving.

I've experienced some of my most joyful moments when giving in secret—when the person or people receiving the blessing have no idea who gave it. They aren't able to thank me or anyone else; they can only praise and thank God for His provision. And that's the best part—He alone gets all the glory!

Jesus even taught about this kind of giving:

> "Give your gifts in private, and your Father, who sees every-
> thing, will reward you."
>
> —Matthew 6:4 NLT

When we give in a way that removes our name from the equation, it shifts all the attention, gratitude, and worship to God. That's the goal—not to be seen, but to point people to Him.

It doesn't get any better than that!

Make sure to read 2 Corinthians 9—it's so good when it comes to giving and it covers much about giving without others knowing! I especially love the final verse:

> "Thank God for this gift too wonderful for words!"
>
> —2 Corinthians 9:15 NLT

When we understand and walk in God's principles of tithing and giving, we experience His faithfulness firsthand. We become vessels of blessing to others, and in the end, God gets all the glory and thanks!

I wanted to lay a solid foundation on finances right from the start in the beginning of this chapter, and that foundation has to begin with tithing and giving. These principles shape the way we handle money, teaching us to put God first, trust Him fully, and develop a heart of generosity.

Now, let's take a quick look at some other key financial topics that we'll explore in more depth as we walk through various life journey topics in the following chapters.

Each of these areas impacts real-life decisions, and we'll explore them in depth in future chapters. For now, here are a few to start considering:

- **Budgeting** – Managing money wisely so we're prepared for both daily needs and future goals.

"Good planning and hard work lead to prosperity, but hasty shortcuts lead to poverty."
—Proverbs 21:5 NLT

- **Saving and Investing** – Learning to be financially responsible while trusting God's provision.

"The wise have wealth and luxury, but fools spend whatever they get."
—Proverbs 21:20 NLT

- **Debt and Financial Freedom** – Avoiding financial traps and making wise choices.

"Just as the rich rule the poor, so the borrower is servant to the lender."

—Proverbs 22:7 NLT

- **Work Ethic and Income** – Honoring God through diligence and integrity in our work.

"Work willingly at whatever you do, as though you were working for the Lord rather than for people."

—Colossians 3:23 NLT

- **Contentment vs. Materialism** – Learning to live with gratitude rather than chasing more.

"Not that I was ever in need, for I have learned how to be content with whatever I have."

—Philippians 4:11-12 NLT

Money Mic Drop

Some people, when they first encounter the concept of tithing and giving, experience an immediate pushback in their hearts. Often, this resistance comes from viewing finances through a worldly lens rather than a Kingdom one.

They wonder, *"How can I possibly give 10% when I'm already struggling to make ends meet with 100%?"*

But tithing isn't about what we can or can't afford—it's about understanding, trusting, and obeying God. In *Malachi 3*, God doesn't say *"give the tithe"*—He says, *"bring the tithe into the storehouse."* That language matters. It reminds us that the tithe already belongs to Him. We're not giving Him something that's ours; we're returning something that is rightfully His.

Think of it like this: if you find a lost wallet on the street, you have a choice. You can keep it for yourself—or you can return it to its owner. Returning it is the right thing to do because it was never yours to begin with.

Tithing and giving is ultimately a heart issue. When we align our hearts with God's Word and understand His design for stewardship, tithing becomes an act of worship, not a burden. In fact, God is so serious about this that He invites us—commands us, even—to *test Him* in this. He promises that if we do, He will open the windows of Heaven and pour out a blessing so great, we won't have room enough to contain it (*Malachi 3:10*).

Many who take this step of faith quickly discover something remarkable: they can live better on 90% with God's blessing than they ever could on 100% without it.

If we can't trust God with our finances, how can we truly trust Him with the rest of our lives? Our money is often one of the last things we surrender—but it's foundational. God has already given us His very best—His Son. We've inherited His Kingdom freely. How can we not trust Him with what He's entrusted to us?

Once we begin walking in the truth about tithing and giving, we must also walk in wisdom and apply faithful stewardship to the remaining 90% that God has entrusted to us.

As we go through this journey, we'll see how finances are connected to so many areas of life. When we apply God's wisdom, we'll not only have financial stability but also peace, purpose, and the ability to be a blessing to others.

Let's dive in!

Budgeting
Your Wallet Wants a Plan

How Much Will You Make in a Lifetime?

Have you ever stopped to do the math on how much money you'll actually earn in your lifetime? Most people go to work week after week, paycheck after paycheck, without ever calculating what all those hours will add up to by the time they retire. But stepping back and looking at the big picture—fifty years of working—can offer some serious perspective. It can shape how you think about your career, your goals, and the kind of life you want to build.

Let's start with a simple baseline: imagine someone working full-time—40 hours a week, 52 weeks a year—for 50 years straight. That's 2,080 hours a year, and over 50 years, that's 104,000 total hours of work. But the real question is: what are those hours worth?

Let's compare three different paths, all assuming a modest 3% cost-of-living raise each year, which is pretty standard over time.

1. Minimum-Wage Worker ($10/hour starting wage)

Someone working at a low-paying job for $10 an hour, like in retail, food service, or custodial work, would earn:

- Starting wage: **$10/hour**

- Total over 50 years (with 3% annual raises): **~$2.35 million**

That's a lifetime of hard work, and though the number may sound big, it's modest when stretched over five decades—especially considering taxes, rent, groceries, medical costs, and raising a family.

2. Average College Graduate (starting around $60,000/year)

Someone with a college degree might start at around $60,000 per year and see steady increases over their career. With a similar cost-of-living raise, plus modest promotions and raises along the way, their lifetime earnings might look more like:

- Starting salary: **$60,000/year**

- Total over 50 years (with 3% annual raises): **~$14 million**

This doesn't mean life is easy, but it does show how much education and skill-building can impact your long-term financial picture.

3. Medical Doctor (starting around $150,000/year)

A doctor might not start earning until their early 30s due to years of schooling and training, but their income quickly outpaces most careers. Even starting later, their lifetime earnings can be staggering:

- Starting salary: **$150,000/year**

- Total over 50 years (with 3% annual raises): **~$35 million**

Of course, doctors work extremely hard and take on years of debt and training, but the long-term return on that investment is clear.

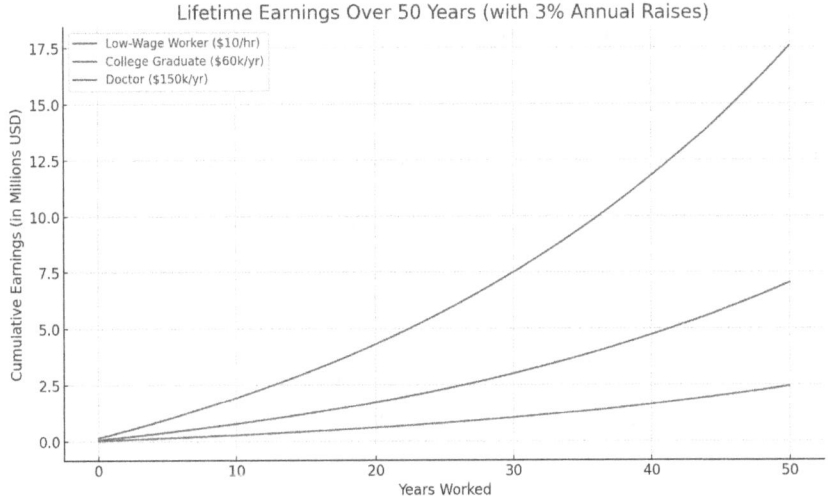

Imagine someone walks up to you today and says, "You can work in any career field you want—low-wage, college graduate, or doctor—and I'll give you all the money you'd earn over your lifetime upfront, today. The only catch? You have to commit to that job for the next 50 years, and you won't receive another dime beyond what I give you right now."

Wouldn't that instantly change how you think about your money? You'd probably pause, start calculating, and get real serious about budgeting, planning, and making wise decisions to stretch those dollars over a lifetime. Suddenly, every purchase, every goal, and every moment matters more—because you've been given a fixed amount, and it's up to you to manage it well.

That's exactly what God is offering you—not just with money, but with everything you've been given: your time, your talents, your resources, your energy. It's called stewardship. It's the idea that you are responsible for managing what God has entrusted to you.

The ball is in your court. God invites you to seek Him as you choose your career path and set your goals. Your work, your choices, your direction—it's all part of how you steward the life He's given you.

These numbers aren't just about money—they're about choices, sacrifices, and planning. Whether you're just starting out or reassessing your path, understanding what your time is worth over a lifetime can help you make wiser decisions today.

So What's A Budget?

A budget is just a plan for how to manage your money. Think of it like a roadmap that helps you decide how to spend and save your money wisely over a set period—whether that's a week, a month, or even a year. It helps you know exactly how much money you have coming in and where it needs to go, so you don't have to guess or worry about running out.

Here's how it works: You start by looking at how much money you're expecting to make (your income), and then you figure out how much you need to spend on things like bills, food, and other important stuff (your expenses). After that, you can see if there's any money left over that you can use to save or treat yourself!

The benefits? Well, for starters, having a budget gives you peace of mind. It keeps you from overspending, helps you stay on track with your goals (like saving for a vacation or paying off debt), and gives you a clearer picture of where your money's going. Plus, it can help you feel more in control of your finances, so you're not caught off guard by unexpected expenses.

So, if you're thinking about creating a budget, it's a great step toward feeling more confident and secure with your money, and it doesn't have to be complicated. It's just about finding what works for you!

There are two main types of budgets that you can consider when managing your money:

1. **Zero-Based Budget**: This type of budget is all about giving every dollar a job. At the beginning of the month (or any period), you plan out exactly how you'll use every dollar of your income. This means that your income minus your expenses should equal zero. The goal is to make sure each dollar is working for you, whether it's going toward savings, paying bills, or fun activities. This type of budget helps you stay intentional with your money and ensures you aren't wasting any of it.

2. **Flexible Budget**: This budget adjusts based on actual income or expenses. It's more adaptable and can change throughout the period depending on how things go. If you end up earning more or spending less, you can reallocate that extra money to savings,

debt, or other areas. While it's not as rigid as the zero-based budget, it still helps you keep control over your finances by adjusting to what's actually happening, rather than sticking to an estimate.

Both types help you stay organized with your money, but the zero-based budget is great if you want to be very intentional about every dollar you earn, while the flexible budget gives you room to adjust based on how things are going.

There are many options for budgeting software and you can find more online. Here are just a few software options for each type of budget:

For Zero-Based Budgeting:

1. **You Need a Budget (YNAB)**: YNAB is specifically designed for zero-based budgeting. It helps you assign every dollar a job, making sure your income is fully allocated to expenses, savings, and debt repayment. It also helps track your progress toward your financial goals.

2. **EveryDollar**: Created by Dave Ramsey, EveryDollar follows a zero-based budgeting approach. It's easy to use and helps you plan where every dollar goes, whether that's bills, savings, or even fun expenses. It offers a free version with basic features and a paid version with more advanced tools.

3. **GoodBudget**: GoodBudget is a digital envelope budgeting app that helps you assign funds to different categories. While it doesn't sync with your bank account, it allows you to plan for

your spending ahead of time and track your progress, making it a great tool for zero-based budgeting.

For Flexible Budgeting:

1. **Mint**: Mint is a popular budgeting tool that offers flexibility in tracking income and expenses. It automatically categorizes your spending and allows you to adjust your budget as needed. It syncs with your bank accounts and credit cards, making it easy to track your finances in real-time.

2. **Quicken:** Quicken is a comprehensive personal finance software with a long history and many advanced features. It's more robust than many other budgeting tools and offers a wide range of financial management tools.

3. **Personal Capital**: Personal Capital is great for managing both a flexible budget and your investments. It allows you to track income and expenses, while also helping you adjust based on how things are going throughout the month. It provides insights into your overall financial health, including retirement planning.

These tools make it easier to manage your budget, whether you're sticking strictly to a zero-based approach or need a more adaptable, flexible system.

My Experience

Over the years, my approach to budgeting has definitely evolved! There were times when I didn't have a budget at all (crazy, right?). I just went with the flow and hoped for the best. Then, I tried something a bit more structured – a cash-only system where I had a box with paper envelopes for each category, and I'd put the cash for each category in the envelope for the month. It was definitely hands-on, but not always the most convenient.

After that, I started using budgeting software like Quicken, Quick-Books, and Mint. While each had its benefits, they didn't quite click with me the way I hoped. I also gave EveryDollar by Dave Ramsey a try. It follows a zero-based budgeting approach and helped me become more intentional with my money, but it still wasn't quite the perfect fit for me.

Then I found YNAB (You Need a Budget), and I've been using it for years now. It's by far the best choice for me! The way it focuses on giving every dollar a job really helped me stay on track and feel more in control of my finances. YNAB's flexibility, simplicity, and emphasis on building better financial habits has made it an essential tool in my journey to financial peace. It's the one I've stuck with, and I can't imagine going back to anything else.

I highly recommend trying out several budgeting software options before settling on one. Many of them offer trial periods, so you can test them out and see if they'll work for you. In fact, you can usually get enough time during the trial to get a good feel for the software's features and whether it suits your needs.

You'll also find that some software is free, while others charge a monthly fee or offer a discounted yearly price. If you decide to go with one that has a cost, trust me, it'll be worth the small investment. The right software can save you a lot of time and effort in the long run.

A few things to consider when choosing a budgeting tool:

- **Platform Compatibility**: What platforms does the software run on? Make sure it's available on the devices you use regularly.

- **Phone App**: Is there a phone app version? It's super helpful to have the ability to access your budget on-the-go.

- **Bank Integration**: Does it connect to your bank and other financial institutions? In my opinion, you'll really enjoy a software that syncs with your accounts automatically. This saves you from having to manually download or enter transactions, making the whole process more seamless and less time-consuming.

Taking the time to explore your options and find the right one will definitely pay off in the long run!

YNAB Sample Budget

Below is a sample budget I created in YNAB to help you understand how a budget might look and how you can use it effectively. Most budgeting software options come with helpful training videos, so I highly recommend investing some time in learning how to use the features properly. This will give you a full picture of how it can work for you and help you get the most out of it.

When I think about a budget, I like to organize it into areas that make sense to me. You can label these categories however works best for your life.

	CATEGORY	ASSIGNED	ACTIVITY	AVAILABLE
>	Giving	$140.00	-$135.00	$5.00
>	Monthy Bills	$455.00	-$390.00	$65.00
>	Daily Life	$205.00	$0.00	$205.00
>	Non-Monthly	$45.00	$0.00	$45.00
>	Goals	$2,502.00	$0.00	$2,502.00
>	Quality of Life	$0.00	$0.00	$0.00

Budget Category Groups

1. Giving

This is always at the top of my list, and I start with the tithe. It's important to prioritize giving before anything else.

2. Monthly Bills

These are the regular, predictable expenses like rent, water, electricity, phone, and gas. They are the expenses that happen every month without fail.

3. Living Expenses

Next, we have the day-to-day expenses for living—groceries, fuel, eating out, and other daily needs.

4. Non-Monthly Items

These are the unexpected or irregular expenses that pop up throughout the year, such as car repairs, gifts for birthdays or holidays, and other random costs.

5. Goals

This is where you'll set aside money for your future—whether that's for an emergency fund, vacation savings, education, or other long-term goals. This helps you plan ahead and save for what's important.

6. Quality of Life

This section is for hobbies, entertainment, fitness, and anything else that enhances your lifestyle and well-being.

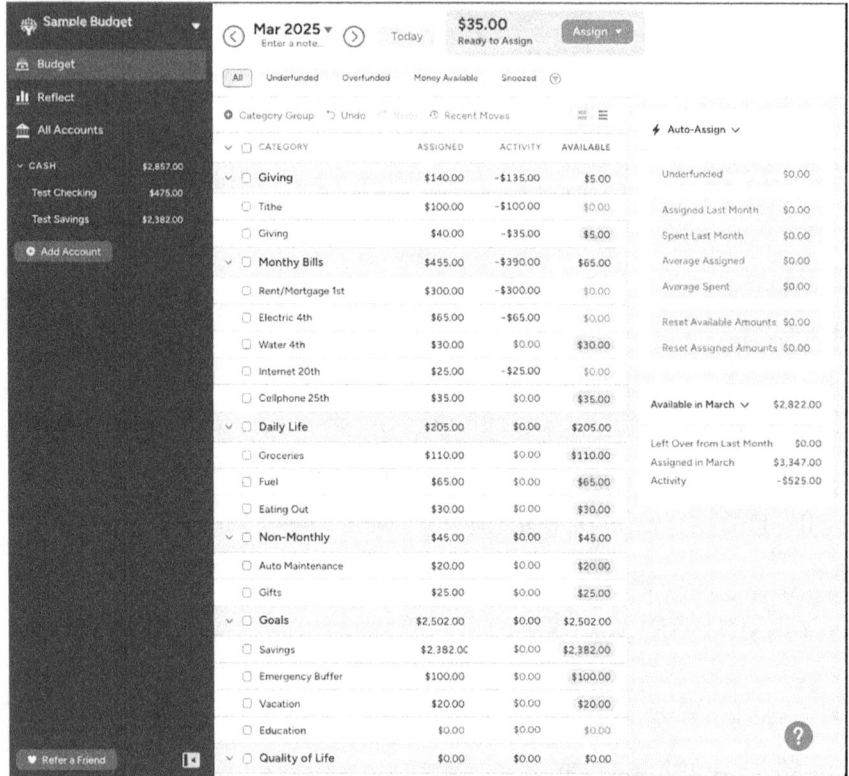

Budget Categories

This is just a sample structure, and the beauty of a budget is that it's flexible. You can design the categories and subcategories to fit your needs and goals. You're in control!

The most important thing is to get started now, even if your income isn't much. Learning to use the software will help you get into the habit of planning where your money goes as soon as you receive it. As you spend money, make sure to record every transaction in your budget software's checking register. It's an essential step in staying on track.

Sometimes, you might need to spend more in one category than you had planned. No worries! You can move funds from other categories to cover the extra expense. Budgets aren't set in stone—they're flexible and meant to work for you.

Don't give up if things feel challenging at first. With practice, you'll become a pro at managing your budget. Over time, you'll see the benefits of sticking with it. Budgeting now will save you stress later when unexpected needs or changes arise.

Remember the saying, "He who aims at nothing, hits it every time." Setting a financial plan and sticking to it is the best way to ensure you're moving in the right direction.

So, make sure to add "get on a budget" to your to-do list today! You won't regret it, and it's a great way to be a good steward of the resources you have.

Bank It Like You Really Mean It

Ditch the Shoebox—It's Bank Time

If you're starting to earn money, opening a bank account is a smart move. It keeps your cash safe, helps you stay organized, and makes everyday stuff—like getting paid or paying for things—a lot easier. Many employers use direct deposit, which means your paycheck goes straight into your account on payday, no extra steps needed. It saves time, effort, and a trip to the bank. Here are a few great reasons to get your money into a real bank.

1. It Keeps Your Money Safe

Stashing your cash in a sock drawer or under your mattress might sound old-school and simple, but it's actually pretty risky. Fire, theft, or even just forgetfulness can wipe out your savings in an instant. A bank, on the other hand, offers a level of protection that homemade hiding spots simply can't. Banks and credit unions are insured—up to $250,000 per account—by the FDIC or NCUA, which means even if your bank goes belly up, your money is still protected.

Keeping your money in the bank also removes the temptation to spend everything you see. When it's not physically sitting in front of you, it's easier to pause and think before making a purchase. Safe storage plus built-in discipline? That's a win-win.

2. It Gives You Access and Control

A bank account isn't just a place to stash your money—it's a full-on money-management toolkit. With a debit card in hand, you can shop in stores or online without needing cash. You can pay bills automatically, transfer money to friends or family using apps like Venmo or Zelle, and even deposit checks just by snapping a picture with your phone.

Mobile banking apps also give you real-time access to your money. You can see what's come in, what's gone out, and what's left. It's like carrying around a financial dashboard in your pocket. With a bank account, you stay in control—and you don't have to guess what your balance looks like.

3. Makes Getting Paid (and Paying Others) Super Easy

Having a bank account is basically a must when it comes to getting paid. Most employers use direct deposit, which means your paycheck goes straight into your account on payday. No more waiting for a paper check, heading to the bank, or worrying about it getting lost. It's fast, easy, and automatic.

And it's not just about getting paid. If you ever need to rent an apartment, apply for a loan, or finance a big purchase, people will want to see proof that you can handle money—and that usually starts with a bank statement. A bank account helps you build that financial history and credibility, even if you're just getting started.

4. It Helps You Build Healthy Habits

Managing your money through a bank account makes it easier to stay organized and intentional. You can separate your spending money from your savings, set up automatic transfers to build up your emergency fund, and use your transaction history to see where your money is really going.

It also helps curb impulse spending. Swiping a debit card tied to your budget (instead of pulling cash from your pocket) can give you a moment to pause. Plus, seeing your balance regularly helps you stay aware of your spending—and awareness is the first step toward self-control. It's a great way to build smart financial habits without needing a finance degree.

5. It's Safer and Smarter Than Cash

Losing $100 in cash means it's gone forever. But if you lose your debit card, you can lock it instantly using your bank's app—and order a replacement with just a few taps. That's one of the big advantages of using a bank account: it adds layers of protection that cash simply can't offer.

Banks also offer fraud protection, transaction tracking, and alerts that let you know if something suspicious is going on. You can monitor everything from your phone, and many banks will even text or email you about activity on your account. Peace of mind is worth a lot—and a bank helps you hold on to it.

6. The $35 Coffee: How Overdraft Fees Sneak Up on You

One thing to keep an eye on when you're starting out is overdraft fees—they can hit hard if you're not careful. If your account doesn't have enough money to cover a charge, the bank might still let it go through and then charge you $30–$35 for the favor. The worst part? One small charge can start a chain reaction. That $4 coffee goes through, and then a gas stop, a subscription, and lunch do too—each triggering its own fee. Suddenly, you're out over $100 and didn't even realize your balance was low.

Some banks will bounce the payment instead (that's called a non-sufficient funds or NSF fee), but they still charge you. Others offer to link your savings account so they can transfer money automatically to cover the shortage. That's better—but they'll often charge $5–$10 just to move your money around.

The best way to avoid all of it? Budget, check your balance regularly, and set up low-balance alerts. If you're watching your money and planning ahead, you won't get caught off guard. A little attention now can save you a lot of frustration—and a ton of fees—later on.

A First-Time Guide to Personal Banking

This checklist will help you figure out if you've got everything you need to open a bank account. Just be sure to check with the bank you go with—some might ask for slightly different stuff.

Life Stuff

- **I'm earning money or about to start a job**
  If you're getting paid—whether it's from a part-time job, freelance gig, or summer internship—it's time to think about where that money will go. Most employers prefer to use direct deposit, which means your paycheck goes straight into your bank account. No paper checks, no waiting in line. Just money, right where you need it.

- **I need a safe place to keep money (and not just a jar)**
  Keeping your cash hidden in your room might sound old-school and simple, but it's risky. Cash can be lost, stolen, or even accidentally spent. A bank keeps your money safe and insured, and it gives you tools to track, protect, and manage it. You're no longer relying on memory or hiding spots—you've got a secure financial system.

- **I want to pay for things with a debit card**
  A debit card lets you make purchases in stores or online directly from your checking account. It's safer than carrying cash, more convenient than writing checks, and essential for digital life (think streaming subscriptions, online shopping, or buying

lunch without fishing for bills). With a bank account, you'll be swiping like a pro.

- **I plan to pay bills, buy things online, or get direct deposit**
Whether it's splitting rent, paying your phone bill, or ordering something from Amazon, many everyday transactions are easiest (and sometimes only possible) with a bank account. You can schedule payments, avoid late fees, and move money with just a few taps. No more waiting on checks or making awkward cash drop-offs.

- **I want to build good money habits and financial history**
A bank account helps you develop real-life financial habits: budgeting, saving, tracking spending, and staying organized. It also lays the groundwork for building credit and qualifying for future things like car loans, apartments, or even mortgages. Your bank account is like a training ground for financial adulthood—and you'll thank yourself later.

Paperwork Needed to Open Account

- **A valid photo ID (driver's license, state ID, or passport)**
Banks need to verify your identity to open an account, so make sure you have a valid photo ID. This is typically a driver's license or passport, but some banks also accept state-issued IDs or student IDs in certain cases. If you don't have one yet, take care of that first—it's a grown-up essential beyond banking, too.

- **Your Social Security number**
Your Social Security number is how banks identify you for tax

and legal purposes. They use it to report any interest earned on your savings and to help prevent identity fraud. You don't need to carry your Social Security card around, but you do need to know the number when opening your account.

- **Proof of address (a utility bill, lease, or something official)**

  To meet government regulations, banks also need to know where you live. A recent utility bill, lease agreement, or even a school document with your name and address can usually do the trick. If you're living with family, some banks allow you to use their proof of address with a signed note or shared bill.

- **A small amount of money to deposit ($25 or less in most cases)**

  Most accounts require a small opening deposit, often just $25 or less. Some banks even offer accounts with no minimum deposit at all, especially if you're a student. You can bring this in cash if you're opening the account in person, or transfer it electronically if you're opening online.

- **Access to a smartphone or computer (if opening online)**

  Online and mobile banking are the norm now. With a smartphone or computer, you can open and manage your account from anywhere. You'll also be able to check your balance, transfer funds, and deposit checks through your bank's app—so having access to technology makes everything smoother.

Final Decision Checklist

- **I've compared at least two banks or credit unions**
  Not all banks are created equal. Some offer better interest rates, others have fewer fees, and some are more tech-savvy or community-oriented. Take the time to compare two or three banks or credit unions to see what fits your needs. It's like shopping for shoes—you want something that fits your life, not just your feet.

- **I understand basic account types (checking / savings)**
  Checking accounts are for everyday money movement—spending, paying bills, and getting paid. Savings accounts are for setting aside money for future needs or emergencies. You'll want both eventually, and knowing how they work helps you decide where your money should live and how it should move.

- **I've checked for fees, minimum balances, and ATM access**
  Some banks charge fees for having a low balance, using the wrong ATM, or even just existing (kidding—but barely). It's worth reading the fine print to understand what costs you might run into and how to avoid them. Look for accounts with no monthly fees, free ATM access, and low or no minimum balance requirements.

- **I know how to use mobile banking tools and set up alerts**
  Once your account is set up, it's smart to use your bank's app to stay on top of things. You can set up alerts for low balances, large transactions, or deposits. These tools give you eyes on your money, so you're never caught off guard by a surprise withdraw-

al or overdraft.

- **I feel ready to ask questions or get help if I need it**

  You don't have to know everything before you walk in or click "Open Account." What matters is being willing to ask questions. Bank employees are used to helping first-timers, and they'll walk you through it. There's no shame in learning—asking smart questions is part of being wise with money.

These are just a few things to consider when deciding whether to open a bank account. The truth is, in today's world, having one isn't just helpful—it's practically essential for doing anything financial. Beyond the convenience, it's also a powerful step toward becoming a better steward of the money you have.

Credit: Helpful Tool or Dangerous Trap?

(Spoiler: It Can Be Both)

Whated Even *Is* Credit? Credit is basically borrowing money that you promise to pay back later—usually with interest. You'll run into credit in a lot of places: credit cards, car loans, student loans, and more. At first, it might sound like free money (spoiler: it's not). Used wisely, credit can open doors. Used carelessly, it can dig deep holes. This chapter will help you figure out when credit helps and when it hurts.

The Upside: When Credit Can Be a Good Thing

1. It Builds Your Credit History

Your credit score is like your financial GPA. It tells lenders, landlords, and sometimes even employers how trustworthy you are with money. A good score can help you qualify for better loans, lower interest rates, and even get approved for an apartment. Using credit wisely from the start helps you build that score over time.

2. It's Convenient

Credit cards are widely accepted and often more secure than carrying cash. They're helpful in emergencies or when traveling, and they can be used online without needing to reload or transfer money like a debit card sometimes requires.

3. Rewards and Perks

Some credit cards offer cashback, travel points, discounts, and purchase protection. If you pay your balance in full each month, these perks are essentially free benefits. Just be sure the rewards aren't tempting you to overspend.

4. More Financial Flexibility

Using credit can help cover unexpected expenses if you don't have the cash on hand right away. If you have a flat tire or an emergency doctor visit, a credit card can be a helpful bridge—as long as you have a plan to pay it off soon.

5. Teaches Financial Responsibility

Using credit the right way helps you practice managing payments, tracking expenses, and understanding interest and billing cycles. It's like a grown-up version of training wheels for bigger financial decisions later.

The Downside: When Credit Turns Into Trouble

1. It's Easy to Overspend

Swiping a card doesn't feel the same as handing over cash. You might not feel the cost as much in the moment, which makes it easy to go over budget—especially on little things like snacks, apps, or subscriptions.

2. High Interest Can Add Up Fast

If you don't pay your credit card off in full, you'll start paying interest—and credit card interest is some of the highest out there. You could end up spending way more than the item actually cost.

3. Missed Payments Hurt Your Credit

Missing even one payment can seriously hurt your credit score. It can also lead to late fees and penalties, which make it even harder to catch up. And those missed payments can stay on your credit report for years.

4. Debt Can Spiral Quickly

If you're using credit to cover everyday expenses, you can quickly rack up a balance you can't manage. Without a plan, it can feel like you're digging a hole and throwing money in.

5. It Can Delay Your Goals

Carrying debt can hold you back from saving for things that matter—a car, a home, travel, or starting a business. Interest payments eat into your budget, and high balances can weigh on your mental load too.

My Thoughts on Credit: Lessons from Real Life

In my experience, credit can get out of balance really quickly. What starts as a small charge here or there can snowball into something you're stuck with for years—especially once interest starts piling up. Those high interest rates stretch out your payoff timeline and make you pay way more than what you originally spent.

One of the best practices I've learned?

Never put anything on a credit card that you can't pay off in full by the end of the month.

That one simple rule has saved me from a lot of financial stress. If you're going to use a credit card, make it work *for* you. Look for cards that offer cash back or rewards, and always aim to pay the balance completely—on time, every time.

A lot of people don't realize that making just the minimum payment each month can trap you in debt for years. You could end up paying two or three times more than you originally charged, just because of interest. That's not a good trade.

Honestly, I believe it's usually better to save up and pay cash for the things you need. Credit can be useful—but only as a tool to build a strong credit history so you qualify for better interest rates when you need to finance something big, like a car or a home. Outside of that? Use cash whenever you can, stay within the budget you've set for yourself, and think long-term.

Credit can work for you, but only if you use it with intention, discipline, and a plan.

What Does Credit Really Cost?

One of the biggest things people miss when they first start using credit is just how expensive it can get if you're not careful. And a lot of it comes down to one number: your interest rate.

Average Interest Rates by Credit Score

Your interest rate (or APR—Annual Percentage Rate) depends on your credit score. Here's a general idea of what people pay:

- **Excellent Credit (750+):** 14%–18% APR

- **Average Credit (650–749):** 19%–25% APR

- **Poor or No Credit (<650 or none):** 26%–30%+ APR

If you're just getting started or rebuilding your credit, you'll likely start on the higher end of that range. That's why understanding how interest works is a must before you rely on credit.

Real-Life Example: What Happens When You Only Make the Minimum Payment

Let's say you charge $3,000 to your credit card and make only the minimum monthly payment (usually around 2% of your balance). Here's how that plays out based on your credit rating:

Excellent Credit – 15% APR

- **Time to Pay Off:** 79 months (about 6.5 years)

- **Total Paid:** $4,740

- **Total Interest Paid:** $1,740

Even with a good interest rate, making just the minimum payment can cost you thousands more and take years to pay off.

Poor Credit – 28% APR (But Adding $20 Extra Each Month)

- **Time to Pay Off:** 209 months (over 17 years!)

- **Total Paid:** $11,174.91

- **Total Interest Paid:** $8,174.91

Yes, you read that right. Even with an extra $20 on top of the minimum each month, the debt drags on for nearly two decades and ends up costing almost three times the original purchase.

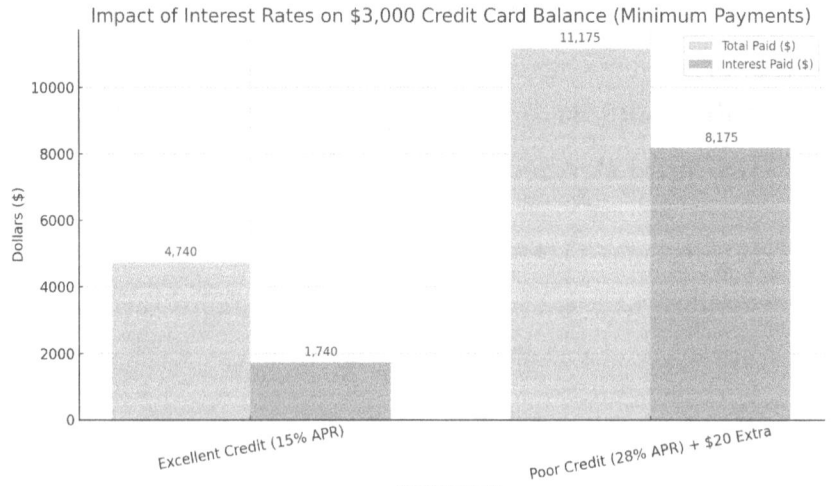

The Smart Move

To avoid this trap:

- Only charge what you can afford to pay off in full each month.

- Pay on time, every time.

- Use credit to build your score, not bury yourself in debt.

- If you do carry a balance, pay more than the minimum—every time.

Interest doesn't have to be scary if you understand how it works and stay ahead of it. Use credit as a tool, not a crutch—and let it serve your future instead of holding you back.

Bottom Line: Use It, Don't Let It Use You

Credit isn't good or bad on its own—it depends on how you use it. When used thoughtfully, it can help you build a strong financial foundation and open up future opportunities. But if you use it carelessly, it can leave you stressed, stuck, and in serious debt.

The key? Stay informed, stay in control, and treat credit like a tool, not a toy. You don't have to be afraid of it—just respect it.

You've got this.

Insurance

S tarting out on your own comes with a lot of milestones—your first place, your own car, maybe a steady paycheck. It's exciting to have more freedom and responsibility! But life doesn't always go according to plan. What if your car gets wrecked? Or your laptop disappears? Or you slip and land in the ER? That's where insurance comes in. It's a way to protect your money (and your peace of mind) when unexpected things happen. You pay a set amount on a regular basis so that if something big goes wrong, you're not stuck trying to cover the full cost by yourself.

Insurance isn't about expecting bad things to happen—it's about being prepared just in case they do. It gives you a backup plan when life doesn't go as planned, which is actually a pretty wise move. Whether it's covering hospital bills, replacing stolen items, or helping your family if something serious happens, insurance is one of those behind-the-scenes tools that helps you keep moving forward with confidence.

Why You're Paying for Stuff You Hope Never Happens

At its core, insurance is a way to share risk with a big group of people. Instead of facing the full cost of a major accident or emergency on your own, you (and lots of other people) pay a smaller, set amount regularly—called a premium—into a shared pool of money. Then, when someone in that group has an unexpected event—a car crash, a house fire, a medical emergency—they can file a claim, and the insurance company uses money from that pool to help cover the cost.

It works because not everyone needs help at the same time. Most people pay their premiums and don't have a major emergency in a given year, which means their money helps cover the few who do. In return, when it's your turn to face something unexpected, the system is there to back you up. Insurance companies use a lot of data to predict how many claims they'll likely pay out each year, and they set premiums high enough to cover those costs (plus their own expenses and a profit). That's why you might feel like you're paying for something you don't use—but when you *do* need it, it can save you from financial disaster.

There are different types of insurance for different parts of life, and each one plays a role in keeping you covered. Here's your checklist—how many of these do you have?

Health Insurance – Covers doctor visits, emergencies, and helps you avoid medical debt.

Auto Insurance – Keeps you legal on the road and helps if you crash your ride (or someone crashes into you).

Renters Insurance – Protects your stuff from theft, fire, or unexpected disasters in your apartment.

Life Insurance – If something happens to you, this takes care of your people (especially important if you have dependents or debt).

Disability Insurance – Replaces your income if you get hurt or sick and can't work for a while.

Travel Insurance – Optional, but handy if your dream vacation gets canceled, delayed, or derailed.

Insurance might not be flashy, but it's one of the smartest ways to protect your future self. Check the boxes, stay covered, and keep living your best life!

Avoiding the Two Big Mistakes: Over-Insuring and Under-Insuring

Too Little Insurance

If your coverage is too low, you might save money on premiums—but you're taking on a lot of risk. For example:

- **Auto insurance** with low liability limits might not fully cover damages in a serious accident.

- **Health insurance** with a super high deductible might mean you can't actually afford to use it.

- **Renters insurance** that doesn't reflect the value of your stuff might leave you paying out-of-pocket after a theft or fire.

Too Much Insurance

On the flip side, you don't want to over-insure either:

- You probably don't need life insurance if no one depends on your income yet.

- Paying for extra riders or bells and whistles you're unlikely to use can drive up costs without real benefit.

- Insuring things you could easily replace on your own (like a $100 microwave) might not be worth it.

How to Choose the Right Amount

Here are a few tips to find the sweet spot:

- **Know what you're protecting.** Make a quick inventory: your health, income, belongings, car, etc.

- **Use your real numbers.** What would it cost to replace your stuff? How much do you owe on your car? Could you afford a $2,000 deductible?

- **Look at worst-case scenarios.** Insurance is for big losses, not small inconveniences. Ask, *What could financially wreck me?*

- **Follow the guidelines.** Many companies recommend:

  - **Auto**: Liability of at least 100/300/100 (thousands for injury per person/total/property).

  - **Renters**: Enough to cover your stuff (usually $15k–$30k is a good start).

  - **Health**: A plan you can afford to *use*, not just to *have*.

- **Life**: If you need it, aim for up to 10x your income as a basic rule of thumb.

- **Disability**: Enough to replace 60–70% of your income.

Getting the right amount of insurance isn't about having the most—it's about being smart with what you actually need and what you could handle if something unexpected happens. It's all about finding the coverage that protects you *and* fits your budget, so you're prepared without overspending.

Whole Life vs Term Life Insurance

When you're exploring life insurance options, you'll often hear two main terms: whole life and term life. They both provide financial protection for your loved ones, but they work in very different ways. Here's a simple breakdown of what each one means and how to figure out which might be the better fit for your life and budget.

Term life insurance covers you for a set period of time—like 10, 20, or 30 years. If you pass away during that time, your beneficiary receives a payout. It's typically much more affordable and works well for people who want coverage during key seasons of life—like while raising kids, paying off a mortgage, or covering other big responsibilities.

Whole life insurance, on the other hand, lasts your entire life as long as you keep paying the premiums. It also builds something called *cash value* over time, which you can borrow from or use later. It's more expensive but may be worth considering if you're looking for lifelong coverage and an added financial tool.

Choosing the right one comes down to your goals, your stage in life, and your budget. If you mainly want protection for a specific time period and want to keep costs low, **term life** is usually the way to go. If you're looking for long-term security and are okay paying more, **whole life** may be a good fit.

One Policy, Many Prices: Age Makes All the Difference

Insurance—especially life insurance—is cheaper when you're younger because you're statistically less likely to die anytime soon. The risk to the insurance company is lower, so they charge you less. As you age, the chances of health issues, accidents, or death increase, so the cost of coverage rises accordingly.

Let's look at a simplified example of how the monthly premium for a $100,000 term life insurance policy might change every 10 years from age 20 to age 100:

Estimated Monthly Premiums if Purchased by Age

(Non-smoker, good health)

- **Age 20:** $8 – $12 per month

- **Age 30:** $10 – $15 per month

- **Age 40:** $15 – $25 per month

- **Age 50:** $25 – $50 per month

- **Age 60:** $50 – $90 per month

- **Age 70:** $90 – $180 per month

- **Age 80:** $200 – $400+ per month

- **Age 90+:** Often not available or extremely expensive

- **Age 100:** Rarely offered; cost may exceed the value of the coverage

Something to Think About:

The earlier you buy life insurance, the cheaper it is—especially if you lock in a long-term or permanent policy while you're young and healthy. Waiting too long can mean much higher premiums or even being denied coverage altogether.

Buying Home Insurance? Don't Miss the Fine Print

When you're buying home insurance, it's not just about getting *a* policy—it's about getting the *right* policy. Many people assume standard coverage protects them from all types of damage, only to discover (too late) that it didn't cover the thing that went wrong. That's why it's so important to read through the policy details and ask your agent to explain anything that's unclear.

One Big Example: Flood Insurance

Many people live in what's called a "100-year" or "500-year" floodplain—areas that *might not be* legally required to carry flood insurance. But that doesn't mean a flood can't happen. In fact, more than 20% of flood claims come from areas considered low-risk. Imagine losing your entire home in a flood, only to learn your regular home insurance doesn't cover it—and you now have to pay to tear it down and rebuild. Most people simply can't afford that. So even if it's optional, flood insurance might be worth it.

Deductibles: What Are They, and How Much Can You Handle?

A deductible is the amount *you* pay out of pocket before your insurance kicks in. Choosing the right deductible is all about balance:

- A **higher deductible** usually means lower monthly premiums

- A **lower deductible** gives you more help up front, but you'll pay more month to month

Example: Roof Replacement After a Storm

Let's say a hailstorm or hurricane damages your roof, and the average cost to replace it is $12,000.

- **With a $1,000 deductible**, your insurance would cover **$11,000**, and you'd pay **$1,000**.

- **With a $5,000 deductible**, you'd pay **$5,000**, and insurance would cover **$7,000**.

That's a big difference. Make sure the deductible you choose is an amount you could realistically afford to pay at short notice.

Ask About Add-Ons ("Riders" or "Endorsements")

Your basic home insurance might look solid—but it often skips some big stuff. That's where **add-ons** (also called riders or endorsements) come in. They're like ordering extra toppings on your pizza: optional, but sometimes exactly what you need.

Here are a few to ask about:

- **Flood Insurance** – Regular policies *don't* cover floods, and even low-risk areas can get hit. One bad storm, and boom—you're mopping up regrets.

- **Earthquake Coverage** – Shaky ground? Basic policies usually skip this, but it could save you big.

- **Sewer Backup** – If the sewer backs up into your home, the cleanup is gross *and* expensive. This is often an overlooked add-on.

- **Replacement Cost vs. Actual Cash Value** – Ask for replacement cost if you want your stuff replaced at today's prices, not what it was worth 5 years ago.

- **Extended Dwelling Coverage** – Building costs can spike. This covers you if rebuilding your home costs more than your policy's limit.

- **Foundation Water Damage** – Many standard policies *don't* cover water damage caused by a broken pipe under the foundation. That can mean tearing up floors or the slab—super expensive. Ask for coverage that includes broken pipes under the foundation.

- **Foundation Coverage** – Some policies limit or exclude damage to your foundation from shifting, cracking, or leaks. It's worth checking and adding coverage if it's not already included.

Pro Tip: Don't Assume. Ask!

These add-ons aren't always offered upfront. Sometimes they're tucked away in the "Oh yeah, you didn't ask" file. So don't be shy—ask your agent to walk you through what's covered, what's not, and what's available to add.

Because nobody wants to find out they *could* have been covered... after the jackhammer's already in your living room.

Bottom Line

Don't wait until something breaks, floods, or blows away to learn what your policy actually covers. Take time now to read through the details, ask questions, and make sure you have the protection you'll need *before* you need it. Insurance is one of those things you hope you never have to use—but when you do, it makes all the difference.

Auto Insurance: Your Wallet's Airbag

Driving is awesome—windows down, music up, freedom at your fingertips. But let's be honest: cars are expensive, and accidents happen (even if you're a great driver). That's where auto insurance comes in. It's like a financial airbag for your wallet. You pay a set amount each month so that if something goes wrong—like a fender bender, a hailstorm, or a deer out of nowhere—your insurance steps in to help cover the cost.

Auto insurance doesn't just protect *your* car, either. It also covers damage you might cause to other people's cars, property, or even medical bills if someone gets hurt. In most places, it's legally required just to be on the road.

There are a few main parts to know:

- **Liability Coverage** – Covers damage or injuries you cause to other people.

- **Collision Coverage** – Pays to fix or replace your car if you hit something.

- **Comprehensive Coverage** – Covers "everything else"—like theft, weather damage, vandalism, or a rogue shopping cart.

- **Personal Injury Protection (PIP)** or **Medical Payments** – Helps with medical bills for you and your passengers.

- **Uninsured/Underinsured Motorist Coverage** – Protects you if *they* don't have enough insurance.

Auto insurance is one of those things you hope you never need—but when you do, you'll be glad you have it. Because no one wants to be stuck paying thousands out of pocket just because someone ran a red light or a tree decided to take a nap on your hood.

When "Totaled" Means Totally Unexpected

This really happened to us—twice. My wife has had *two* cars totaled in accidents, and neither one was her fault.

The first time, she was driving the speed limit (35 mph) when a large king cab pickup came flying up behind her and slammed into her car. The impact was so strong, it turned into a five-car pile-up. Each car got pushed into the one in front of it like a giant metal domino chain. The truck that hit her didn't have enough coverage to pay for all the damage it caused, and to make things worse, my wife was injured.

The biggest blow (besides the literal one)? Her car was totaled.

What does it mean when a car is "totaled"?

When the cost to repair a car is more than what the car is worth, the insurance company declares it a "total loss" or "totaled." Instead of fixing it, they pay you what they believe the car is worth—not what you paid for it or what it would cost to replace it.

Then It Happened Again...

A few years later, we had just bought a brand new car. I mean *just*—we hadn't even made the first payment yet. My wife was pulling out of a grocery store parking spot when another big truck came speeding through the lot and T-boned her on the passenger side. All the airbags went off, and once again, the car was totaled.

The other driver's insurance eventually paid, but they only paid what they said the car was worth—which was less than what we paid for it. That's especially common with new cars.

Why Do New Cars Lose So Much Value So Fast?

You might've heard this before: *"A car loses $8,000 in value the moment you drive it off the lot."*

That's called depreciation—the drop in value that happens the second your car becomes "used." Even if it's only got 10 miles on it, it's no longer "new," and the resale value plummets. Insurance companies pay out based on *actual cash value*, which means what the car is worth now—not what you paid, and definitely not what you owe on your loan.

Enter: Gap Insurance

This is where gap insurance can save the day.

What is gap insurance?

Gap insurance covers the "gap" between what your car is worth (what insurance will pay) and what you still owe on your loan or lease. So if your brand new $30,000 car is totaled and insurance only pays $22,000, gap insurance covers that missing $8,000.

It's especially useful when:

- You bought a brand new car

- You made a small down payment

- You're financing with a long-term loan

- Your car is rapidly depreciating (which, let's face it, most are)

Lessons Learned the Hard Way

Both times, my wife did everything right—but the crashes still happened. And both times, the cars were declared total losses. If we hadn't had good coverage—and added on the gap insurance coverage when we purchased the new cars—we could've been stuck paying thousands of dollars *for cars we no longer had.*

So if you're buying a new car (or even a fairly new used one), ask about gap insurance. It's one of those "just in case" add-ons that you hope you never need... but if you do, you'll be *so* glad it's there.

Travel Insurance – Real Life Example

The Disney Dream That Detoured

Last year, our son, his wife and their children had been planning the ultimate Disney vacation in Florida. For nearly a year, they carefully researched, saved, and booked the most magical experiences they could find. One of the crown jewels of their trip? A coveted dinner reservation at Cinderella's Castle—something you have to try for at least a year in advance just to *maybe* get. Somehow, they got it. Everyone was beyond excited as the trip drew near.

But just a day or two before they were scheduled to hit the road, a storm started brewing in the Gulf. As they traveled south, it strengthened and shifted course—heading straight for Disney. They paused in Georgia, hoping the forecast would improve, but eventually had to face the facts: Disney was shutting down for safety.

Disappointed but flexible, they activated *Plan B* and rerouted to Tennessee, visiting another park there instead. While it didn't match the magic of Disney, they still made memories and made the most of what could have been a total loss.

But here's what made all the difference: they had purchased travel insurance.

Because of that wise planning, they were eventually able to get refunds for most of their vacation costs, including those hard-to-get Disney bookings. What could have been a costly disappointment turned into a manageable reroute—because they were covered.

Do You *Really* Need Travel Insurance?

If you don't purchase travel insurance, you could lose all the money you've paid upfront for flights, hotels, or events if something forces you to cancel your trip.

So how do you know when it's worth it to buy travel insurance?

Start by asking yourself this simple question:

"If my trip gets canceled, can I live with losing the money I've already paid?"

That might include flight costs, hotel reservations, theme park tickets, or special experiences like tours or dinners you had to book in advance. If you've invested a lot of money to guarantee those parts of your trip, travel insurance might be a smart safety net.

On the other hand, if you haven't paid much upfront—or if your reservations are refundable—it might not be worth the extra expense of travel insurance.

A Quick Note About Airline Tickets

Some airlines offer refundable tickets, but they typically cost quite a bit more—and not all flights offer them. So if flexibility matters to you, it's worth checking whether the added cost makes sense for your situation.

Also, here's something many people don't realize: it's common for airlines to overbook flights. That may seem wrong, but it's a business strategy. Airlines know that a certain percentage of passengers won't show up or will switch flights at the last minute. Rather than fly with empty seats, they overbook based on historical no-show data.

Of course, that's a bit of a gamble. When more people show up than there are seats, the airline offers travel vouchers—sometimes $200 or more—to anyone willing to give up their seat and take the next available flight. If you're not in a rush, this can be a great way to save money on future travel.

The airline and travel industry is constantly changing—updating rules, policies, and procedures more often than most people realize. That's why it's so important to do your homework. Take time to research, read the fine print, and ask the right questions before you book. You'll be glad you did when unexpected things come up—and they often do.

Buying a Car

There's nothing quite like the thrill of buying your first car. It's a mix of freedom, responsibility, and the smell of slightly questionable air fresheners. One minute you're dreaming of sleek designs and roaring engines, and the next you're knee-deep in confusing paperwork, mysterious fees, and a salesman named Dave who keeps calling you "champ."

It's a wild ride—and that's before you even get behind the wheel. But with a little knowledge (and a lot of patience), buying a car can actually be fun. Or at least... not terrifying.

Let me share my experience when I first went to buy a car.

That New Car Smell (And Other Traps)

I still remember my first vehicle. It was a little Ford Courier pickup truck—a small, four-cylinder machine that wasn't flashy, but it got me where I needed to go. My parents bought it for me, and at the time, it felt like the greatest gift in the world. It had some miles on it, but it was reliable and perfect for a first car.

Eventually, though, the old truck started to show its age. The engine began breaking down, and I knew it wouldn't last much longer. I was working at the time, making around $650 a month, and I had no idea how to actually *buy* a car. I'd never done it before. I didn't really have much credit at this point in my life and what I had wasn't much to speak of, and I didn't really know where to begin.

I went to a local dealership, wandered around the lot, and eventually found a car I really liked. It looked sharp, felt like a big upgrade from my old truck, and I could already imagine myself driving it. I sat down with the salesman, my first real experience doing this sort of thing. He was friendly, confident, and had a way of making me feel like I was handling it all just right.

As we talked numbers, he leaned in a little and said something like, "Now, I'm going to go into the back and talk with my sales manager—see if I can get you a better deal." Off he went, into the mysterious *back room,* while I sat there feeling like he was fighting for me, working out some kind of behind-the-scenes magic to get me the deal of the century.

When he came back, he acted like he'd pulled off a miracle—slashed prices, better financing, the whole works. I remember thinking, "Wow, I must be getting the best deal anyone's ever gotten here."

Later, I found out this is actually a pretty common sales tactic. It's meant to make the buyer feel like they're getting something special, like the dealership is doing them a personal favor. In reality, it's all part of the process.

That's the tricky part about buying a car: you know the dealership needs to make money—they're a business, after all—but it's hard to tell if you're getting a fair deal or getting taken for a ride. The numbers can be confusing, and it's easy to feel out of your depth, especially if it's your first time.

That's why *research is your best friend* before you ever set foot on a car lot.

Sites like Kelley Blue Book and others can give you solid information about the value of both new and used cars, depending on the condition, mileage, and features. You can compare prices, see what similar vehicles are selling for in your area, and walk into a dealership already knowing the ballpark figures.

That knowledge gives you confidence. It helps you ask the right questions, spot a deal that's too good to be true, and recognize when something *is* actually a fair offer.

Buying a car doesn't have to be a guessing game. But you've got to do your homework ahead of time. The more you know, the less likely you are to fall for a slick sales pitch—or end up signing up for payments you'll regret later.

We looked at the numbers, figured out what the payments would be, and then compared them to my monthly income. After a quick pause, he said, "Well, you're a little short on qualifying... but if you can get someone to co-sign, I can get you in this car today."

That was the hook.

Now, this was back before everyone had a phone in their pocket, so he handed me the desk phone. I dialed my parents, explained the situation, told them all I needed was a co-signer—and asked if they would help.

I was sure they would say yes. But instead, I heard my dad say, "I'm sorry, we can't do that."

There I sat, still on the salesman's phone, feeling stuck. I looked across the desk at him, holding the receiver, and listened to my dad gently explain that they couldn't take on that responsibility. It was disappointing—and a little embarrassing—but it was also a turning point.

Needless to say, I didn't drive away in that car. And honestly? That was probably a blessing. On my income at the time, those payments would have been a heavy load to carry.

Since then, I've bought and sold quite a few cars. I've learned a lot—lessons I want to pass on to you so you don't have to figure it all out the hard way like I did.

A Few Things to Know Before You Buy

- **New cars lose value fast.** The moment you drive it off the lot, it's worth less. That's not just a saying—it's real. Dealerships have overhead to cover: the big building, the team of employees, the coffee machine in the lobby, the service center. All of that is rolled into what you're paying.

- **If you finance, consider gap insurance.** I tell a story about this in the insurance section—don't skip it. It's important, especially if something happens to your car before it's paid off.

  We had a vehicle totaled once, and gap insurance saved us from paying for a car we no longer had.

- **Know why you want a car.** Most people say, "Well, I need transportation." That's fair. But sometimes other thoughts creep in: "I want something sporty... something that looks cool... something red." Desire can drive decisions before wisdom gets a chance to speak.

- **Think long-term.** A car is not forever. It wears out, needs repairs, and eventually gets replaced. It's not a treasure—it's a tool. You're investing not just the purchase price, but years of maintenance, fuel, insurance, and repairs.

- **Fuel efficiency matters.** I once had a vehicle that got 13 miles per gallon with a 25-gallon tank. Back when gas hit $4 per gallon, I was spending $100 every time I filled up. That adds up fast.

- **Electric vehicles are changing the game.** If you're considering going electric, do your homework. Talk to people who own one. Ask what they like, what they wish they knew beforehand, and how it fits their lifestyle.

A Tale of Two Mattresses: A Modern-Day Parable

To help really get the idea that *price isn't everything,* let's take a little detour from cars... to beds.

Let's say you've had enough of waking up with a stiff back and decide it's finally time for a new mattress. You walk into the local mattress store and—whoa—there are rows and rows of them. Some are super cheap, some are surprisingly pricey, and a bunch are right in the middle. At first glance, they all kind of look the same. So naturally, you think, *"How different can they really be?"*

But instead of just guessing, you do a little homework. You check out reviews, compare brands, and see which ones people love—or regret. You even scope out which store in town has the best service and fair pricing.

When you go back, you're ready. You test a few out and narrow it down to two mattresses. They both feel comfy. They both seem to do the job. But one costs $500, and the other one is $750.

Your first thought might be to save the $250. After all, they feel the same, right?

But here's the twist: because you did your research, you know the $500 mattress usually lasts about five years. The $750 one? It's built to last ten. So now you're faced with a better question—*what's actually the smarter buy?*

Do you pay less now and plan to replace it sooner? Do you stretch your budget a bit and avoid buying again for a decade? Or maybe you find a way to meet in the middle.

That's the heart of it—sometimes spending a little more upfront saves you money (and hassle) down the road.

And the same goes for cars.

When you're car shopping, it's easy to get caught up in the price tag. But just like with mattresses, the real question is: what are you getting *for* that price? A cheaper car that breaks down all the time might cost you more than a solid, reliable one that runs for years.

It's not just about getting the best deal—it's about making the best decision.

I've owned a variety of makes and models, but in recent years, I've stuck with one particular brand for both my wife and me. They aren't the cheapest, but they last. One of mine has nearly 200,000 miles on it and still drives like new. Some of the cars I owned years ago wouldn't have made it to 80,000 without major problems.

The point is this: buying a car doesn't have to be stressful. But it *does* need to be thoughtful. Do your research. Ask around. And make a plan before you ever set foot on a car lot.

It's not just about getting from point A to point B. It's about making a smart decision that fits your life—not just today, but down the road too.

When Buying a New Car Isn't Possible

Let's be real—buying a brand-new car isn't always possible. Maybe your budget is tight, your credit needs some time to grow, or you're just trying to be smart with your money right now.

The good news? You don't have to buy new to get a great car.

Used cars can be an excellent choice. A vehicle that's just a few years old can still be in great shape and cost a whole lot less than something brand new. Someone else already took the hit on depreciation—you get the savings.

But here's the thing: be careful where you buy. Some used car dealerships offer weekly payment plans that seem convenient, especially if you don't have much saved up. But there's a downside. Miss a payment—even just one—and they can tow the car back and sell it to the next person. It's a tough spot to be in, and it happens more than you'd think.

Another option is buying directly from an individual—just a regular person selling their car. That can work out great, but you need to protect yourself. Always get a bill of sale with the seller's name, signature, the date, the sale amount, and any details that make it official. And be sure to transfer the title properly so everything is in your name.

Most private sales are cash deals, so you'll need the full amount upfront. That might mean saving up or arranging financing through a bank or credit union before you go shopping.

If you're looking at more expensive used cars, you'll probably end up back at a dealership where financing options come into play again. And that's fine—just go in prepared. Know your numbers, read the fine print, and don't be afraid to walk away if something doesn't feel right.

At the end of the day, buying a used car can be a really smart move. The key is to stay informed, ask good questions, and make sure the vehicle (and the deal) fits your life and your budget.

When You Can't Afford a Car (Yet!)

Okay, so what if you're in a season of life where buying a car—new *or* used—just isn't happening right now?

You still need to get to work, get to school, pick up groceries, and maybe grab a milkshake every now and then. Life doesn't stop just because you don't have a car. So what do you do?

The answer? You get creative.

Here are some ways to keep moving—even without a car:

- **Catch a ride with a co-worker or friend.**
  Carpooling is a classic move. Just make sure you're a good passenger—be on time, be appreciative, and definitely offer to pitch in for gas. Bonus points if you bring coffee.

- **Ride-sharing apps (like Uber or Lyft).**
  Handy in a pinch, but they'll eat up your wallet fast if you rely on them every day. Think of these like ketchup—not the main meal, just a side when you really need it.

- **Break out the bike.**
  If your destination isn't too far, biking is a budget-friendly (and leg-toning) way to get around. Just keep an eye on the weather. Pedaling through a thunderstorm is *less* fun than it sounds.

- **Hop on the bus.**
  Public transportation might not be glamorous, but it's reliable, affordable, and gets the job done. Plus, you can people-watch or listen to a podcast on your commute—win-win.

- **Check out trains, trolleys, or local transit.**
  Depending on where you live, you might have more options than you think. Some cities have light rail systems or community shuttles that are super convenient once you learn the routes.

Look, sometimes you just have to do what you have to do. It's not forever—it's just for now. You're making smart choices, showing up, doing what it takes, and saving toward the next step—getting your own car.

This might be a detour, but you're still moving forward. Keep going! That set of keys is closer than you think.

So... How Do I Pay for This Thing?

Alright, you've found the car. You've done the research. You've imagined yourself driving it with the windows down and your favorite song playing.

Now comes the big question: How are you going to pay for it?

Whether you're eyeing something brand-new or gently used, there are a few main ways people pay for a car—and each one comes with its own pros, cons, and surprises.

Option 1: Financing – The Monthly Payment Life

This is the route most people take. Financing just means you're borrowing money to buy the car and paying it back over time—with interest. You can finance directly through the dealership, or you can get preapproved through a bank or credit union before you even walk onto the lot. Preapproval gives you a clear idea of what you can afford, your interest rate, and what your monthly payments will look like.

A few things can affect your financing:

- **Down payment:** The more you can put down upfront, the less you have to borrow—and the smaller your monthly payments will be.

- **Credit score:** Your credit rating has a big impact on the interest rate you'll get. Good credit usually means a lower rate (and lower payments), while poor credit means higher interest and a more expensive loan overall.

- **Loan term:** Most car loans are spread over 3 to 6 years. A longer loan gives you smaller monthly payments, but you'll pay more in interest by the end.

And here's something a lot of first-time buyers don't realize: if you finance a car, the lender will require you to carry full coverage insurance. That means more than just basic liability—you'll need comprehensive and collision coverage too. This kind of insurance costs more, and it's something you'll need to factor into your monthly car budget.

To give you a real-world example, let's say you buy a $30,000 car and put $3,000 down. That leaves you financing $27,000. With good credit (around a 4.5% interest rate), your monthly payment on a 5-year loan would be around $503, and you'd pay about $30,200 total by the time the car is yours.

With poor credit (say, 12.5%), your monthly payment jumps to about $607, and you'd end up paying around $36,447 total over the same time. That's over $6,000 more—all because of the interest rate.

Stretching the loan to 6 years can lower your monthly payment, but it also means you're paying interest for a longer time. The car may be more "affordable" each month, but you'll pay more in the long run. So make sure you're looking at the full cost—not just the monthly bite.

Option 2: Leasing – The Short-Term Ride

Leasing a car is kind of like renting, but for a longer stretch—usually two or three years. You get to drive a brand-new (or nearly new) car, make monthly payments, and then return it at the end of the lease term. You're not buying the car—you're just borrowing it for a while.

Leasing can sound pretty appealing, especially if:

- You love driving something new every few years

- You want a lower monthly payment than financing a purchase

- You don't plan to drive a lot of miles

But—there's a "but"—leasing comes with strings attached.

First, most leases have mileage limits, and if you go over, you'll pay extra—sometimes a lot extra. Also, the car has to be returned in good shape. Scratches, dents, or heavy wear and tear? That could mean extra charges when you turn it in.

And remember: at the end of the lease, you don't own the car. All those payments are gone, and you've got nothing to trade in or sell. You just start the process over again.

Some people love leasing because it keeps them in a fresh, worry-free ride under warranty. Others prefer to buy, because at the end of the payments—they own something.

If you're considering a lease, just go in with eyes wide open. Do the math. Know your driving habits. And read the fine print—especially the part about what happens if you want to get out early (spoiler: it's not cheap).

Leasing isn't a bad option—it's just a different one. And it works best when you understand what you're signing up for.

Option 3: Saving Up and Paying Cash

This method takes more time and patience, but it's also the simplest and most cost-effective: you save up the money, then pay cash.

No loan. No interest. No monthly payments.

If you're putting your savings in an interest-bearing account while you wait, you'll even earn a little money along the way. It's not a ton—but hey, free money is free money.

Some people take it a step further and simulate a car payment by "paying themselves" every month. Let's say you decide $400 a month is what you could afford if you had a loan. So, you start putting that into savings instead. After a few years, you've got enough saved to buy a car outright. And yes—it's absolutely possible to save up enough to pay *cash* for a brand-new car. It just takes discipline and a plan.

Cash buyers also have more leverage when negotiating. Dealers love the simplicity of cash deals, and many will offer discounts for not having to deal with financing paperwork.

What's *Really* in the Price?

Let's talk about the sticker price—the big number you see on the car window or on the dealership's website. That's just the starting point.

When you buy from a dealership, there are usually a bunch of extra fees that get tacked on:

- Sales tax (varies by state)

- Title and registration fees

- Documentation or processing fees

- Delivery or transportation fees

- Paint or fabric protection

- Dealer-installed extras like sealants, wheel locks, and window tinting

Even if you're financing, some of these costs (like taxes and title fees) may need to be paid in cash at the time of purchase. So always ask for the "out-the-door" price—that's the total cost including all taxes and fees—before you agree to anything.

What About Trading in My Old Car?

If you already have a vehicle, you've got two options: trade it in at the dealership, or sell it yourself.

Trading in is super convenient. The dealership takes your old car and applies its value to the price of the new one. In some states, you only pay sales tax on the difference between the new car price and the trade-in value—which can save you some money.

On the other hand, selling the car yourself usually brings in more cash. Dealerships need to resell your trade-in for a profit, so they'll offer less than a private buyer might. If you don't mind a little extra work (like posting online, meeting buyers, and handling paperwork), selling it yourself can give you more to put toward your next car.

Oil, Tires, and a Little Bit of Wisdom

Whether you're driving a brand-new car or one that's been with you for years, taking care of it is just part of being a good steward. A car is a big responsibility, and regular maintenance helps it stay safe, dependable, and running well for the long haul. That means keeping up with oil changes, swapping out air filters, checking the brakes, rotating the tires, and handling scheduled things like spark plug replacements or a transmission flush. It might not be the most exciting part of car ownership, but it's one of the smartest. A simple notebook, app, or folder for receipts can help you keep track of what's been done and when. Stick to the manufacturer's recommended schedule, and your car will be more likely to serve you well—without those "why is it making that noise?" moments.

And while you're caring for the engine, don't forget the rest. Keep your tires at the right pressure and rotate them regularly to help them last longer and keep you safer on the road. Some places, like Discount Tire, even offer free tire pressure checks. Swing by every 4 to 8 weeks and have them check it for you—especially when the seasons or temperatures start to change. Weather shifts can cause big changes in tire pressure, and keeping it where it should be makes a huge difference for safety, tire life, and even gas mileage. And yes—go ahead and keep your car clean too! It's a great feeling to hop into a tidy car that doesn't have snack wrappers in the door or mystery spills on the console. Regular washes also protect your paint job, and many car washes offer unlimited monthly plans that cost about the same as a single wash. It's an easy way to stay on top of it and keep your ride looking sharp.

One more thing—budget for it. Repairs and maintenance will come eventually, and it's a whole lot less stressful when you've already set aside the money. Add a line in your monthly budget for car upkeep—even just a little—and you'll be ready when the brakes need attention or new tires roll around. There's something really satisfying about being able to say, "Yep, I've got that covered." That's good stewardship in action—and it'll keep you moving forward without unexpected bumps in the road.

Drive Smart, Pay Smart

Buying a car is a big decision—and how you pay for it is just as important as what you drive away in. Whether you're financing, saving, trading, or selling, the goal is the same: make a wise choice that fits your budget and helps you keep moving forward without unnecessary stress.

The more you understand the numbers, the better prepared you'll be—and the better deal you'll get in the end.

Retirement and Investing

For YOUR Future

This Ain't Your Granddad's Retirement Plan

Your granddad worked one job, wore the same tie for 40 to 50 years, and retired with a pension, a recliner, and maybe a fishing pole. Easy. Predictable. Done.

You? You're playing a whole different game.

Today's retirement isn't handed to you in a neat little envelope—it's something you build, one smart move at a time. You're not waiting for a gold watch. You're stacking wisdom, saving intentionally, and trusting God with the blueprint.

Retirement now is less "kick back forever" and more "live with freedom and purpose." So grab your coffee (or energy drink), and let's figure out how to set future-you up for a life that's paid-for, peaceful, and full of potential.

But times have changed. Big time!

These days, most people will change jobs around eight times in their lifetime—and not just jobs, but entire career fields. You might start out in teaching, shift into tech, and later find yourself launching a side business or doing something you never saw coming.

That's not failure. That's *normal.*

1. Sometimes the job you thought was the dream turns out to be a mismatch.

2. Sometimes you get laid off.

3. Sometimes you get fired.

4. Sometimes God shuts a door you didn't even realize was the wrong one.

And here's the kicker: back then, people relied heavily on pensions—those guaranteed retirement checks that companies used to offer. But today? Pensions are rare. And worse, companies can go bankrupt, and pensions can disappear with them.

That's why now, the responsibility is on YOU to prepare for your future. Instead of a pension, most people now have access to 401(k)s or other self-managed retirement accounts. That sounds scary, but it's actually empowering. It means you're not depending on a company to take care of you—you're learning to steward what God's given you and build your own foundation.

And hey, you're not alone. God is your provider—not your employer. Jobs will change. Companies will fold. But God stays faithful.

He gives wisdom, direction, and daily bread—your part is to be faithful with the season you're in, and prepare for the one that's coming.

"Commit your actions to the Lord, and your plans will succeed."

—Proverbs 16:3 NLT

So don't panic if your path doesn't look like your Granddad's. This isn't the one-job, one-pension world anymore.

It's the trust-God, stay-flexible, and build as you go world. And you were made for it.

Retirement & Investing–Future 'You' Will Thank You

Okay, real talk—retirement sounds like something your grandparents worry about. Right? You've got bills, maybe student loans, and life is just getting started. Why think about something that's 40 years away?

Here's why: future you is totally counting on current you to be wise.

This chapter isn't about being rich or obsessed with money. It's about being smart, steady, and intentional. It's about realizing that *time* is your greatest financial superpower—and every year you wait, you're letting it slip through your fingers.

If you start early, even small amounts can grow into something big. But even if you didn't start early, the good news is: today is the best day to start. No guilt, just grace. Pick up where you are, and move forward with purpose.

> "Take a lesson from the ants, you lazybones. Learn from their ways and become wise! Though they have no prince or governor or ruler to make them work, they labor hard all summer, gathering food for the winter."
>
> —Proverbs 6:6–8 NLT

Ants don't have a boss telling them to save, but they do it anyway. Why? Because they know winter is coming. That's you, being wise and stacking up for your future—one paycheck at a time.

> "The wise have wealth and luxury, but fools spend whatever they get."
>
> —Proverbs 21:20 NLT

Ouch. That one stings a little. But also? It's solid advice. Spend every dollar, and your money disappears. Save and invest wisely, and you give future you some breathing room.

In this chapter, we'll unpack:

- What retirement really is (spoiler: it's not just golfing)

- What Social Security can help with—and what it can't

- Why investing isn't scary, and how to make it work for you

- The Blessing of compound interest (it's like a money snowball)

- And how all of this ties into stewardship—managing what God gave you for the long haul

You don't need to be a financial expert. You just need to be faithful with what's in your hands. So whether you're ahead of the game or just getting started, don't wait.

Let's get future you smiling.

What Retirement Really Is—(spoiler: not just golfing)

Retirement isn't just about sipping iced tea in a rocking chair or playing endless rounds of golf (though hey—if that's your dream, go for it). At its core, retirement is simply the season of life where you no longer have to work for money because your money has started working for you.

It's when your past self has invested, saved, and planned well enough that your future self gets options. You might travel. You might volunteer. You might start a small business or finally write that book. Or yes—you might move to Florida and get really good at pickleball.

But retirement is not the end. It's a shift. It's the payoff of decades of wise decisions, hard work, and faithful stewardship. And the cool part? You don't have to be rich to retire well—you just have to start, be consistent, and stay the course.

What Social Security Can Help With—and What it Can't

Social Security is kind of like the government's way of saying, *"Hey, thanks for working all those years—here's a check to help you out in retirement."* It's a monthly benefit you earn by paying into the system through your job. If you've seen that chunk taken out of your paycheck labeled "FICA"—yep, that's it.

So, what can Social Security do?

- It can give you a steady monthly income once you hit retirement age (as early as 62, but more if you wait until 67 or even 70).

- It can help cover your basic needs like housing, food, and bills—especially if you live simply.

- It can act as a safety net so you're not starting from zero.

But here's what it can't do:

- It can't cover everything you'll likely want or need—especially in a world where prices keep rising.

- It can't replace your full paycheck from your working years—most people get about 40% of their previous income.

- It can't guarantee a comfortable or flexible lifestyle on its own.

In other words: Social Security is a good foundation, but it's not the whole house. If you want freedom, options, and peace of mind, you'll need to build on top of it with your own savings and investments. That's where 401(k)s, IRAs, and compound interest come into play—and why starting early (or starting now!) matters so much.

Why Investing Isn't Scary—and How a 401(k) is a Tool

When you hear the word "investing," it might sound intimidating or even a little worldly. But in reality, investing is simply planning wisely for the future—and that's something God encourages.

> "Good planning and hard work lead to prosperity, but hasty shortcuts lead to poverty."
>
> —Proverbs 21:5 NLT

Jesus even told a parable about servants who were entrusted with resources and expected to multiply and manage them well (Matthew 25:14–30). That's what investing really is—it's taking what God has given you and stewarding it so that it grows over time to meet future needs.

One of the best and most accessible ways to do that is through a 401(k). If your job offers one, it allows you to put a portion of your paycheck into a retirement account automatically—and many employers even match part of what you give. That's a blessing worth taking advantage of.

You don't need to be an expert in finance. Most 401(k) plans allow you to choose simple, well-diversified options that grow over time. What matters is being faithful, consistent, and intentional—not trying to beat the market, but preparing your heart and your household for the future.

The Blessing of Compound Interest:
(God's design for multiplication)

God loves multiplication. From the loaves and fish, to the seeds planted in good soil, to the parables of wise servants—He often shows us that small things, when handled faithfully, can grow into much more.

That's what compound interest does. When you invest money, it grows—not just by what you put in, but by what it earns over time. And then the *growth itself* earns more. It's a quiet but powerful kind of blessing—slow, steady, and fruitful.

Here's a practical example:

If you invest $200/month starting at age 25, by age 67 you could have over $600,000—the Blessing from consistency, time, and God's design for increase.

If you wait until 35 to start? You'll likely end up with less than half that—just because you missed those early years when your money could have been growing.

So whether you feel "behind" or "ahead," the key is this: start where you are, and be faithful with what you've got. Trust God, plan wisely, and give your money time to grow. That's how you build a future that honors Him, blesses others, and brings peace to your life down the road.

How All of This Ties Into Stewardship:
Managing what God Gave You for the Long Haul

Everything we've talked about—investing, saving, planning for retirement—it's not just financial advice. It's spiritual. It's about stewardship.

Stewardship means understanding that everything you have—your money, time, energy, and opportunities—ultimately belongs to God. He's entrusted it to you not to hoard, waste, or fearfully bury in the ground, but to manage faithfully and multiply wisely.

When you invest, when you plan ahead, when you take steps toward financial peace, you're not just being smart—you're being obedient. You're saying, "Lord, I recognize this came from You, and I want to handle it in a way that honors You."

Stewardship doesn't mean you have to be rich. It doesn't mean you'll always get it right. It just means you show up with faithfulness and purpose, trusting that God will bless the work of your hands over time.

> "Now, a person who is put in charge as a manager must be faithful."
>
> —1 Corinthians 4:2 NLT

> "The earth is the Lord's, and everything in it. The world and all its people belong to him."
>
> —Psalm 24:1 NLT

Don't Wait:
Plan Ahead for Medicare and Social Security

As you get closer to retirement age, it's not just about having your finances in order—it's also about making wise decisions around Medicare and Social Security. These systems can be incredibly helpful, but they also come with a lot of fine print and complex choices. That's why it's wise to start planning 3 to 6 months before you retire.

One of the best things you can do is talk with a licensed Medicare agent and also reach out to your local Social Security office. They can help you understand your options, avoid mistakes, and walk you through the timelines and paperwork required.

When it comes to Medicare, there are several paths to take—including Part A, Part B, Part D (prescription coverage), and Medigap supplements like Plan G. Choosing the right plan the first time matters, especially with supplements. For example, if you want a Plan G Medigap policy, it's best to enroll when you first qualify for Medicare. Why? Because changing plans later in life can be extremely difficult—especially if you develop health issues, as insurers can decline coverage based on medical history.

And with Social Security, the timing of when you start collecting benefits will affect how much you receive each month for the rest of your life. The earlier you begin, the smaller your monthly check—but if you wait until full retirement age (or even later), your benefit grows.

So don't go into retirement guessing. Do your homework. Ask questions. Talk to experts. The decisions you make around Medicare and

Social Security can have a lifelong impact on your finances and your peace of mind.

> "Plans succeed through good counsel; don't go to war without wise advice."
>
> —Proverbs 20:18 NLT

Planning ahead is just one more way to steward the life God has given you—with wisdom, care, and trust in His guidance.

One of the Wisest Moves: Be Debt-Free by Retirement

When it comes to preparing for retirement—and really, financial peace at *any* stage of life—few things bring more freedom than being completely debt-free. That means having your home and vehicles fully paid off, yes—but also adopting a mindset that treats debt as the rare exception, not the rule.

The goal is to live debt free all the time, not just at retirement. For most people, the only major purchases typically made on credit are a home and sometimes a vehicle. And even with cars, some people take a different path—they save what would normally be a car payment every month, earn a little interest, and then pay cash when it's time to buy. That kind of discipline not only avoids the burden of interest payments, but it also puts you in a stronger position to negotiate a better deal.

Choosing to avoid debt whenever possible isn't just smart—it's a form of stewardship. It's saying, "I want to honor God with how I manage what

He's given me." Because the less you owe, the more you can give, save, and live with peace.

Imagine stepping into your later years without a mortgage or car payment. That's not just financial relief—that's stewardship in action. It means your retirement income goes further, your stress levels drop, and you have the flexibility to follow where God leads without financial chains holding you back.

But let's be honest—a paid-off home isn't the end of expenses. You'll still have to pay property taxes and homeowners insurance, which can be shockingly high depending on where you live. In some areas, retired homeowners pay $1,000 to $1,500 per month just to cover those two costs.

And it doesn't stop there. Homes wear out. Even if your mortgage is gone, you'll need to budget for big-ticket repairs and replacements, including:

- **New A/C or heating unit** – $5,000 to $12,000

- **Roof replacement** – $8,000 to $20,000

- **Hot water heater** – $1,000 to $2,500

- **New fence** – $3,000 to $8,000

- **Exterior house painting** – $4,000 to $10,000

- **Appliance replacements** – $500 to $3,000 each

These aren't "maybe someday" costs. They're part of the natural wear and tear of owning a home—and wise stewards plan ahead so these expenses don't become crises.

> "But don't begin until you count the cost. For who would begin construction of a building without first calculating the cost to see if there is enough money to finish it?"
>
> —Luke 14:28 NLT

And don't forget the other essential: your vehicle. Once you're retired, the last thing you want is a surprise car breakdown or the pressure of buying something new. A low-mileage, reliable car paid off before retirement can be a huge blessing. It gives you freedom, independence, and peace of mind.

Buying a new car in retirement can be tough. Monthly payments for a new vehicle today often run $500–$600 or more for 72 months—which can take a big bite out of your fixed income. Even if you're driving a fully paid-off car, maintenance and repairs still add up—especially as vehicles age. Tires, brakes, oil changes, batteries, and unexpected issues can cost hundreds or even thousands per year.

That's why it's wise to enter retirement with a dependable car you can drive for years to come—and a budget for repairs set aside.

One Last Gift: Why Everyone Should Have a Will

Let's talk about something important—your will. No, not your willpower (though that's great too). I'm talking about the simple, loving act of writing down your wishes for what happens when you're no longer here.

Now before you skip ahead thinking, *"I'm too young for that,"* or *"That's for people with mansions and yachts,"*—hang on! No matter your age or how much you have, having a will is one of the kindest things you can do for your loved ones.

I've seen what happens when families are left without one. After Mom and Dad pass, siblings who once laughed around the dinner table end up fighting over furniture, money, and memories. What should've been a time of honoring and grieving together turns into a tug-of-war. Sometimes, it even ends up in court for years—with lawyer fees eating away at what was left. It's heartbreaking to watch. And it's so preventable.

A will is simply putting love in writing. It's your way of saying, "Here's how I want things handled. I trust you with this. And I've thought it through so you don't have to wonder."

From a Christian perspective, it's also a final act of stewardship. God has entrusted you with time, talents, finances, and possessions—big or small—and making a will is your way of faithfully managing those blessings even after you're gone.

Here are a few things to think about when your life changes:

- Have insurance benefits? List the beneficiaries.

- Getting married? Update the will.

- Have kids? Definitely update the will.

- Changed jobs, bought a house, sold a house? Update the will.

And here's the thing: It doesn't have to be fancy or expensive. You can start simple. The point is to start.

So whether you're 25 or 75, now's a great time to put it in writing. Because while we don't know the number of our days, we *do* know we can prepare in a way that blesses our family, honors God, and brings peace instead of confusion.

It's one more way to say: "I loved you enough to think ahead."

Finish Strong and Leave No Guesswork

So that's the big picture—retirement, investing, and yes, even writing a will. You don't have to have it all figured out today, but every step you take now is a step toward peace later.

Plan wisely. Invest faithfully. Steward generously. And don't forget to write that will—because someday, your loved ones will thank you (and you won't be hovering over them shouting, *"That was supposed to be Aunt Martha's rocking chair!"*)

This isn't just about money—it's about legacy. It's about making decisions today that reflect your trust in God, your love for your family, and your desire to finish well.

Now go on—look at retirement with joy, invest with purpose, and live each day like you mean it. You've got this!

RELATIONSHIPS

Communication

Let's Talk About Talking (and Writing, and Listening)

C ommunication is kind of a big deal. Whether you're ordering coffee, writing an email, having a deep conversation with a friend, or texting your mom back (finally), you're communicating. And guess what? You're going to be doing a lot more of it as life goes on.

The good news? You can absolutely get better at it. Communication is a *skill*—not just something you're born with or not. And even better? God wants to help you grow in it. He cares about how you connect with people, express yourself, and build strong, healthy relationships.

Most of us aren't born great communicators. It takes practice—and some courage. Sometimes we're afraid of saying the wrong thing, looking silly, or starting conflict. But God doesn't want fear to hold you back.

"For God has not given us a spirit of fear and timidity, but of power, love, and self-discipline."

—2 Timothy 1:7 NLT

He's not asking you to be perfect—just to be brave and intentional. That's what He told Joshua when he was stepping into a brand-new role of leadership:

> "This is my command—be strong and courageous! Do not be afraid or discouraged. For the Lord your God is with you wherever you go."
>
> —Joshua 1:9 NLT

You don't have to have it all figured out. Just be willing to grow. Let's walk through how.

The Big 3 of Communication

You're constantly doing one (or more) of these: Speaking. Writing. Listening. Here's how to strengthen each one—with simple, practical ideas.

Speaking: Talk Like a Pro (Without Being One)

Think Before You Talk

Before you launch into a conversation, take a second to pause. What's the main thing you want to say? Being clear up front will help you speak with confidence instead of spiraling into a ramble.

Say It Simply

You don't need fancy vocabulary or a long explanation. Speak clearly and honestly. People are more interested in hearing your heart than being impressed with your words.

Adjust Based on Who You're Talking To

Your tone, words, and body language should shift depending on who you're speaking with. The way you talk to your best friend isn't how you'd speak to a teacher or manager—and that's a good thing.

Try This: Before your next important conversation, say what you want to say out loud first. You'll feel more ready when the time comes.

Writing: Make Your Words Work

Start With the Point

Whether it's a text, a note, or an email, try not to bury your message under too many words. People appreciate clarity.

Instead of writing:

"I was just wondering if maybe it would work better for you if we possibly considered..."

Try this: "Hey! Would it work to move our meeting to 2pm?"

Be Clear and Kind

You can be direct and still be friendly. There's no need to sound overly formal or robotic. Just be respectful and sincere. Emojis or exclamation points can help, as long as they fit your style and the relationship.

Reread Before You Send

Take a moment to check what you wrote before hitting send. Is it clear? Could it be misunderstood? Would it sound confusing if you were reading it for the first time?

Try This: Send a kind, encouraging message to someone today. Keep it short and real.

Listening: Your Secret Superpower

Give People Your Full Attention

Put your phone away. Close your laptop. Listening well starts with being fully present. When you give someone your undivided attention, it communicates respect and value.

Listen to Understand, Not Just to Reply

Try to hear what the other person is really saying—not just their words, but their feelings behind the words. Ask follow-up questions or repeat back what you heard to make sure you understand.

Let Them Finish

Don't interrupt, even if you're excited or feel like you already know where they're going. Letting someone finish helps them feel heard, which builds trust.

Try This: Have one screen-free conversation today. Ask someone how they're doing, and just listen.

5 Easy Ways to Practice This Week

Here are some real-life ways to grow in communication—starting today:

1. Call someone instead of texting.

2. Write a thank-you note by hand.

3. Have one conversation without any screens nearby.

4. Rehearse what you want to say before a big talk.

5. Ask a friend how they're doing—and really listen.

Why This Matters

Your words have power. They can build someone up, help solve a problem, open the door to healing, or start a new opportunity. That's why Scripture says:

> "The tongue can bring death or life; those who love to talk
> will reap the consequences."
>
> —Proverbs 18:21 NLT

So let's use our words to bring life—to encourage, connect, and strengthen the people around us. Communication isn't about being perfect—it's about being thoughtful, clear, and kind. You can grow in this. God is with you. So take a breath, lean in, and keep learning. You've got this.

Communication isn't just what comes out of your mouth.

That might sound obvious, but it's easy to forget. We often think of communication as the conversations we have or the messages we send. But what about the things we *don't* say? What about our body language, facial expressions, follow-through, and daily habits?

The truth is, we are always communicating—*especially* through our actions. As followers of Jesus, our entire life is supposed to reflect Him. That includes the way we talk, the way we live, and the way we treat others. Communication is more than just speaking clearly. It's living intentionally.

The Greatest Communication of All

Jesus was once asked, "What's the greatest commandment?" And His answer was all about love—not just spoken love, He lived it!

> "You must love the Lord your God with all your heart, all your soul, and all your mind." This is the first and greatest commandment. A second is equally important: "Love your neighbor as yourself."
>
> —Matthew 22:37–39 NLT

Love isn't just something you say. It's something you *show!* When our lives reflect this kind of love—toward God and others—we're communicating something powerful. And it doesn't require a microphone or a platform. Just a willingness to let your actions line up with your heart.

When Actions Speak Louder Than Words

Let's explore a few key areas where your actions communicate just as loudly (or louder) than your words.

In Relationships: Show What You Mean

You can say, "I care about you," but if you're never available, don't respond, or always cancel plans, the message people receive is very different.

Actions that build trust:

- Remembering details they've shared

- Listening without interrupting

- Showing up when it matters

- Being consistent, even when it's inconvenient

Sometimes love looks like putting your phone down. Sometimes it's asking, "How can I help?" instead of saying, "Let me know if you need anything." You don't need a big speech to make someone feel valued—just be there and be real.

At Work: Earn Trust by Living It

You can tell your boss you're a team player, but if you grumble about every task, miss deadlines, or act entitled, the message gets lost.

Actions that communicate excellence and integrity:

- Showing up on time

- Doing your work with care—even when no one's watching

- Owning your mistakes and learning from them

- Treating everyone with respect, regardless of title

Paul wrote:

> "Work willingly at whatever you do, as though you were working for the Lord rather than for people."
>
> —Colossians 3:23 NLT

That kind of mindset changes everything. It turns ordinary work into worship—and makes your work ethic a testimony all on its own.

In Everyday Life: Communicate Christ Through Consistency

The way you handle small, everyday moments says a lot about what you value.

What you communicate by your actions:

- Patience when things don't go your way

- Kindness to people who can't "pay you back"

- Integrity when no one else will know

- Grace when someone's rude or ungrateful

You don't have to announce you're a Christian to be a light. You just have to live like one.

And when your actions align with the heart of Jesus, people will notice. They may not say it out loud, but they'll wonder what makes you different. And often, that opens the door to conversations that *do* use words—but by then, your actions have already prepared the way.

When Words and Actions Work Together

Words are important. But words backed by action? That's powerful.

- It's one thing to say, "I forgive you." It's another to treat that person with kindness the next time you see them.

- It's one thing to say, "I'm praying for you." It's another to *actually* do it—and maybe even follow up later.

- It's one thing to say, "I love Jesus." It's another to live in a way that reflects His grace, compassion, humility, and truth.

The best communication happens when your words and your life match.

The way we communicate has the power to build strong, lasting connections—or to damage them. It can either open doors in relationships or quietly close them. That's why communication is such a vital part of our life journey.

Take a few quiet moments with God and reflect on the questions below. You might choose to journal your thoughts, pray through them, or talk them out with a trusted mentor or friend.

1. What is my life currently communicating to others?

Are there areas where my actions don't line up with what I believe or say?

2. Who in my life needs more than just words right now?

Is there someone who needs love shown in action—through time, service, a listening ear, or follow-through?

3. Where do I struggle to be consistent?

Is it in how I handle frustration? Work? Friendships? What would it look like to invite God into that?

4. What would it look like this week for my life to reflect Jesus more clearly?

Try to think of one simple, practical step you can take—something small, but intentional.

I've been noticing a growing challenge that a lot of young people are facing today—it's getting harder for them to communicate well. I found something about this that I think is worth including. Check this out!

Fear of Talking on the Phone: Telephobia

I recently came across an article about something called "Telephobia"—a growing challenge for many young people. It's the fear of making phone calls, especially to businesses, like setting up appointments. They often worry about saying the wrong thing or not knowing how to respond, so they avoid the call entirely. But learning to push past that fear is important—it's a skill they'll need to navigate real-life situations with confidence.

Recent studies show that nearly 90% of young people feel anxious about talking on the phone, and around 70% of adults aged 18 to 35 rarely answer incoming calls. In response to this growing issue, colleges are now offering courses to help students overcome telephobia—the fear of using the phone. These courses aim to teach students how to confidently make and take phone calls without fear. The goal is to equip them with the skills to handle phone conversations, whether for professional or personal purposes, and help them feel more comfortable with real-time phone interactions.

The pressure of real-time interactions in phone calls can be overwhelming, often driven by anxiety about making mistakes, not knowing what to say, or being judged. Many Gen Z individuals prefer the control texting offers, where they can take their time crafting responses without the pressure of speaking on the spot.

This shift in communication habits reflects how younger generations engage with technology. With phones mainly used for texting and online interactions, voice calls are becoming less familiar, and phone phobia is becoming a real challenge, affecting both personal and professional communication.

In response, businesses have made things easier by allowing customers to book appointments or place orders without speaking to a live person. Many now use AI bots that handle these tasks more efficiently than humans, saving time and money.

While this tech is great for businesses, it also reduces face-to-face or even phone interactions. This is a problem because, according to God, we were made for connection. That's why He created relationships and community. Family and human connection are important to God, but it seems like the world is pulling us apart more than ever.

As it says in the book of Hebrews:

> "Let us think of ways to motivate one another to acts of love and good works. And let us not neglect our meeting together, as some people do, but encourage one another, especially now that the day of His return is drawing near."
> —Hebrews 10:24-25 NLT

We're created for connection, and it's essential to keep those relationships alive, even in a world full of technology.

How to Conquer Telephobia

Telephobia is real, but don't worry—here are a few fun and practical steps to help you conquer it:

1. **Start with Little Steps**: Begin by making easy calls, like to a friend or family member. Think of it as practice before you tackle the big ones!

2. **Prep Like a Pro**: Jot down a quick script or bullet points so you don't have to guess what to say. It's like having a cheat sheet for your phone call!

3. **Breathe, Relax, Repeat**: Before dialing, take a few deep breaths. It's a simple way to calm those nerves and get into the right headspace.

4. **Picture the Win**: Close your eyes and imagine the call going perfectly. A little positive visualization can go a long way in making you feel more confident.

5. **Challenge Your Inner Critic**: Remind yourself that making mistakes is totally normal—and hey, the person on the other end is just another human being, not a phone call judge!

Saying the Right Thing, the Right Way, Every Time

Jesus was the best communicator the world has ever known. And He had the most important message to share—one that would change eternity. But interestingly, He didn't always speak directly. Many times, He used parables—short, vivid stories that taught deep spiritual truths.

To some, it may have seemed like He was being unclear, almost like He was hiding the message. But that was intentional. Jesus knew that stories had a way of getting into people's hearts—and He also knew that true understanding would come only through the Father.

He explained it this way:

> "They look, but they don't really see. They hear, but they don't really listen or understand."
>
> —Matthew 13:13 NLT

And then He said this to His disciples:

> "You are permitted to understand the secrets of the Kingdom of Heaven, but others are not."
>
> —Matthew 13:11 NLT

Jesus knew that communication wasn't just about information—it was about transformation. And He also knew that people would need spiritual eyes and ears to truly receive the message. That kind of understanding can only come from God.

Now, we carry that same message. Jesus passed it on to us—to go into all the world and share the good news. And just like Jesus, we don't communicate it only through our words. We communicate it through our actions, our character, our daily choices, and the way we love.

Everything we say and everything we do should flow from the same foundation that Jesus built His life on: love.

When people encounter you, they should catch a glimpse of Him. Not because you're perfect—but because you live with purpose, speak with grace, and love with the same compassion that Jesus showed us.

Communicating in Love

As you walk through life, you'll encounter many people and form many relationships—some lasting a lifetime, others brief and sometimes even painful. Each one carries purpose and potential. Some will be built on strong, godly foundations and grow deep over time. Others may challenge you, stretch you, or even hurt you.

Regardless of the outcome, every relationship is an opportunity to love others well—especially those God places in your path. When you choose to steward these connections with care and intention, they can bear great fruit in your life and in the lives of others.

I've been blessed with friendships that have lasted over 50 years. Even though we rarely talk or see each other now because of distance, the connection is still strong. When we do reconnect, it feels like no time has passed. That kind of bond is a gift.

At the same time, not every relationship is from God. Some may even be used by the enemy to distract or harm you. Thankfully, God is faithful to give wisdom and discernment. He'll show you when someone isn't meant to stay in your life. In those moments, you'll learn how to set healthy boundaries—and when necessary, how to walk away. We'll talk more about that later.

For now, cherish each person you meet. Sometimes when I meet someone new, I pause and ask God, "Why are you connecting us?" The Holy Spirit often answers in surprising and beautiful ways, guiding the relationship from the very beginning.

Let's take a 30,000-foot view of some of the relationships you'll likely encounter in life—and explore the purpose and foundation of each.

Let's Talk About It: Communication in Real Life

Communication is everywhere. Whether you're at work, hanging out with friends, in a relationship, texting your roommate, or dealing with a stranger at the grocery store—how you communicate matters. It builds bridges or puts up walls. It brings clarity or creates confusion. Good communication is a superpower that makes life smoother, relationships stronger, and conflict easier to navigate.

So how do you actually *communicate well*? Start by being clear, kind, and honest. Say what you mean—without being mean. Ask questions instead of jumping to conclusions. Listen more than you talk. And when you do talk, aim to understand before trying to be understood. Whether you're dealing with a frustrating co-worker or having a heart-to-heart with a close friend, the basics are the same: be present, be respectful, and speak with intention.

Of course, communication challenges are going to happen. Misunderstandings, awkward silences, emotional reactions—it's part of being human. People have different personalities, communication styles, and expectations. But when things go sideways, you don't have to stay stuck. You can reset the tone, clear up confusion, and try again. Sometimes all it takes is a simple, "Hey, can we talk about what happened earlier?" or "I think I misunderstood you—can we start over?"

Here's the good news: when you *invest* in healthy communication, it always pays off. It leads to stronger friendships, better teamwork, fewer regrets, and deeper trust. You become someone people feel safe talking to—and that's a gift in any setting. And yes, that includes having the hard conversations. Growth doesn't come from avoiding conflict; it comes from working through it. So keep showing up, keep learning, and keep choosing connection over comfort. That's where the fruit is.

Now let's take a closer look at some key things to keep in mind when communicating with different types of people in your life. Each group—family, friends, coworkers, and beyond—brings its own unique dynamics. It helps to know what matters most in each relationship.

Family

Family relationships are often where Christian love and humility are most deeply tested and practiced. Whether in a child-parent relationship or among siblings, God calls Christians to honor, forgive, support, and serve one another. Even when family dynamics are difficult or broken, Christians are called to seek peace and show Christlike love, while establishing healthy boundaries when necessary. The family is a primary context for discipleship and spiritual growth.

Unique Dynamics of Family Communication

1. Communicate Across Generations

In most families, you're not just talking to people your age—you're communicating with parents, grandparents, younger siblings, aunts, uncles, and sometimes even great-grandparents. Every generation brings a different perspective and communication style. Learn to adapt. Speak respectfully to older family members, even when you disagree, and be patient when younger ones don't always "get it" right away.

> "Always be humble and gentle. Be patient with each other, making allowance for each other's faults because of your love. Make every effort to keep yourselves united in the Spirit, binding yourselves together with peace."
>
> —Ephesians 4:2–3 NLT

This verse speaks directly to the tone we need in family communication—humility, gentleness, patience, and a deep commitment to unity.

2. Don't Assume—Clarify

Because we know our family so well, it's easy to assume what someone means—or what they're *really* feeling. But assumptions can lead to misunderstanding or unnecessary tension.

Try saying, "Can you help me understand what you meant by that?" or "Hey, just to be clear, did you mean...?"

"A gentle answer deflects anger, but harsh words make tempers flare."

—Proverbs 15:1 NLT

This is a powerful reminder, especially when tensions rise at home. The way we respond in family conversations—especially during conflict—can either calm things down or make them worse.

3. Use Non-Conflict Moments to Build Connection

Don't let all your meaningful conversations happen *only* during conflict. Family communication thrives when you also talk during the peaceful, everyday moments—on a walk, in the kitchen, or during a car ride. Build connection outside of crisis. It makes the hard talks easier when they come.

4. Know Their Love Languages

Yes, this one ties into communication! Some family members feel most loved through words, while others need time, acts of service, or physical touch. Learning and using each other's love languages can dramatically improve how you communicate care and affection.

5. Use Humor—but Carefully

Inside jokes and laughter can bring a family closer, but sarcasm or teasing—especially if it targets someone's insecurities—can do quiet damage. Make sure your humor builds up, not tears down. When in doubt, err on the side of kindness.

6. Set Boundaries with Grace

Sometimes healthy communication means knowing when *not* to engage, or how to say "no" kindly. In families, emotions run deep and roles can get blurry. Learning how to communicate your needs and limits—with respect and love—is essential to long-term peace.

7. Don't Just Talk—Follow Up

It's easy to say, "I'm here if you need anything." But real family connection grows when you check back in. "Hey, I've been thinking about what you said the other day—how are you doing now?" That kind of follow-up shows people they matter and weren't forgotten.

Friends

Friendship is a gift from God, providing companionship, encouragement, and shared joy in life's journey. Christian friendships are marked by authenticity, grace, mutual sharpening, and spiritual support. True friends point each other to Christ, celebrate victories, and walk together through trials. They are safe places for vulnerability and growth, built on trust and commitment rather than convenience.

Communicating with Friends

1. Don't Ghost—Be Honest

Friendships thrive on openness, not silence. When life gets busy or something feels off, don't disappear. If you need space, say so. If something hurt you, talk about it. True friends can handle honesty better than silence.

2. Speak Life Into Each Other

Friendships aren't just about fun—they're also about encouragement. Take time to call out the good you see in your friends. Text them that they're doing a great job. Tell them how they've helped you grow. Regular encouragement builds trust and emotional connection.

3. Keep Short Accounts

Offense can sneak in fast between close friends. Don't let little things fester. If something bothers you, address it in love. "Hey, this probably wasn't a big deal to you, but I wanted to talk about it." Dealing with things early helps preserve long-term friendship.

4. Ask Deeper Questions

Real communication isn't just "What are you up to?" It's "How are you *really* doing?" Strong friendships grow through intentional conversations—about faith, struggles, dreams, and even doubts. Show your friends you care by asking thoughtful questions and really wanting to know the answer.

5. Be a Safe Place

The best friendships are built on safety—knowing your heart won't be mocked, gossiped about, or dismissed. If a friend opens up, treat their words like gold. Show empathy, keep it confidential, and don't try to fix everything right away. Sometimes the best response is just "I'm here for you."

6. Celebrate the Wins

Communication in friendship isn't just about support during hard times—it's also about celebrating the good. Be the friend who claps the loudest when they win. A promotion, a healing, a breakthrough—cheer them on like it's your own victory.

7. Make Time to Talk

Friendship needs regular, meaningful communication to stay strong.

Life gets full, but make space for check-ins. Send a voice message. Plan a coffee catch-up. Do a "life update" phone call. A little intentional time goes a long way.

Best Friends: The Inner Circle

Best friends hold a unique place of closeness and influence. For a Christian, a best friend is someone who knows your soul deeply and loves you with both truth and tenderness. They see your strengths and weaknesses and walk with you in accountability, prayer, and encouragement. This kind of friendship often lasts through seasons, deepens over time, and reflects the loyalty and love Christ showed His disciples.

Let's be real—best friends are different. They're not just the people you hang out with. They're the ones who know your awkward middle school phase, your go-to coffee order, and your biggest dreams. They're the ones you can call at 2 a.m. and not feel bad about it. Most people, if they're lucky, will only have *one or two* true best friends throughout their entire life—and that's okay. Best friends aren't about quantity. They're about depth.

A best friend is someone who sticks with you through every version of yourself. They know your mess and still choose you. They call you out *and* call you up. They celebrate your weirdness, challenge your excuses, and remind you of who you really are when you forget.

"A friend is always loyal, and a brother is born to help in time of need."

—Proverbs 17:17 NLT

How to Be a Best Friend

Being a best friend isn't about always having the right words—it's about showing up, staying consistent, and loving deeply. Here are a few ways to be a next-level best friend:

1. Remember the Details
Best friends remember the little things. The job interview. The anniversary of a hard loss. The new song they've been obsessed with. Remembering shows you *care*, and it makes people feel deeply known.

2. Say the Hard Stuff (With Love)
Best friends don't just tell you what you want to hear. They tell you the truth—even when it's uncomfortable. But they do it in a way that builds you up, not tears you down. If something's off, speak up *with love*.

3. Be Unshockable
One of the greatest gifts you can give your best friend is your non-judgmental presence. When they confess something raw or vulnerable, don't flinch. Don't freak out. Be their steady place when everything feels shaky.

4. Protect the Friendship
Gossip kills trust. So does comparison and silent resentment. Best friends protect the relationship fiercely. If something's off, *talk* about it. Don't let hurt feelings sit in the dark. Clean it up, clear it out, and move forward.

5. Invest Time—Even When Life Gets Busy
Life moves fast. But best friendships need regular care to stay healthy. Send the random "thinking of you" message. Share a meme that made

you laugh. Set up a time to talk—even if it's just for 15 minutes. Show them they matter.

The Gift of Best Friendship

Best friends are rare—and that's what makes them so valuable. If you've got one, thank God for them. If you're becoming one to someone else, keep going. Being a best friend isn't about perfection—it's about presence. Loyalty. Grace. Honesty. And showing up again and again, no matter what.

Talking Shop: Communication with Co-Workers

In the workplace, Christians are called to be diligent, respectful, and honest, serving as unto the Lord and not just for human approval. Relationships with co-workers should be marked by kindness, integrity, and a willingness to collaborate. While maintaining professionalism, Christians are also called to be lights in their workplace, showing Christ's character through their actions and attitudes.

Work relationships can be tricky. You're not necessarily friends, but you spend a huge chunk of your week together. That's why clear, respectful communication is essential in the workplace. Whether you're working on a team project, dealing with a tough customer, or just trying to survive Monday meetings, how you speak and listen matters. Being honest, dependable, and kind sets the tone—not just for you, but for the whole environment around you.

Good communication at work means more than just saying the right thing. It's about being approachable, responding on time, giving credit where it's due, and handling conflict without drama. If something goes wrong, don't blame—own it. If there's a problem, don't complain—communicate. Great workplace communication is built on professionalism, emotional intelligence, and a whole lot of grace. When you bring that into your job, you become someone people trust and want to work with.

Communicating with Your Manager

Authority figures in the workplace deserve respect and honor, even when they are difficult. A Christian employee is called to submit to leadership with humility, unless asked to do something contrary to God's commands. Speaking with respect, taking feedback graciously, and serving with excellence reflects Christ and builds trust. When trust is broken, Christians are still called to respond with grace and wisdom.

Communicating with a manager or supervisor can sometimes feel intimidating, but it doesn't have to be. Great communication with leadership starts with respect, clarity, and confidence. Be honest about what you need, take responsibility for your work, and don't be afraid to ask questions. Most supervisors appreciate proactive communication—like when you give updates before they have to ask or bring a solution along with a problem.

It's also important to understand your manager's communication style. Some prefer quick check-ins; others want detailed updates. Pay attention to how they like to receive information, and match that style when you can. And if you need feedback or support, don't wait for your annual review—speak up. Clear, respectful communication builds trust and shows that you care about doing your job well—and that goes a long way in any workplace.

Guys and Girls: Communicating with the Opposite Sex

Friendships with the opposite sex require intentionality, honesty, and healthy boundaries. Christians are called to treat one another with purity, respect, and brotherly or sisterly love. These relationships can be enriching and mutually encouraging, but they must be handled with care, especially when one or both people are married or dating someone else. Clarity, accountability, and wisdom help ensure these friendships remain God-honoring.

Healthy communication between guys and girls is an incredibly valuable part of life. It helps us grow, learn from each other, and see the world from different perspectives. Often, guys bring straightforwardness and directness to the table, while girls might bring emotional depth and sensitivity—and both are a gift. When we communicate well across genders, we develop stronger friendships, work better together, and gain a deeper understanding of how to relate to people who are different from us. These skills are helpful not just in personal life, but in church, school, work, and future relationships.

The good news is, it's totally possible to have respectful, honest, and uplifting conversations with the opposite sex. Encouraging one another, cheering each other on, learning how to listen well, and offering advice or support when it's welcomed—these are all awesome ways to strengthen your communication. You can absolutely enjoy meaningful conversations without awkwardness or confusion when you lead with kindness, humility, and clarity. Plus, learning how to communicate with both genders helps build emotional intelligence, maturity, and confidence in every area of life.

Of course, there are a few things to be aware of. It's easy for messages to be misunderstood—especially when conversations get overly personal, emotionally intense, or consistent without clear purpose. If there's no romantic interest, don't lead someone on through deep emotional connection. Watch for tone, touch, and teasing—sometimes what feels playful to one person can feel very different to the other. The goal is to stay grounded in respect and be intentional with your words and actions. When handled well, communication between guys and girls can be encouraging, fun, and spiritually strengthening—without any confusion in the mix.

Marriage Talk: Communicating with Your Spouse

Marriage is a sacred covenant designed to reflect Christ's love for the Church. A Christian spouse is called to love sacrificially, serve joyfully, and grow spiritually together with their partner. Marriage is about mutual submission, forgiveness, and shared vision. It's a place of safety, refinement, intimacy, and partnership in both life and ministry. In the ups and downs, love remains a choice and a commitment grounded in God's grace.

Communication in marriage is one of the most powerful tools for connection—and one of the easiest areas to neglect. When it's good, it creates safety, intimacy, and deep trust. When it's off, even small misunderstandings can grow into frustration and distance. The best kind of communication in marriage is open, honest, and full of grace. That means listening to understand (not just to respond), speaking with kindness even when you're upset, and checking in regularly—not just about schedules and to-do lists, but about how your spouse is really doing.

Marriage communication thrives on intentionality. The little things matter—eye contact, tone of voice, patience, and presence. Make time for real conversations, not just surface-level check-ins. Laugh together. Pray together. Be brave enough to talk about the hard stuff before it turns into something bigger. And remember: you're not on opposing teams. The goal isn't to win an argument—it's to grow closer and understand each other better.

There *will* be challenges. You won't always feel heard. You won't always agree. And you might have completely different communication styles. But when both spouses commit to being honest, humble, and willing to grow, communication becomes a beautiful way to reflect God's love—and build a marriage that's both strong and joyful.

Speaking Life: Communicating with Your Children

Children are a blessing from the Lord and a profound responsibility. Christian parents are called to raise their children in the knowledge and love of God, training them with truth, patience, and grace. Parenting involves both discipline and delight—modeling a life of faith, prayer, and integrity. The goal is not just good behavior, but helping children know Jesus and walk in His ways.

Communicating with your children is one of the most important ways you build connection, trust, and influence that lasts. Whether they're toddlers or teens, kids need to know they're heard, valued, and safe to express themselves. That means creating a home environment where questions are welcome, feelings are acknowledged, and your words are filled with patience and grace. Talk with them, not just *at* them. And when they do open up, listen fully—eye contact, undivided attention, no interruptions.

Of course, there are challenges. Kids don't always know how to express themselves clearly, and emotions can run high—especially during stressful or developmental seasons. It's easy to either shut things down with quick answers or overreact to behavior without understanding the heart behind it. But fruitful communication happens when parents slow down, stay calm, and ask thoughtful questions. Give them language to express what they're feeling. Teach them how to speak respectfully by modeling it first. And don't be afraid to admit when you've gotten it wrong—humility goes a long way in building trust.

Ultimately, consistent, loving communication with your children helps them feel secure and understood. It models how to handle emotions, solve problems, and build healthy relationships by showing them what that looks like in real life. And more than anything, it reminds them that their voice matters—and that they have a parent who's always in their corner.

Loving Deeply, Communicating Clearly

These are just a few insights to help open your heart to the importance of godly communication, especially within your closest relationships. As you continue to grow in your walk with Christ, He will teach you how to communicate with love, patience, and purpose—especially in your marriage, with your children, and in the daily rhythms of family life.

You won't get it perfect every time, and that's okay. What matters is that you keep seeking the Lord and asking Him to shape your words, your tone, and your timing. He is faithful to give wisdom when you ask, and He'll help you build a home where communication reflects His heart.

In the chapters ahead, we'll go deeper into communication within marriage, parenting, and family life—because these relationships are sacred, and they deserve intentional, Spirit-led communication that brings unity, peace, and lasting love.

Dating

ating can be both exciting and confusing, especially when you're
trying to follow Jesus in a world that often sees relationships very
differently. Culture tends to focus on feelings, fun, and finding "the
one," with an emphasis on chemistry, convenience, and instant gratifi-
cation. But when you're pursuing a life of faith, it's natural to wonder if
there's more to it than swiping right or chasing butterflies. Is it possible
to date in a way that's still joyful and genuine, but also honors God and
leads to something lasting? Absolutely. God's way isn't about missing
out—it's about discovering a deeper kind of connection that starts with
character, wisdom, and trust.

This chapter isn't about giving you a list of rules or making you feel
pressured to get it all right. Instead, it's about shifting your perspective—seeing dating not just as something fun (though it can be!), but
as part of a bigger picture. It's a chance to grow, learn, and love well,
whether or not a relationship leads to marriage. We'll talk through the
differences between how culture views dating and how Scripture invites
us to approach it, and offer some honest, practical encouragement for
the journey. Whether you're new to dating, feeling burned out, or just
wondering how to honor God with your relationships, you're in the
right place.

Purpose of Dating

What the World Says

In today's culture, dating is often treated like a casual activity—something you do for fun, comfort, or to avoid feeling alone. It's centered on personal enjoyment, chemistry, or even sexual exploration, with commitment seen as something that can wait or might not happen at all. The idea is to follow your heart, go with the flow, and see where things lead, often with little thought to the long-term impact. While this approach may feel freeing at first, it can lead to confusion, heartbreak, and patterns that don't build a solid foundation for love that lasts.

What God Says

God offers a better way—one that's full of intention, purpose, and peace. From a biblical perspective, dating isn't just about having fun or finding someone who makes you feel good. It's about learning whether the person you're with could be a godly spouse and building a relationship that honors Him from the start. It's not about pressure—it's about wisdom and direction. Scripture reminds us,

> "So whether you eat or drink, or whatever you do, do it all
> for the glory of God"
>
> —1 Corinthians 10:31 NLT

That includes dating. When God is at the center of your relationships, it shifts everything—for your good and His glory.

Foundation of the Relationship

What the World Says

In today's culture, the foundation of a relationship is often built on attraction, emotions, and chemistry. If the spark is there, that's usually enough to jump in. But the problem with this approach is that feelings can change, and emotional highs eventually fade. When the excitement wears off or challenges arise, many relationships fall apart because there wasn't anything deeper holding them together. The world tells you to chase passion, prioritize your own happiness, and move on when it no longer feels good.

What God Says

God calls us to build relationships on something much stronger than emotions—on shared faith, godly character, mutual respect, and spiritual maturity. These qualities create a lasting foundation that can weather life's ups and downs. It's not that attraction and emotions don't matter, but they're not the main thing. God wants your relationship to be rooted in Him, growing from a place of unity in purpose and belief.

> "Don't team up with those who are unbelievers. How can righteousness be a partner with wickedness? How can light live with darkness?"
>
> —2 Corinthians 6:14 NLT

When you're both walking with Jesus, you can build something strong, steady, and full of purpose.

Boundaries and Purity

What the World Says

In today's dating culture, physical boundaries are often ignored or seen as old-fashioned. Sexual activity is not just expected—it's often assumed to be a normal part of getting to know someone. The idea of purity is rarely talked about, and if it is, it's usually dismissed as unnecessary or restrictive. Culture tends to say, "If you love each other, why wait?" or "If it feels right, go for it." But this mindset can lead to heartache, confusion, and regret, because it treats something sacred as casual.

What God Says

God's way is different—and better. He designed sex to be a beautiful, powerful expression of love within marriage, not something to be rushed or taken lightly. Physical boundaries matter, not because God wants to limit your joy, but because He wants to protect your heart.

> "God's will is for you to be holy, so stay away from all sexual sin"
>
> —1 Thessalonians 4:3 NLT

Purity isn't about shame or a list of rules—it's about honoring God with your body, your heart, and your future. And if you've crossed lines in the past, there's still hope.

> "But if we confess our sins to him, he is faithful and just to forgive us our sins and to cleanse us from all wickedness"
>
> —1 John 1:9 NLT

You don't have to carry guilt. You can start fresh today, choosing to move forward with God at the center. When you date His way, you not only protect your heart—you show love and honor to the person you're with, building a relationship that's pure, strong, and full of purpose.

Accountability

What the World Says

In the culture around us, dating is often treated as a personal, private matter. It's common to keep relationships under wraps or only share the fun parts with friends who may not always offer the best advice. Sometimes, those closest to us cheer on decisions that feel good in the moment but don't align with godly wisdom. There's a strong message that says, "Follow your heart" or "It's your life—do what makes you happy." But this approach can lead to blind spots, missed red flags, and choices that bring pain instead of peace.

What God Says

God never meant for us to do life—or dating—alone. In fact, His Word encourages us to lean on the wisdom of others. Dating in a healthy, Christ-centered way means inviting trusted people into your journey: mentors, pastors, parents, and friends who love God and want what's best for you. Their insight can help you see things clearly and make decisions rooted in truth.

"Get all the advice and instruction you can, so you will be wise the rest of your life"

—Proverbs 19:20 NLT

When you date with accountability, you're surrounding yourself with support, clarity, and encouragement—laying the groundwork for a relationship built on wisdom and trust.

Identity and Security

What the World Says

Culture often teaches that your worth is tied to your relationship status. If you're dating someone, you're seen as valuable, wanted, and successful. If you're single, it can feel like something's wrong or missing. Many people turn to dating as a way to find identity, boost self-esteem, or feel complete. The world says, "You need someone to make you happy," and encourages looking to another person for validation, purpose, and fulfillment. But no human relationship—no matter how great—can fully satisfy the deep need we all have to be known and loved.

What God Says

God wants you to know that your identity is not found in who you date, but in who you belong to. If you're in Christ, you are already loved, chosen, and complete.

> "For you are all children of God through faith in Christ Jesus"
>
> —Galatians 3:26 NLT

That truth should be the foundation of your heart before you step into any relationship. A godly relationship isn't meant to fill a void—it should come alongside your walk with Christ, not compete with it. When your security is rooted in Him, you're free to love someone else from a place of strength and wholeness, not need or insecurity.

5 Signs You're Dating the Wrong Person

Back in November 2022, I took notes on a message by Craig Groeschel, pastor of Life.Church, titled *"Save the Date: 5 Signs You're Dating the Wrong Person."* [1]

In this message, Pastor Craig Groeschel shares five clear, biblical warning signs to help you spot red flags in dating—before they turn into relationship regrets. It's a mix of straight truth, real-life insight, and solid Scripture that challenges you to look past the butterflies and the surface-level chemistry. Instead of getting swept up in emotion, he encourages you to slow down, pay attention, and be spiritually discerning.

Because let's be honest—dating can be tricky. It's easy to let feelings lead the way, but God calls us to date with wisdom, not just emotion. This message gives you practical tools to recognize when something's off and the spiritual clarity to walk in God's best for your relationships. It's eye-opening, honest, and packed with wisdom that could save you a lot of heartache.

Here's a summary of the notes I had from that teaching:

5 Signs You're Dating the Wrong Person:

1. **They're not consistently pursuing Jesus.**
   If Jesus isn't first in their life, they won't know how to love you well. Don't give your heart to someone who hasn't given theirs to God.

(*2 Corinthians 6:14-15, Amos 3:3*)

2. Your loved ones don't love who you're dating.

Wise friends and family often see what you can't. Don't ignore godly counsel.

(*Proverbs 27:9, Proverbs 12:15*)

3. You don't experience healthy conflict.

Healthy relationships include listening, understanding, and managing anger in godly ways.

(*James 1:19-20*)

4. You struggle to trust them.

A foundation of love includes trust, protection, and perseverance.

(*1 Corinthians 13:7*)

5. They're leading you away from Jesus.

Anyone who pulls you away from God's path isn't someone to build your future with.

(*Matthew 24:4, Psalm 119:115*)

For more resources on dating and relationships, visit www.life.church, or watch the full message through the Life.Church app.

YouVersion Bible Plan

For those wanting to explore this topic further, the YouVersion Bible App offers an excellent reading plan titled "Wisdom for Dating", which dives into additional thoughts and scriptures from God's Word. You can find it here: https://www.bible.com/reading-plans/33729-wisdom-for -dating[2]

This plan walks through foundational biblical principles on relationships and dating with wisdom and clarity—something that's so needed in today's culture.

And that's just the beginning! The YouVersion app has many other Bible reading plans that can help you grow in your understanding of God's design for relationships, marriage, and personal growth. Dig in—you'll be amazed at how much insight God's Word has to offer on this topic.

The Way of Wisdom: Honoring God in Who and How You Date

In today's culture, dating is often centered around self-fulfillment—what feels good, what makes *me* happy, what *I* want in the moment. But God's way flips the script completely. Instead of being driven by selfish desires, biblical dating is rooted in selflessness, love, patience, and a desire to honor God in every step. It invites you to approach relationships with purpose, humility, and a heart that asks, "How can I love this person well and glorify God through this?"

It won't always be easy. In fact, it might look completely different from what the world says is normal. But it will be worth it. When you build a relationship God's way—on a foundation of faith, purity, wisdom, and trust—you're not just preparing for a strong relationship, you're growing into the kind of person who can build a strong, lasting love. And that's the kind of relationship that not only brings joy but also reflects the heart of Christ.

Marriage

Marriage, from God's perspective, is a sacred covenant—a holy promise made before Him—that joins one man and one woman together for life. It's not just a legal agreement or a romantic partnership; it's a spiritual union where two become one in body, soul, and purpose. This relationship is designed by God to reflect His faithfulness, His sacrificial love, and His desire for deep, lasting intimacy with His people. Within marriage, God invites both husband and wife to grow in character, humility, and love, refining one another and walking side by side in obedience to Him.

Unfortunately, the world we live in today often paints a very different picture. Current statistics show that about half of all marriages in the U.S. end in divorce, and many young couples are choosing to live together without ever marrying, often seeing marriage as unnecessary, outdated, or even risky. TV shows, movies, and social media frequently glamorize casual relationships, cohabitation, and even infidelity, while rarely portraying the beauty and strength of a marriage built on God's design. As a result, the purpose and sacredness of marriage have been distorted.

But God's Word gives us a different story. As Paul wrote

"As the Scriptures say, 'A man leaves his father and mother and is joined to his wife, and the two are united into one.' This is a great mystery, but it is an illustration of the way Christ and the church are one."

—Ephesians 5:31–32 NLT

He calls this a "great mystery" because it mirrors Christ's love for the Church. A God-centered marriage isn't just about personal happiness—it's a living testimony of God's faithfulness, love, and covenant with His people.

Seek Confirmation Through Prayer and Counsel

When you start to feel that spark—that "this might be *the one*" kind of feeling—it's easy to get swept up in the joy and momentum. But before you start planning the playlist for the wedding reception, it's time to pump the brakes just a little—not because you're unsure, but because wisdom says to pause and seek God even more.

This is your chance to really lean in and ask Him, "God, is this Your best for me?" and "Are we stronger for Your Kingdom together than apart?" These aren't just good questions—they're heart-level invitations for God to shape your future.

While you're praying, don't forget to bring some wise, trusted voices into the mix. Chat with that mentor who always keeps it real. Sit down with your pastor, the one who's been there through your spiritual highs and lows. Grab coffee with that married couple whose relationship you admire—the ones who laugh, pray, and serve like a team.

And talk with your parents or family, let them in on what you're discerning. They've probably seen a few things you haven't. Proverbs shares this truth:

> "Plans succeed through good counsel; don't go to war without wise advice."
>
> —Proverbs 20:18 NLT

And let's be honest—marriage is one of life's greatest adventures, so you want to go in with all the clarity, support, and godly guidance you can get.

Pursue Purity and Intentionality

If this really is the one God has for you, that's exciting—but don't sprint ahead of His timing. Love doesn't have to be rushed. In fact, one of the most powerful things you can do in this season is slow down and build something that lasts. Protect your physical and emotional boundaries. This is your time to grow a solid foundation of friendship, trust, and spiritual unity—things that carry far more weight than temporary feelings.

God's not trying to withhold anything good from you; He's inviting you to build something beautiful, His way as He tells us in 1 Thessalonians,

> "God's will is for you to be holy, so stay away from all sexual sin."
>
> —1 Thessalonians 4:3 NLT.

That might not be a popular message in today's culture, but it's one of the most freeing, life-giving choices you can make. Purity isn't about shame—it's about honoring each other and inviting God's blessing into your relationship.

Premarital Mentorship and Counseling

As your relationship deepens and marriage feels closer on the horizon, don't try to figure it all out on your own. This is the perfect time to find a couple you trust and a solid church that offers premarital guidance. Look for people who are ahead of you in the journey—those who've walked through the highs and lows and still choose love daily. Let them walk with you as you talk through real-life stuff like communication styles, financial habits, intimacy and expectations, how you'll handle conflict, and what spiritual leadership will look like in your future home.

These conversations may feel big, but they're essential. You're not just planning a wedding—you're laying the groundwork for a lifelong partnership. And the good news is, you don't have to do it alone.

As God says in the book of Ecclesiastes.

> "Though one may be overpowered, two can defend themselves. A cord of three strands is not quickly broken."
> —Ecclesiastes 4:12 NLT

When I used to hike and camp a lot, there was always a rope or nylon cord in my pack. It had a hundred uses—keeping a tent secure in the wind, tying gear down, or even anchoring me when I was climbing the side of a cliff. But one thing I learned early on: a single strand of rope doesn't hold up very well under pressure. It frays, snaps, and gives way. The real strength comes when multiple strands are woven and twisted together. When that happens, the rope becomes exponentially stronger, able to carry weight, tension, and stress that would tear a single strand apart.

Marriage is the same way. The verse in *Ecclesiastes 4:12* that talks about the threefold cord has been a core truth my wife Sherri and I have held onto—even before we got married. In fact, her wedding ring is designed with three cord-like bands that are woven together and meet right where the diamond is set. It's a visual reminder for us every day that the strength in our marriage doesn't come from just the two of us. It comes from God at the center—His love, His grace, His strength woven into both of our lives. Without Him, we're just two individual strands doing our best. But with Him, we're bound together in something unbreakable, something sacred, something strong enough to face whatever comes.

With you, your future spouse, and God at the center, you're building something that can stand the test of time.

Ask God for a Vision for Your Marriage

Marriage isn't just about happiness—it's also about growing together, becoming more like Jesus, and living out a mission as a team. Sure, there will be romance, inside jokes, road trips, and cozy evenings on the couch—but there's a deeper purpose woven into it all. God designed marriage to shape us, stretch us, and send us out together to make a difference in the world. It's about loving each other well *and* being a light to others around you.

"Commit everything you do to the Lord. Trust him, and he will help you."

—Psalm 37:5 NLT

So as you move forward, take time to dream and pray together. Ask each other: *How can our relationship glorify God? How might He be calling us to serve together? What kind of legacy do we want to leave?* These questions help anchor your relationship in purpose, not just feelings. And when your love is built on God's foundation, it only gets stronger, richer, and more meaningful with time.

Before You Say 'I Do': Building a Marriage That Lasts

First, as mentioned earlier—start with counseling from a pastor at your church. If you don't have a church, it's a great time to find one that you can both be part of together, even before getting married. Being connected to a healthy church family isn't just a nice addition—it's a critical part of your foundation. In a strong church, you'll have the chance to worship in many ways, grow spiritually, and form lifelong relationships. In fact, my best friend of over 50 years is someone I met at one of the first churches I attended right around the time I got married. That kind of connection is a gift only God can orchestrate.

As you journey into marriage, make sure to surround yourselves with mentors—people who have walked with God through both the struggles and victories of married life. These are the people you can be real with, who will listen, speak truth, and share their own challenges and lessons. God often uses wise mentors to help guide us when we feel stuck, discouraged, or unsure. And as the years go by, it's equally important to turn around and ask God who He's calling *you* to mentor. Your experiences, your growth, and your testimony will be exactly what someone else needs as they start their journey.

One common mistake people make early in dating—and sometimes carry into marriage—is the belief that they can "fix" the other person after the wedding. That's a big red flag. If you see something in the other person's life that doesn't align with God's ways or feels off, don't ignore it or assume it'll change later. Talk about it honestly. Invite mentors and godly counselors into the conversation. If the issue can be worked through in a healthy, biblical way—that's a huge win. But if it remains unresolved, it may be God's way of showing you that moving forward isn't wise.

Over the years, I've come to believe there are two foundational things every strong marriage needs. First, it takes two healthy individuals. That doesn't mean perfect—but it does mean spiritually, mentally, and emotionally whole. If either person is carrying deep wounds, unaddressed baggage, or lacks a rooted identity in Christ, those things will eventually surface in the marriage. Taking time to grow and heal before you say "I do" will protect your relationship in the long run.

Second, one of the most important core values is this: marry someone who loves God more than they love you. When hard times come—and they will—you both need to run to God first. When things are good, you still keep Him first. I've learned that the more I truly understand how deeply God loves me, the more I'm able to love Him back—and love others well, especially my spouse.

One of the most beautiful things I've experienced in my marriage is something my wife does often. No matter when she goes to bed, she usually wakes around 4 a.m. I'm an early riser too, but not *that* early. There have been so many mornings when I walk down the hall and stop before entering the living room because I hear her praying. I see her on her knees, crying out to God for our family, for friends, for the burdens on her heart. Other times she's quietly worshiping with music in her ears, or deep in Scripture with her Bible open, listening for what God wants to speak to her that day.

In those moments, I step back quietly. She never sees me—but I see her. And what I see is breathtaking: a woman who deeply loves her Abba Father. Watching her pursue Him has inspired and encouraged me more than words can say.

From the very first time we connected—our first conversation on the phone—we didn't talk about surface stuff. We immediately dove into what God was showing each of us that day, what we had read in the Word. From day one, our relationship was built on Him and our shared love for Him. And now, all these years later, our marriage is still held together by that same love—our individual walks with God, woven together like the three strands in that unbreakable cord. He is the center, the strength, and the heartbeat of our marriage.

Foundations First: We're Just Getting Started

There's an almost infinite number of things I could include in a book about marriage. The truth is, no single book, sermon, or conversation can cover it all, because every individual and every couple is uniquely crafted by God. That's why it's so important to surround yourself with godly people—mentors, friends, pastors—who can speak into your specific journey. You were never meant to figure this out on your own. When you walk closely with a healthy, faith-filled community, you'll receive wisdom, encouragement, and accountability as you grow into the person—and the spouse—God has called you to be.

Let's be real: no one is ever *completely* ready for marriage. You'll be living day in and day out with another human being—your spouse—and over time, you'll discover things you didn't see before. Some of those things will be wonderful surprises. Others... not so much. That's why it's so vital to approach dating and engagement with intention, preparing for marriage by seeking God's wisdom through prayer, Scripture, and godly counsel. You'll quickly learn your spouse isn't perfect—but they'll discover that you aren't either. And that's where the beauty begins: two imperfect people learning to love, forgive, and grow together with God at the center.

I once heard a pastor say the purpose of marriage is simple: *"To die."* People laughed at first, but all the married folks in the room understood. Because the essence of marriage is not about getting your way—it's about laying down your life. It's about dying to selfishness, pride, and control, and choosing to serve, love, and forgive—again and again. And while it may sound heavy, it's actually one of the most beautiful invitations God gives us. Because when we choose to love like Jesus, God meets us there and builds something strong, lasting, and deeply fulfilling.

After all, marriage is a picture—remember the verse at the top of this chapter? *"As the Scriptures say, 'A man leaves his father and mother and is joined to his wife, and the two are united into one.' This is a great mystery,*

but it is an illustration of the way Christ and the church are one." —
Ephesians 5:31–32 NLT.

Marriage is a living illustration of Jesus and His church—*us*. So when
you're unsure what marriage should look like, look to Jesus. He laid
down His life for us. He gave up everything so we could gain everything. And we never deserved it. If you carry that heart into your marriage—for your spouse, and even for your children if God blesses you
with them—you will be walking in the kind of love that transforms
everything. That's the kind of marriage God can bless beyond what you
could ever ask or imagine.

Things That Don't Fix Themselves

Here's the truth: many couples walk into marriage without working
through a few essential areas—and it ends up causing a lot of pain. In
some cases, the issues were never discussed, and in others, they were
simply ignored. Either way, the damage is real. Some marriages have
struggled deeply because of these things, and others haven't survived at
all. That's why it's so important to talk through these topics ahead of
time and decide how you will walk together in unity.

Money Matters (So Talk About It!)

Finances are one of the biggest issues couples face. It's not just about
money—it's about values, communication, trust, and priorities. You or
your future spouse might be early in your career and still learning how to
handle money. Maybe one of you is bringing debt into the relationship.
Maybe neither of you has ever learned how to budget, and spending
just happens—often with credit cards and no plan. These patterns won't

magically disappear once you're married. In fact, marriage often magnifies financial stress if it isn't addressed intentionally.

When it comes to money, both of us are totally capable of balancing the budget—but I've kind of taken the lead on doing the weekly updates and keeping things organized. I actually enjoy it (most days), and it's become part of our routine. Once I've done the mechanical side—reconciling the accounts and making sure everything lines up—we sit down together and talk through the real decisions. Where we're spending, how we want to give, and what we're saving for are things we always decide as a team.

One thing we try to do regularly is pray over our giving. Whether it's our tithe or support for other ministries and giving, we take a moment and ask God to bless it and use it for His kingdom. It's a way to keep our finances grounded in purpose, not just numbers.

Even though I'm the one doing most of the day-to-day tracking, Sherri and I meet several times a month to look at the budget together. We talk about where we are, what's coming up, and what things look like going forward. It keeps us on the same page and reminds us we're in this together—budget and all.

Make sure to check out the chapter on budgeting in this book—you'll find practical tools and biblical perspective to help you succeed financially, not just survive.

Another common mistake that couples make is deciding to keep their finances separate. They maintain different bank accounts, split bills down the middle, and treat money as if it belongs to two individuals rather than one united couple. I've even seen spouses writing each other checks for half the rent or utilities—handling their finances more like business partners or roommates than a husband and wife in covenant with one another.

So what's really happening here? At the core, it often comes down to either control or distrust. One person may want to manage their money independently without having to explain or be questioned, or there may be a fear of fully opening up and sharing financial responsibility. Regardless of the reason, this approach is a mistake. In fact, I believe it directly contradicts God's design for marriage. When a couple chooses not to become one in their finances, it reveals something much deeper—it often means they're not fully committed to the covenant of marriage.

That might sound harsh, but think about it: if you're holding back in one of the most practical, daily parts of life—your money—it sends a powerful message: *"I don't completely trust you,"* or *"I'm keeping one foot out the door just in case."* That's not the unity God describes. That's just cohabitation with paperwork.

And it's not just about separate accounts—hidden money can be just as damaging. Secret spending, undisclosed debt, or hidden accounts all break trust and create division. Marriage was never meant to operate in secrecy. It's meant to be a place of full transparency and unity. When financial secrets exist, they're usually symptoms of deeper issues—fear, control, shame, or unresolved wounds. And whether spoken or not, those secrets communicate: *"This part of my life isn't yours."*

But God's design is clear. In Ephesians 5:31, He says, *"A man leaves his father and mother and is joined to his wife, and the two are united into one."* That unity covers every part of life—spiritually, emotionally, physically, and yes, financially. Money isn't separate from the rest of your marriage; it's one of the most revealing and practical ways you live out your oneness.

This isn't something to brush aside or leave for "someday." It's something that needs to be addressed early—with honesty, prayer, and wise counsel. Because marriage, at its core, is about full unity, full trust, and full surrender to God's design. And that includes how you handle every dollar, together.

Remember what Scripture says: *"...the two are united into one."* It doesn't say they become two under one roof. It says they become one—spiritually, physically, emotionally, and yes, financially. That unity is a picture of Christ and His church, fully surrendered, fully trusting, fully committed. Your finances are part of that picture. When you choose oneness in every area—including money—you honor God's design, and you open the door for His blessing on your marriage.

Lack of Spiritual Unity

When couples aren't pursuing God together—praying, worshiping, reading Scripture, or seeking His will—it's easy to slowly drift apart. The relationship might still look fine on the surface, but underneath, there's a growing disconnect. Spiritual unity is the heartbeat of a strong, God-centered marriage. Without it, trust weakens, shared purpose fades, and the vision for your life together can get cloudy. You may still function as a couple, but the bond God intended you to have—rooted in Him—isn't fully there.

Without Christ at the center, marriage loses its anchor. When the storms of life hit (and they will), you need something stronger than emotions or good intentions to hold you together. Spiritual unity isn't about being perfect or super religious—it's about regularly inviting God into your relationship, together. Praying for one another, seeking Him in decision-making, worshiping side by side, and keeping your hearts aligned with His. A couple that pursues God together creates a foundation that is not easily shaken. When both hearts are surrendered to Him, there's a deep sense of peace, direction, and unity that nothing else can replace.

Poor Communication

Whether it's constant arguing or complete silence, poor communication is one of the fastest ways a marriage can begin to unravel. Communication isn't just about talking—it's about understanding. When couples fail to express their thoughts, feelings, or needs in a healthy way, small frustrations can quickly build into major walls. Sometimes one person dominates the conversation while the other shuts down. Other times, both partners avoid conflict altogether, stuffing their feelings until they eventually explode or drift apart.

The absence of grace, honesty, and active listening opens the door for misunderstandings to grow. Assumptions are made, tone is misread, and intentions are questioned. Resentment doesn't usually come in loud—it creeps in quietly, over time. You start to feel unheard, unseen, or unloved, even if your spouse has no idea. Healthy communication requires both people to slow down, listen well, and speak truth in love. It also requires humility and a willingness to say, "I was wrong" or "Help me understand."

If this sounds familiar, don't panic—but don't ignore it either. Communication struggles are incredibly common, but they're also incredibly fixable with God's help and the right tools. Take time to check out the chapter on communication in this book. It's full of practical ideas, godly wisdom, and real-life encouragement to help you strengthen one of the most vital parts of your marriage. A healthy, grace-filled conversation might just change everything.

Unresolved Conflict and Lack of Forgiveness

No marriage is perfect. Every couple will face conflict—big or small—because two imperfect people living closely together are bound to disagree at times. But the danger isn't in the conflict itself; it's in how we handle it. When arguments are swept under the rug, avoided entirely, or worse, brought back later as ammunition, the wounds don't just disappear—they linger. Over time, they become harder to heal. What was once a small offense turns into a wall of distance between hearts that were meant to grow closer.

Forgiveness isn't just a nice idea in a godly marriage—it's essential. Jesus calls us to forgive as we've been forgiven (Colossians 3:13), and that's no small thing. Forgiveness doesn't mean forgetting or pretending it didn't hurt—it means choosing to release the offense and offer grace instead of holding it over your spouse's head. When forgiveness is missing, bitterness creeps in. And bitterness, left unchecked, slowly chokes out love, joy, and intimacy. What could have been worked through with humility and prayer becomes a wedge that divides.

A healthy marriage doesn't avoid conflict—it faces it with grace, truth, and the desire for peace. That takes intentional effort, honest conversations, and a deep dependence on God. The ability to say "I forgive you" and mean it, even when it's hard, is one of the strongest signs of a spiritually mature relationship. When you make forgiveness a regular rhythm in your home, you create space for love to flourish, even in the face of failure.

Leaving and Cleaving: Setting Boundaries with Parents

One area of conflict that shows up in some marriages is when a spouse hasn't truly let go of their parents. It can look like constantly seeking their approval, bringing them into every decision, or—even worse—using them as leverage during disagreements. While parents can be a blessing, when they're placed *in* your marriage instead of *outside* it, it creates confusion, tension, and division.

God's design is clear: *"A man leaves his father and mother and is joined to his wife, and the two are united into one."* (Ephesians 5:31 NLT) That doesn't mean you dishonor or cut off your parents—it means your priorities shift. You are still part of your parents' family, but you and your spouse now form a new family unit with a new spiritual covering. Your responsibility is first and foremost to one another and to God.

Sometimes it's not the spouse dragging their parents into the marriage—it's the parents who won't let go, trying to influence, control, or intrude. In either case, the solution is the same: healthy, prayerfully decided boundaries. You and your spouse must protect the emotional and spiritual safety of your home. That may mean limiting certain conversations, deciding what kind of involvement is appropriate, or agreeing on how to respond when pressure or interference arises.

If your relationship with your parents is healthy, they can be an incredible resource—offering wisdom, encouragement, and shared experience. But even then, they must never take the place of the unity and decision-making that belongs to you and your spouse. You can honor their counsel while remembering that you and your spouse are ultimately responsible before God for your life, your relationship, and your family. Healthy boundaries don't reject your parents—they simply protect your marriage.

Self-Centeredness

At the heart of many struggling marriages is a simple but powerful truth: one or both people have stopped serving each other. Marriage isn't meant to revolve around personal happiness or convenience—it's a daily act of love, humility, and sacrifice. When one person begins to focus more on what they're *getting* than what they're *giving*, the relationship becomes lopsided and unhealthy. Over time, selfishness chips away at intimacy, respect, and trust. What once felt like a team effort slowly becomes two individuals pulling in different directions.

Self-centeredness often sneaks in quietly. It may show up as an unwillingness to compromise, constant criticism, always needing to be right, or simply ignoring the needs of the other person. It can also manifest in more passive ways—like checking out emotionally, withholding affection, or refusing to engage in meaningful conversations. No matter how it appears, the root is the same: a heart that's more focused on self than on serving. And when that becomes the norm, it's not long before distance grows and disconnection takes hold.

In many cases, the struggle with selfishness isn't intentional—it's the result of someone not having matured in certain areas of life. Maybe they never learned how to consider others, how to handle conflict in healthy ways, or how to give without expecting something in return. These gaps in maturity, if unaddressed, can be disastrous in marriage. What's left unresolved in singleness doesn't disappear after the wedding—it usually grows louder. That's why it's so important to allow God to grow and stretch you in these areas before and during marriage, and to invite trusted mentors to speak into your blind spots.

The truth is, like I mentioned before, marriage will constantly invite you to die to yourself—not in a way that erases who you are, but in a way that transforms you into someone more like Jesus. When both spouses approach each other with the heart of a servant, something beautiful happens: love deepens, trust builds, and unity flourishes. But it takes daily, intentional choices to put the other person first—not because they deserve it every day, but because God calls you to love like He does. And that kind of love has the power to transform any marriage.

There's Always Room to Grow

No matter where your marriage stands—whether it's strong and thriving or going through a tough season—there's always room to grow. Marriage, like anything meaningful, takes ongoing effort, humility, and a willingness to keep learning. Thankfully, there are many incredible ministries out there that offer support, encouragement, and practical tools to help couples thrive.

One ministry I highly recommend is XO Marriage [1]. Founded by Jimmy and Karen Evans, XO Marriage has helped millions of couples around the world experience hope, healing, and deeper connection. Their own story started with a struggling marriage—one filled with brokenness and difficulty. But through God's grace and their willingness to surrender, they experienced powerful restoration. Out of that journey came a calling to help others, and over the years, their ministry has become a global resource for marriages in every stage.

Whether you're looking for encouragement, teaching, conferences, or real-life wisdom from couples who've walked through the fire and come out stronger, XO Marriage is worth checking out. You can learn more at their website: xomarriage.com. It's a great step toward strengthening your relationship and building a marriage that reflects God's heart.

When You Know It's Time

So, you've been dating with purpose, seeking God together, getting wise counsel, and somewhere along the way... you just know. This is it. God is bringing your lives together, and it's time to take that next step toward marriage. It's an exciting season—filled with deep conversations, joyful anticipation, and yes, a few butterflies in your stomach. So where do you go from here? Let's walk through it—from the "I think this is the one," all the way to "I do."

If you're the guy, start by doing something both bold and respect-ful—talk to her parents. It's not just a nod to tradition; it's a way to honor them and the role they've played in her life. Asking for her father's (or parents') blessing before you propose says, "I don't just love your daughter—I honor your family too." It might feel nerve-wracking, but it's a powerful moment that sets a tone of love and respect from the beginning.

Next, it's time to pick out the ring and plan the proposal. This can be as big or as simple as you'd like. Some plan an elaborate setup with friends hiding nearby to capture it all on camera—maybe at a favorite restaurant or scenic spot. Others opt for something more private and personal, like a quiet walk in the park or a heartfelt moment at home. Whatever fits your relationship best is what's perfect. Just make sure it reflects your heart and gives you both a memory to treasure forever.

Once you've got a yes, the planning officially begins! But before you get caught up in Pinterest boards and seating charts, take a deep breath and set a budget. Seriously. Weddings can get expensive fast, and the last thing you want is to start your marriage in debt. Some of the most beautiful weddings I've seen were simple, affordable, and full of love. Use wisdom, not pressure, to guide your spending. It's far better to invest in your future together than to blow everything on one day.

Take care of the legal stuff, too—like applying for your marriage license. Some states have a waiting period, so don't wait until the last minute. From there, start building your to-do list: pick a date, book your pastor or officiant, and complete premarital counseling (preferably at least a month or two before the wedding). Choose your venue, plan your reception, and think through food, music, and decorations. Don't forget to pick out songs for the pre-ceremony, the walk down the aisle, and the celebration afterward—music sets the mood, so choose what moves your hearts.

One of the most touching moments of any wedding is when the bride walks down the aisle. If her dad is present and able, it's a beautiful tradition for him to walk her down and give her away—it's emotional and sacred and yes, cue the tissues. You can also invite younger family members to be a flower girl or ring bearer to add a little sweetness to the day.

Then comes the heart of the ceremony—the vows. Whether you choose the time-tested traditional words ("for better or worse, for richer or poorer..."), or write your own personal, contemporary vows, just remember: this isn't just about saying something sweet. Your vows are a sacred promise—a covenant. You're not only speaking them to your future spouse—you're speaking them before God. Picture Him standing right there with you, listening as you make this lifelong commitment. That's what a vow is. So choose your words carefully, speak them sincerely, and take them seriously. This moment isn't just romantic—it's holy.

Consider building in a moment of prayer during the ceremony—a time to pray over each other out loud, asking God to bless and protect your new life together. If your parents are present and supportive, you can also invite them to come forward and pray over both of you. It's a beautiful way to begin your marriage surrounded by love, faith, and generational blessing. Many couples also choose a symbolic act—like lighting a unity candle or pouring unity sand—to visually represent two lives becoming one.

And of course... the honeymoon! After all the planning and celebration, it's time to rest and enjoy each other. Plan something fun, relaxing, and within your budget. Whether it's a beach escape, a cozy cabin, or a peaceful staycation, the goal is simple: connect, rest, and celebrate the beautiful beginning of your life as husband and wife. Just don't forget to request time off work and book the essentials ahead of time—nothing like scrambling for plane tickets two days before the wedding!

In the end, your wedding day is one very special day—but your marriage is the adventure of a lifetime. So plan the details with care, but keep your hearts fixed on what truly matters: honoring God, loving each other deeply, and stepping into this covenant with joy, peace, and purpose. With God at the center, the day will be unforgettable—but the marriage will be unshakable.

Don't Just Be Married—Be Madly in Love

Just because you're married doesn't mean the pursuit is over—*keep dating each other!* Never stop planning little adventures, laughing over coffee, and stealing away time to simply be together. It doesn't have to be fancy; it just has to be *intentional.* My wife and I have a fun tradition she absolutely loves: whenever we step onto an elevator—just the two of us—we look at each other and say, "Elevator kiss!" and then I kiss her right there. Every time, her face lights up with excitement and joy, like it's our first kiss all over again. It's those simple, everyday moments that keep the spark alive and remind you both that your love is still fresh and worth celebrating.

Hold hands often. Give long hugs that say, *"I'm still crazy about you."* Speak your love out loud to each other—daily. A text, a whispered "I love you," a note on the fridge—it matters. Little acts of love aren't little at all; they're the glue that keeps hearts close over the years. Keep doing the small things that tell your spouse, *"You're still the one."* Men, open her doors—not just the car door, but every door you can. Show her she's cherished, not just once in a while, but as a way of life. And ladies—honor your husbands. Cheer them on, believe in them, speak words of respect and life into them, and watch how it strengthens their hearts.

God's design for marriage is simple and powerful:

> "So again I say, each man must love his wife as he loves himself, and the wife must respect her husband."
> —Ephesians 5:33 NLT

When love, honor, laughter, and affection are woven into your everyday rhythm, your marriage won't just survive—it'll flourish into something even better than you dreamed.

The Joy of Becoming One

We've walked through some of the tricky stuff—those potential land-mines that can cause stress or even damage in a marriage if you're not paying attention. And it's good to name those things. Being honest and prepared helps build a strong foundation. But don't let the challenges steal the spotlight—because the other side of marriage is filled with laughter, love, purpose, and some of the most meaningful moments of your life.

Marriage, when built on the foundation of God's love, is one of the most beautiful relationships you'll ever experience. It's not just sharing a house with your best friend—it's sharing a life, a calling, and a heart. It's whispered prayers over coffee, holding hands in the waiting room, cracking up over inside jokes, and learning how to dance in the kitchen when no one's watching. It's someone who knows your quirks, your flaws, and your fears—and keeps choosing you anyway. That kind of love? That's where the good stuff lives.

A Christ-centered marriage isn't just about making each other hap-py—it's about walking in purpose together. You're not just building a home; you're building a legacy. Whether you're raising kids or simply in-vesting in the people around you, your marriage can be a living, breathing picture of God's faithfulness. In a world full of temporary, your covenant love stands as a powerful witness to the kind of love that lasts.

And let's be real—you'll both mess up. You'll both have days where you don't bring your A-game. But when grace keeps flowing, when humility and forgiveness fill your home, and when laughter sticks around even after a rough day—that's when marriage becomes more than good. It becomes holy. A real-life picture of how Jesus loves His Church—steadfast, sacrificial, and full of mercy.

So if you're looking at marriage and thinking, "There's still so much I don't know," don't sweat it. That's true for everyone. Marriage isn't about getting it perfect—it's about choosing each other daily, walking with God together, and letting Him shape you both along the way.

Here's to becoming one. To learning, laughing, growing, and loving with everything you've got. And to the wild, wonderful, God-written adventure that begins with "I do."

Children

You're Having a What?!

L et me tell you right now—you will never be totally prepared to have children. No matter how many books you read, classes you attend, or YouTube videos you watch, nothing truly prepares you for the moment you realize you're going to be a parent.

I still remember the exact moment I found out we were expecting our first child, my son Chris. It was like something straight out of a movie—the kind of scene where someone gets such shocking news they almost fall over. Time slowed down. The world got quiet. A surreal wave of joy (and a tiny dose of panic) washed over me.

My mind was racing: *I'm going to be a dad!*
Then, almost immediately: *Wait... how do I be a dad?*

It was equal parts thrill and terror, like being strapped into a roller coaster that you just realized you helped build. I had nine months—T-minus nine and counting—to figure out how to be a dad. And let me tell you, there was a lot I didn't have a clue about.

We dove into the excitement: painting the nursery, attending birth classes, buying tiny onesies, and learning the mysterious art of diaper changing (which, up to this point, I had never successfully attempted—or at least remembered doing). We circled the due date on the calendar in bright red. And sure enough, like a punctual little gentleman, Chris arrived right on schedule.

I was in the delivery room, gowned up and wide-eyed, my heart pounding with anticipation. When he finally arrived, he made his grand entrance with a solid, deep newborn cry that let us all know he was here and ready to be noticed. And then, there he was—my son. I looked into his tiny, beautiful face and saw the innocence, wonder, and the undeniable truth that God had given us a gift.

My best friend Don, who has the superpower of being insanely thoughtful, had waited at the hospital. He came up to me with a huge grin and handed me... a roll of quarters.

Now, for the younger crowd reading this—this was before cell phones were a thing. The hospital had what was known as a pay phone (Google it, you'll be amazed), and each call cost twenty-five cents. I had family and friends to call, and Don, somehow thinking ahead of my scattered, sleep-deprived mind, gave me the means to share the news.

That roll of quarters meant more than he'll ever know. It was a small act of thoughtfulness that spoke volumes in that moment of joy and emotional overwhelm.

A few days later, we packed up our precious newborn and drove home like we were carrying a crown jewel across a battlefield. I was the most careful driver on the road, glaring at anyone who got too close.

And by God's grace, Chris was an amazing sleeper. After the third night, he was snoozing straight through. We had been advised not to keep things silent but to let normal sounds—TV, talking, life—continue. It worked. He slept like... well, like a baby should.

The years ahead? Unbelievable. The joy, the wonder, the surprises—they can't be put into words. Being a dad has been one of the greatest, most humbling, and most rewarding adventures of my life.

That was easy—let's do this again!

Well... 21 months later, our second little blessing arrived. Just enough time to get slightly less terrified, mildly more confident, and fully convinced that this whole parenting thing was the greatest (and most exhausting) adventure in the world.

Now, I should mention—back when our kids were born, they couldn't tell you the gender ahead of time. Nope. There were no fancy 3D ultrasounds or baby reveal parties with pink or blue smoke bombs. You just showed up, waited, and met your child for the first time like opening the best surprise gift of your life. Personally, I think that's how it should be—not knowing just made it all the more exciting.

So the big day came—a little later than the due date, but right on God's schedule. We were about to meet our second child.

Once again, I was gowned up, heart racing, full of anticipation and excitement. We didn't know if we were having a son or daughter, and that only added to the wonder of the moment.

Labor took longer this time—long enough for me to start memorizing the wallpaper pattern—but finally, it was time. And then... silence.

No cry. No sound.

The doctor quickly lifted our baby up and said, "You have a girl!" but her little body was quiet, still, and not breathing. A nurse hit a red button on the wall, and within seconds a NICU doctor came flying in. They put a little rubber bulb over her face and started giving her air—squeezing gently, pump after pump, trying to get her lungs to wake up. They were giving her compressions too, trying to help her exhale.

As a dad, I just stood there, frozen. I was scared—completely helpless, watching my daughter fight to live, and there was absolutely nothing I could do. That's a moment you never forget.

Finally, after what felt like eternity, she let out a loud, beautiful cry—the most musical sound I've ever heard.

They told us the umbilical cord had wrapped around her neck during delivery and had slowed the oxygen to her body. She simply didn't have the strength to breathe when she arrived. But the team worked fast, and thank God, they were able to give her the help she needed to come back strong.

She spent three days in the NICU while they ran tests, monitored oxygen and CO_2 levels, and made sure everything was functioning well.

And in those first few moments, I was learning something new as a dad: our children are God's. We get to love them, care for them, raise them—but ultimately, their lives are in His hands, not ours. And that's a good thing, because He's the best Abba there is.

After a few long days, we finally brought our beautiful little girl home.

That's when I learned another truth: God makes every child so uniquely.

"You made all the delicate, inner parts of my body and knit me together in my mother's womb. Thank you for making me so wonderfully complex! Your workmanship is marvelous—how well I know it."

—Psalm 139:13–14 NLT

It took nearly nine more months before I got my first full night of sleep again. I was a struggling to stay awake at times. Being a dad of two was stretching me in ways I never expected, but oh the joy! It was beyond words!

Now I had a son and a daughter—and I was completely smitten by both. My heart was fuller, my coffee stronger, and my sleep schedule permanently altered.

And I wouldn't trade it for the world.

Parenting on Purpose – Building The Foundation

Just like every other part of life, raising kids comes with some basics—things to learn, practice, and grow into over time. You don't have to know it all up front (no one does), but it helps to be intentional.

Think of these early years like laying a foundation. It doesn't have to be fancy—it just needs to be solid. And the secret ingredient? Consistency.

It's the day-after-day faithfulness that makes the biggest impact. Not the big moments, but the little ones. When you're consistent in your love, your values, and your walk with God—even when life is hard—your kids will notice.

They'll see you at your best, and they'll see you in your most challenging times. And when they do, they'll learn that faith isn't just something you talk about—it's something you live.

As your faith grows, so will theirs. They'll gain courage and confidence by watching you trust God, rely on Him, and see Him come through—again and again. That kind of example sticks with them long after they leave home.

And when they do? That's when you hand them their own copy of this book. (*Shameless book plug—because they'll need it, and you'll want them to have it.*)

> "Direct your children onto the right path, and when they are older, they will not leave it."
>
> —Proverbs 22:6 NLT

So let's talk about some of those foundational areas—practical, spiritual, emotional—and how to build them well, one day at a time.

Spiritual Foundations

When it comes to raising kids, this is the deepest foundation you can lay—helping them know that they are fully loved by God and that they can know Him personally. And it starts simply. Pray with them. Sing with them. Talk about God like He's right there with you—because He is. You don't need a degree in theology to show your kids what it looks like to walk with Jesus. You just need a real relationship with Him yourself.

Make space for spiritual moments in everyday life—bedtime prayers, thank-you Jesus moments at the dinner table, pointing out how God helped you through a tough day. These simple rhythms teach more than any formal lesson ever could. Kids learn by watching, and the more naturally you live out your faith, the more naturally they'll absorb it.

And remember, you don't have to be perfect. You just have to be real. When they see you trust God, especially when things aren't easy, they'll start to understand what faith really looks like. Over time, as they grow, their understanding will grow too—and one day, they'll take those seeds of faith and start walking out their own journey with God.

Even in the Bible, God modeled how to teach children His heart. He didn't give Israel one big info dump and call it a day. Instead, He built teaching into the rhythm of their year—through stories, songs, and celebrations. The feasts like Passover weren't just about tradition; they were vivid, hands-on reminders of who God is, what He had done, and what He wanted His people—including the children—to never forget.

Why? Because He's a good Father. The very best Abba. He knew repetition, rhythm, and relationship would shape hearts over time. It was never about checking religious boxes—it was about protecting His kids and keeping them close to His heart. And that's our job, too. To pass on the goodness of God in a way our children can understand, remember, and carry with them for life.

Emotional Foundations

Helping your child grow emotionally doesn't mean shielding them from every hard feeling—it means giving them tools to understand what they're feeling and how to handle it. And it starts with simple things like naming emotions: "You seem sad," or "It looks like you're frustrated." These moments might feel small, but they help your child realize that emotions aren't something to hide or fear—they're part of being human.

One of the best ways to build emotional health is by being a safe space yourself. When your child has a meltdown (and they will), try not to shut it down too quickly. Instead, offer calm, connection, and comfort. Your steady presence teaches them that emotions don't have to be overwhelming or scary. Over time, they'll learn to work through feelings rather than being ruled by them.

And here's something important: each child is unique. You'll notice it early on—how God has wired them differently in every part of life. One might be quiet and thoughtful, the other full of energy and words. One might love routine and early bedtimes, while another seems to come alive at midnight. Some kids want to talk through everything; others need time and space before they open up. These differences aren't mistakes—they're part of God's intentional design.

That means the way you walk with each child emotionally may look different. You'll need to tune in, adjust, and learn alongside them. But at the same time, there are foundational things—like helping them feel seen, safe, and loved—that every child needs. You might teach them in different ways, but the core truths stay the same.

Modeling is powerful here. If you're upset, take a breath and talk through it in a way they can see: "I'm feeling a little stressed right now, so I'm going to take a moment and pray." Or, "I overreacted just now—I'm sorry." When you show them how to deal with emotions in a healthy way, you're not only helping them in the moment—you're giving them tools for the rest of their lives.

Most of all, remind them often that they are loved, no matter what they're feeling. God does that for us—we can cry, yell, get overwhelmed, and He still holds us close. When your child knows they're safe with you in their hardest moments, they'll begin to believe that they're safe with God too.

Physical Foundations

Raising kids means tending to their physical world just as much as their spiritual and emotional one. That starts with the basics—food, sleep, play, and safety. These everyday things might seem simple, but they matter deeply. A consistent rhythm helps children feel secure. Mealtimes, bath times, naps, and bedtime routines create a sense of peace and predictability in a world that's brand new to them.

Physical touch is another huge part of this foundation. Hugs, snuggles, hand-holding, rocking them to sleep—it's not just comforting, it's wiring their brains to feel loved, safe, and connected. Don't underestimate the power of being present in the physical moments, even the messy ones. Diapers, midnight wakeups, sticky fingers—these are sacred spaces where trust is built.

And just like everything else, each child is different. One might sleep like clockwork. Another might resist bedtime like it's a battle every night. Some kids need tons of physical activity to stay regulated, while others are content to curl up with a book or toy. Learning what helps your child feel their best physically takes time, patience, and a little creativity. But even with those differences, the foundation stays the same: teach them that their bodies are valuable, made by God, and worth caring for.

You're not just raising a child who eats vegetables and gets enough rest (though that's a win!). You're helping them learn what it means to be a whole, healthy human being. And one day, they'll carry these habits into their own adult lives, remembering how you showed them what it looks like to care for themselves with love.

Provision Foundations

One of the quiet but powerful parts of parenting is providing for your child's needs. It's more than just putting food on the table or clothes in the drawer—it's creating an environment where your child knows they are safe, cared for, and covered. Provision is an expression of love, and it builds deep security in a child's heart.

From the very beginning, your child is learning to trust that you'll be there—that there will be milk when they're hungry, a blanket when they're cold, and a hand to hold when they're unsure. Over time, this becomes part of how they learn to trust that God is also a provider. The way you meet their everyday needs can shape how they see His heart.

And again—every child is different. One child might thrive with a simple wardrobe and a few favorite toys. Another might be more sensitive to textures, food variety, or change in routine. You'll learn as you go what each one needs—not just materially, but also in the way they feel provided for emotionally and practically. But the core is the same: provision rooted in love, not pressure.

As they grow, invite them into conversations about gratitude, generosity, and contentment. Show them how you budget, save, and pray about decisions. Model living within your means and trusting God when things are tight. These everyday choices will help them understand that provision isn't just about what you have—it's about who you're trusting.

And here's the gift: when you live with open hands before God, your kids will see that. They'll learn that provision ultimately comes from Him—and that He's always faithful.

Educational Foundations

Learning doesn't just happen in school—it starts way before that and continues every day in the little things. Kids are naturally curious, and as a parent, you get the front-row seat to their wonder. From the moment they start asking, "Why?" (a thousand times a day!), you're shaping how they see the world and how they approach learning.

The key here is to create an environment where learning feels fun, doable, and part of everyday life. Read books together. Answer their questions, even when they come out of nowhere. Let them explore, experiment, and make mistakes. Some kids will be hands-on learners. Others will process quietly. One might want to take everything apart to see how it works, while another might prefer to draw, build, or imagine. It won't look the same for each child—but the goal is the same: helping them love learning.

Education is also a chance to teach values like responsibility, curiosity, and persistence. Whether it's learning how to tie shoes, write their name, or handle a tough homework assignment, your steady encouragement tells them: "You can do this." And when they see you learning too—reading, trying new things, asking for help—they'll learn that education isn't just for kids. It's a lifelong journey.

Most of all, let them know that their minds are a gift from God. Remind them often that they are smart, capable, and full of potential—not just because of what they know, but because of how God made them.

Character Foundations

Character is about who your child is becoming on the inside. It's the stuff that holds up when no one's watching—things like honesty, kindness, humility, and integrity. And the best way for your child to learn character? By watching you live it. The way you treat others, the way you speak, how you respond under pressure—all of it is shaping their view of what's normal, and what's right.

The beauty (and challenge) of character-building is that it happens in the everyday stuff. When your child tells a half-truth and you gently correct it. When they share their toy without being asked, and you notice. When you mess up and say, "I was wrong. Will you forgive me?"—you're modeling humility and honesty, and they're taking it in.

And just like every other part of parenting, each child will need something a little different here. One child might struggle with self-control. Another might need help learning to speak up. You'll find yourself repeating things a hundred times (okay, maybe more)—but it's in that patient repetition, that steady presence, that real growth happens. What's important is that your home is a place where values are not just taught, but lived out.

The goal isn't to raise a "perfectly behaved kid." The goal is to raise someone who knows what's right, desires to do good, and is willing to grow. Someone who learns to care about others, own their mistakes, and keep choosing what's right even when it's hard.

And through it all, remind them that God is growing their heart just like you're growing their body and mind. He's not asking for perfection—He's shaping character over time, just like He's doing in you.

Right and Wrong / Values Foundations

Teaching right from wrong isn't just about making rules—it's about shaping values that will guide your child long after they leave your home. Kids need clear, consistent boundaries, yes—but more than that, they need to understand why those boundaries matter. You're not just correcting behavior—you're forming a heart that knows how to choose what's good, even when it's hard.

This part of parenting takes time, repetition, and a whole lot of grace. You'll be saying the same things over and over: "Tell the truth." "Be kind." "Think about how that made someone else feel." It might feel like it's not sinking in, but trust me—it is. And when you live those values out in your own life, it speaks even louder. Your child will learn more from what you do than what you say.

Every child will respond differently here, too. Some are naturally tenderhearted and want to do the right thing. Others might challenge the rules just to make sure they still matter tomorrow. That's okay. The goal isn't blind obedience—it's heart transformation. Teach them that actions have consequences, but also that God is full of grace and second chances.

And in the middle of all that teaching, don't forget to share God's heart. The values we hold—truth, justice, compassion, forgiveness—aren't random. They reflect who God is. And as your children see those values at work in your family, they'll begin to understand that choosing what's right isn't just about "being good"—it's about becoming more like Jesus.

Let God Lead, Not the Culture

Don't let culture and society be the ones to teach you how to raise your children. Trends shift, opinions change, and what's popular isn't always what's right. Go to the Word of God. Let Scripture shape your parenting, not Instagram posts or loud voices online. God's Word is steady, wise, and full of truth for every season of parenting.

Look for parents who are doing it well—who love their kids deeply, raise them with purpose, and walk closely with God. Ask questions. Learn from them. And yes, also pay attention to what not to do. If you see patterns in parenting that seem to lead to chaos, distance, or pain, ask God to help you see the difference.

His Bible is a love letter to us, and in it we find everything we need to raise our children with wisdom and grace. At the end of the day, we're not just parenting for our kids—we're parenting before God. These children are His first, and we are stewards of the precious lives He's placed in our hands.

Life Lessons in the Check Out Line

I remember a time when my daughter Heather was probably around five years old. We had gone to the mall together to pick something up from a department store. While we waited in the checkout line, we found ourselves surrounded by the classic marketing trap: those little tables full of "impulse buys" they set near the registers—just close enough to grab while you wait.

Heather spotted something on one of those tables that instantly caught her eye. She picked it up, turned to me with that bright, beautiful smile of hers, and said, "Dad, can we get this?" Most of the time, if it was something she needed—or even something small—I wouldn't think twice. But that day, I decided it wasn't something we needed, and I told her no.

She asked again. And again. But I stuck with it. "Sorry, sweetheart, we're not getting that today."

She wasn't angry—just deeply disappointed. And in that honest little way kids do, she plopped right down on the floor, crossed her arms and legs, and made the saddest face she could manage.

And without missing a beat... I did the exact same thing.

I dropped to the floor, sat cross-legged with my arms folded and my bottom lip stuck way out, mimicking her expression with the most dramatic sad face I could muster. I looked her right in the eyes and didn't say a word.

She immediately snapped out of it. "Dad! Stop! You're embarrassing me!"

We both laughed, stood up, and went on with our day. But that moment has stayed with me for a lifetime. I can still see her precious little face, working through the real emotions of life—from her point of view, in her small but sincere world.

I've truly loved being a dad. Through every high and low, the serious and the silly, parenting has been one of the greatest gifts God has ever given me. And now, with grandchildren in my life too, I feel even more blessed. What an incredible joy to experience the love of God through our children—and then to watch that love multiply into the next generation.

There were so many times in my life while raising my children when I would stop and talk with God and say, "Okay, Father... now I know how You must feel when I do the same things my children do." It was like I got a glimpse into His perspective—the way He truly loves me, gently, patiently, and completely. And I began to understand that the way I love my children is one of the ways God helps me see how deeply He loves me.

Lessons from the Journey: Parenting from the Heart

My mom once told me something that stuck with me for life. She said, "Children, when they're young, step on your toes. But when they're older, they step on your heart."

At first, I thought about the ways I might've stepped on her heart—unintentionally, of course. I would've never wanted to hurt her. But now that I've raised my own children, I understand exactly what she meant. There are moments that sting—things our kids say or do that hit deeper than they realize. But like God's love for us, those moments don't push love away. In fact, they make us love even more. Our hearts grow with this deep desire for them to be free, whole, and walking closely with the Lord.

Don't Spoil Them—Teach Them to Value Things

One of the biggest parenting lessons. Don't spoil your kids. And no, that's not just about money. Spoiling is really an attitude and a heart thing—when a child starts to feel entitled and stops appreciating what they've been given.

Whether you're raising your kids on a tight budget or with plenty of resources, the goal is the same: teach them gratitude, not entitlement. Let them see what it takes to earn something. If they want something, let them save for it or work for it. Help them see the connection between time, effort, and reward. That's how they begin to understand value—of things, of people, and of God's blessings.

Be Watchful of Who They Spend Time With

Another big one? Keep an eye on their friends. As your kids start spending time outside of the house—school, neighborhood, church—pay attention. Ask questions. Trust your gut.

Sometimes kids won't see what you see. But if something feels off, or a certain friend seems to bring out behaviors that don't line up with what you've taught them, speak up. When they're young, it's easier to set those boundaries. As they get older, it's more of a conversation—but your input still matters.

"Bad company corrupts good character."

—1 Corinthians 15:33 NLT

Choices Have Consequences

This is one of those parenting basics that matters at every age: choices have consequences. When my kids were little, I tried to be consistent. I'd explain the expectation, make sure they understood, and if they chose to disobey, there was a consequence. Not harsh or angry—just consistent and loving.

And after the consequence, I'd always sit with them, talk it through, remind them that I loved them, and help them understand why it mattered. It wasn't about punishment—it was about learning. Those moments became some of the most meaningful ones in our relationship.

Teach Obedience as Protection

When my kids were preschool age, I'd teach them to obey instantly—not because I wanted control, but because I wanted them to be safe. I'd give the example to them: if we're getting out of the car and they dart behind it into the parking lot, I need them to stop the moment I say, "STOP!" No debate. No delay. Just stop.

Sometimes I'd even take their hand, walk them to the back of the car, and practice looking both ways. I wanted them to understand that my rules weren't about being mean—they were about keeping them safe. And isn't that so much like God? He tells us to stop or wait or go another way—not because He's trying to ruin our fun, but because He's protecting us from something we can't see.

Respect Matters

Teach your kids to respect people—especially their elders. This one seems to be fading in some parts of our culture, but it's still close to God's heart.

"Honor your father and mother."

—Exodus 20:12 NLT

Show them what honor looks like in real life. Speak kindly. Listen well. Give others the benefit of the doubt. When your kids see that lived out, they'll start to do the same.

A Glimpse Into God's Heart

There were so many moments when I found myself saying, "Okay, God... now I get it. Now I see how You must feel when I do that." Parenting gave me a small glimpse into God's heart for me. His patience. His grace. His deep, unwavering love—even when we mess up. Even when we don't get it. And it reminded me that I wasn't parenting alone—He was walking with me every step of the way.

Different Seasons, Different Strategies

As your kids grow, parenting shifts. The toddler years are different from the teen years—and both are different from when they leave the house. With each new season, you'll need to adjust your approach.

There comes a time to let the rope out a little. Give them room to make choices. Trust them to live out the values you've taught. And yes, sometimes they'll fall. But when they do, you'll be there to help them up—not to shame them, but to remind them who they are and where their strength comes from. These are the moments when your faith in them helps build their faith in God.

Wrapping It All Up

This chapter isn't a complete checklist or a how-to manual—just a handful of foundational things to build on. There's so much more you'll learn along the way, and so much of it will come through experience, prayer, and trusting God day by day. The truth is, the only one who can really teach you how to raise your child is the One who created them. Stay close to Him. Pray and ask. Seek and find. Knock—and He will open the door.

You won't be a perfect parent. I sure wasn't and I don't think those exist. You'll make mistakes (probably more than you'd like), but if everything is rooted in love, and you keep coming back to God for direction, you're going to do great. He gave you this child on purpose, and He's walking with you every step of the way.

And then, one day, your kids will grow up and leave home. You'll always be Mom or Dad, but your role will shift. You've poured out your heart, planted seeds, taught and modeled and prayed—and now they'll take what you've given them and walk it out themselves. The good stuff, the not-so-good stuff—it all travels with them. But more importantly, so does God. He's been with them from the very beginning, and He'll keep guiding them just like He did with you.

My parents had a simple prayer for us growing up: that we would know God, love God, and serve God all the days of our lives. I've prayed that over my children, too. I've also prayed for their future spouse and even their future children—long before their spouse or children ever stepped into their lives. Because parenting isn't just about the now—It's generational.

And when your kids move out, you don't stop being a parent—you just become more of an advisor. They'll still come to you for thoughts, stories, recipes, and wisdom (sometimes). But ultimately, they'll make their own decisions. And that's okay. You'll find peace knowing they're on their own journey, and the same God who met you in yours will meet them in theirs.

If God blesses you with grandkids—what a gift. As someone once joked on an old bumper sticker from the '80s:

"If I knew grandkids were this much fun, I would've had them first!"

So take joy in this journey. Keep loving, keep praying, and keep cheering them on. You've done your part—and after all the best Abba has had them from the beginning.

TACOS, APARTMENT
& HOME OWNERSHIP

Pot Roast to Tacos
Learning Through Meals

G rowing up, dinner was almost sacred in our home. My mom had dinner ready around 5 p.m. each day, and we almost always sat together as a family. Sundays were especially memorable. She'd make pot roast in a pressure cooker—one of those special pots that locks in steam and cooks food fast and full of flavor. She'd set it on the stove before church, and by the time we came home, the aroma alone was enough to draw us straight to the table.

Later, as I raised my own children, we tried to create those same kinds of mealtime rhythms. One of our favorite things was grilling out. I loved to fire up the grill and we'd often do chicken two or three nights a week. Mealtime wasn't just about eating—it was about being together.

As the kids got older and started learning to cook, there were plenty of trial-and-error moments—some of them hilarious. One night, my daughter Heather decided she was going to make tacos for dinner. She was so excited and proud, setting everything out on the table just right: taco shells, seasoned meat, fresh veggies.

But when I went to fill a taco shell, I noticed something... off. The meat was soupy—liquid ran off the spoon like a taco soup. We asked

Heather how she prepared the meat, and she confidently explained that she followed the instructions on the taco seasoning packet exactly.

That's when we hit the moment of discovery.

She said, "It said to add 3 or 4 cups of water... so I added 4 as I thought it would be better than just 3."

We checked the packet. It actually said ¾ cup.

Cue the family laughter.

We strained the meat with a slotted spoon, made our tacos, and honestly? They were delicious. But the memory? Even better.

Today, Heather is an *incredible* cook—she's healthy, organized, and creative. She's a master meal planner, an avid cyclist, and one of the most disciplined eaters I know. That taco moment was just one step in a journey of learning, laughing, and growing up—one meal at a time.

So imagine yourself in your own place and that first evening is such a mix of freedom, excitement, and "wait... what now?"

Here's how I imagine it going: It's your first night. The boxes are mostly still unpacked. The kitchen feels unfamiliar—like I'm borrowing someone else's space. But it's mine. Quiet. A little echoey. And the fridge hums like it's glad I'm here. I'm getting hungry and mom isn't here, so what do I do?

Option 1: *Order In*

The temptation is real. I'm tired, maybe a little emotionally spent from the move. Ordering in sounds easy. A slice of comfort in a cardboard box. But deep down... it also feels like a missed opportunity.

Option 2: *Go Out*

There's that new pizza place around the corner. Could be a nice way to explore the neighborhood. But something about going out alone feels more "someday" than "today."

Option 3: *Cook Something*

I look around. I've got eggs. Bread. Maybe a little butter and some salt. I could make toast and scrambled eggs. Not fancy—but warm, satisfying, and homemade. There's something grounding about cooking, even something simple. It's like saying, "I live here now. I belong here."

So I decide to cook. I turn on some music, open the window, and crack the eggs into the pan. The smell fills the space. I sit at my little table—or maybe a moving box—and eat my first real meal here. Simple. Imperfect. But deeply mine.

That first meal isn't really about the food. It's about *presence*. It's about taking that first tiny step toward being on your own. And maybe, just maybe, it's the beginning of learning that cooking—even just a little—is a powerful way of caring for yourself.

Let's Talk Food: The Everyday Essential

You may already know how to cook—or maybe not. Maybe you're scared to try because that one time you did, something burned... or boiled over... or ended up tasting like cardboard. Maybe you've been living off cereal, frozen waffles, and takeout menus.

No shame here. Seriously. Everyone starts somewhere. But no matter where you're at, we're going to talk through some practical, real-life topics that will give you the wisdom, confidence, and rhythm to master and improve this part of your life—because eating is something you'll do every single day.

Let's make it fun. Let's keep it real. You *can* learn to feed yourself well. You *can* cook food that's simple, satisfying, and even kind of awesome.

Getting Started: Making a Food Plan from Scratch

So imagine yourself standing in your new kitchen. You want to "do this food thing" the right way—but you're not sure where to begin.

Here's the secret: start simple. This is something you'll get better at over time. What feels clumsy at first will eventually become second nature. But to grow into it, you need to start. And one of the best ways to start is by making a plan.

Let's say your pantry is empty. Your refrigerator is too. You're basically at square one. Here's what to do:

Step 1: Write Down What You Like to Eat

Grab a piece of paper or open a blank document on your computer. List meals and foods you enjoy—breakfast, lunch, dinner, snacks, desserts—whatever comes to mind. Don't worry if you don't know how to make them yet or what ingredients they require. This step is about *vision*, not perfection.

Step 2: Do Some Recipe Research

Let's side-step for a second—because this part can be fun.

One thing my wife Sherri and I love to do is look up recipes online. There are *so many* good options out there—blogs, cooking sites, videos, you name it.

We use an app called Paprika, and it's been a total game-changer for our kitchen flow. (There are other great apps too—feel free to explore—but I'll use Paprika as an example here.)

Step 3: Use a Tool Like Paprika to Organize

Here's what's awesome about Paprika:

- You can browse for recipes online, and when you find one you like, just tap *Download*—it saves automatically into the app.

- You can categorize recipes into your own folders (like breakfast, chicken dishes, quick meals, etc.).

- It shows you prep time, cook time, and difficulty level.

- It saves both the ingredients and the instructions in one place.

- You can adjust serving sizes, and the ingredient list will update automatically.

- And here's the best part: you can create a grocery list straight from the recipe and check items off your phone while shopping.

Sounds easy, right? That's because it is. Technology can help take the pressure off and let you focus on learning and enjoying the process.

Basic Pantry, Refrigerator and Freezer Starter List

Here's a starter list to kick off your kitchen adventure! Think of it as your "new place, new pantry" starter pack—just enough to get you cooking without feeling overwhelmed. These basics will give you a solid food foundation to build on as you find your rhythm and get your *chef legs* under you. Feel free to adjust to your liking.

Pantry Essentials

☐ Rice

☐ Pasta

☐ Rolled oats

☐ All-purpose flour

☐ Sugar (white or brown)

☐ Canned beans (black, kidney, chickpeas)

☐ Canned tomatoes (diced, crushed, or sauce)

☐ Canned tuna or chicken

☐ Peanut butter

☐ Pasta sauce

☐ Cooking oil (olive or vegetable)

☐ Salt

☐ Black pepper

☐ Baking powder

☐ Baking soda

☐ Garlic powder

☐ Onion powder

☐ Chili powder

☐ Italian seasoning

☐ Cinnamon

☐ Bread (store in freezer if not used quickly)

☐ Tortillas

☐ Instant or dry potatoes

☐ Chicken or vegetable broth (carton or bouillon)

Fridge Essentials

☐ Eggs

☐ Milk or plant-based milk

☐ Cheese (shredded or block)

☐ Butter or margarine

☐ Yogurt

☐ Fresh vegetables (carrots, lettuce, etc.)

☐ Fresh fruit (apples, oranges, berries)

☐ Condiments (ketchup, mustard, mayo)

☐ Salad dressing

☐ Deli meat or sandwich fillings

Freezer Essentials

☐ Frozen vegetables (mixed, broccoli, etc.)

☐ Frozen fruit (for smoothies/snacks)

☐ Meat (chicken, ground beef, etc.)

☐ Bread (freezes well if not used quickly)

☐ Leftovers or batch-cooked meals

☐ Frozen pizza or easy meals

☐ Ice packs or ice cube trays

☐ Waffles, pancakes, or frozen breakfast

☐ Tortillas (freeze well!)

☐ Extra cheese or shredded items

Here's a short list of basic kitchen tools you might want to have on hand when setting up your kitchen for the first time. These essentials will help you handle everyday cooking with ease and confidence.

Starter Kitchen Tools

☐ Chef's knife

☐ Cutting board

☐ Saucepan

☐ Frying pan / skillet

☐ Spatula

☐ Mixing bowl

☐ Measuring cups

☐ Measuring spoons

☐ Can opener

☐ Baking sheet

Here's a simple list of items you'll need to eat your meals, including basic dishes and silverware. If you're on a tight budget, consider using paper plates, plastic utensils, and cups as a temporary solution.

You can also buy individual forks, knives, spoons, plates, and cups at affordable prices from stores like Walmart or dollar stores to build your collection gradually.

Plates, Cups & Silverware

☐ Dinner plates

☐ Salad or side plates

☐ Bowls (for cereal, soup, etc.)

☐ Drinking glasses

☐ Coffee mugs

☐ Forks

☐ Knives

☐ Spoons

☐ Teaspoons

☐ Serving utensils (like a large spoon or tongs)

Meal Planning Without Stress

Meal planning simply means thinking ahead. Start by picking 3–4 dinners for the week, plan to eat leftovers, and stay flexible. Use what you already have, and don't overthink it. Tip: try theme nights like Taco Tuesday or Pasta Friday to keep it fun and easy.

Getting Started with Meal Planning

A great way to meal plan is by using online resources or apps like Paprika, which I mentioned earlier. You can also find free weekly menus and planning templates with a quick online search.

But don't overcomplicate it—start simple. All you need is a piece of paper. Write down the days of the week, and next to each day, jot down what you'd like to eat. Focus on planning dinner only at first—breakfast and lunch are often easier to keep simple with things like cereal, eggs, sandwiches, or leftovers.

Once your dinner plan is set:

1. List the ingredients needed for each meal.

2. Look up recipes if you're not sure how to make something.

3. Check your kitchen and cross off anything you already have.

Now for the shameless plug: apps like Paprika can do all this for you—save recipes, generate shopping lists, and simplify the whole process.

Once your list is ready and it's confirmed that you have money in your grocery budget, head to the store, grab your items, and bring them home to stock your kitchen. Just like that—you're on your way!

Shopping Smart & Keeping It Fun

As you grow in meal planning and grocery shopping, you'll naturally get better at stretching your dollars and making smarter choices. You'll learn where to shop for certain items, what to buy in bulk, and how to spot deals that actually save you money.

For example, in our family, we regularly shop at three stores. I'm not promoting any store here—this is just what works for us.

- Sam's Club or Costco: Great for buying staple items in bulk. Yes, the price tag is higher up front, but the cost per unit is often much cheaper in the long run.

- Walmart and Aldi: We shop here for most of our weekly groceries. Each store has its strengths, and over time you'll figure out what's best to buy where.

Tips for Smart Shopping:

- Compare prices between stores—often you can check online before you go.

- Look for specials, in-store coupons, or mailers.

- Stick to your grocery budget, but leave space to treat yourself. Maybe that's a special dessert, your favorite coffee creamer, or a fun ingredient to try something new.

Keep Creativity in the Mix

Meal planning can fall into a rut if you're not careful. When it starts to feel stale:

- Browse online for fresh recipe ideas.

- Ask friends what meals they love and try something new.

- Don't be afraid to experiment—even a simple twist on a classic can be fun!

Make It About Community

One of the best ways to keep cooking and eating joyful is to share it.

- Invite a friend over.

- Cook with a roommate.

- Fire up the grill if you've got one.

Meals were never meant to be stressful—they're meant to be shared, enjoyed, and remembered.

In Acts 2, we see a beautiful picture of the early church—they met together daily, shared meals, and encouraged one another in their faith and everyday life. Breaking bread wasn't just about eating; it was about *belonging, fellowship,* and *living life together* in the presence of God.

And think about Jesus—He so often met with people over meals. Whether it was feeding the 5,000, eating at Zacchaeus's house, or reclining at the table with His disciples, He used those shared moments to teach, to connect, to heal, and to love.

Can you imagine what it would've been like to sit at one of those tables? To hear Him speak firsthand—over roasted fish or fresh bread? The laughter, the questions, the stories, the quiet moments... I would've loved to be there.

Meals can still be sacred moments today—opportunities to pause, to be present, to listen well, and to encourage one another in the journey of faith and life.

So keep it real. Keep it simple. Keep it joyful.

Clean Up Counts

Last but definitely not least—learn to clean up behind yourself as you cook. It's one of those habits that's *really* easy to skip, especially when you're tired or in a rush. But trust me: over time, you'll thank yourself (and maybe even thank me too!).

A clean kitchen makes the next meal so much easier, and it helps keep your space peaceful and functional.

Here's the key:

- Clean as you go — Wipe counters, put things back, and rinse tools while your food is cooking. It'll save you from feeling overwhelmed later.

- Do dishes after the meal — Even if it's just a few plates and a pan, get it done before the food hardens and the motivation disappears.

- Reset your kitchen — Put everything back in its place. That way, the next time you cook, you're starting fresh.

Doing the dishes is part of being responsible—it's not always fun, but it doesn't have to be miserable. Turn on music, set a timer, or treat it like a wind-down ritual. You'll feel more in control and way more motivated to cook again when your kitchen's ready to go.

Final Wisdom for Stewarding Food

Let's wrap this up with a few tried-and-true nuggets of food wisdom—stuff you'll learn and sharpen over time as you grow in responsibility, resourcefulness, and faithfulness.

- Make a list before you shop. Wandering into the store without a plan is like going on a treasure hunt with no map. Suddenly, you've got snacks galore and nothing for dinner. A list keeps you focused, saves money, and helps avoid those "how did this get in my cart?" moments.

- Plan your meals first. It doesn't have to be complicated—just jot down a few dinners for the week. This makes grocery shopping a breeze and helps cut down on waste. Start with dinners, and once you get the hang of it, expand to breakfasts and lunches too.

- Buy in bulk—when it makes sense. Staples like rice, oats, pasta, and frozen veggies are great to grab in larger quantities. Just be cautious with fresh stuff. Ten pounds of bananas may seem like a good idea... until they all turn brown on the same day.

- Learn to compare unit prices. Don't let the big price tag scare you—check the cost per ounce or pound. That's where the real savings live. It's a sneaky-smart way to shop like a pro.

- Don't be afraid of store brands. They're usually just as tasty as name brands (sometimes identical!) and way easier on your wallet. Your spaghetti sauce doesn't need a designer label.

- Batch cook like a boss. Make a big pot of chili or soup and freeze some for later. It's like creating your own personal stash of home-cooked frozen meals. You'll thank yourself on those busy nights.

- Leftovers = treasure. Seriously. Plan to eat them for lunch, or transform them into something new. Don't let good food go to waste. Your fridge is basically a storage locker of delicious potential.

- Limit the eating out and delivery. It's convenient, yes, but the cost adds up fast. I once watched delivery drivers pick up cup after cup of coffee while sitting in a coffee shop. That $6 drink turned into a $15–$20 expense after fees, tips, and time. Make your own coffee—it's cozy, satisfying, and wildly cheaper.

- Set a food budget that works. $50–$75 a week per person is a decent starting point, but adjust based on your area and needs. Track your spending with cash envelopes or an app like YNAB. You'll feel more in control and less surprised when the bank app dings.

- Plan for fun food too! You don't have to cut out coffee shops or snacks entirely. Just budget for them. That way, you can enjoy your treats guilt-free instead of pretending they don't exist (we all know they do).

- Balance your plate. Try to include some protein, a veggie or two, carbs, and a bit of healthy fat. It doesn't have to be perfect—it just has to fuel you well.

- Watch out for sneaky sugars and processed foods. They're easy, yes, but too much can leave you feeling sluggish. Keep 'em in check and save room for the good stuff.

- Drink water. Lots of it. It's the cheapest, healthiest thing you can put in your body. Don't let sugary drinks steal your energy (or your grocery budget).

- Never put groceries on a credit card. If you're short on funds, ask for help. Call a friend. Talk to family. Most churches have food pantries that would love to help you bridge the gap. Needing help isn't failure—it's being human. And remember, giving and receiving are both part of walking with Jesus.

Food is a daily need and a daily opportunity to grow. Be wise, be creative, and keep it fun. You're learning how to steward your meals, your money, and your time—and that's a big deal.

Bon appétit! You've got this!

Creating A 5 Day Menu

Here's an example of a simple 5-day dinner menu for one person on a $50 budget, using affordable ingredients from Aldi, Walmart or similar stores.

Example of a Simple 5-Day Menu

1. **Monday: Spaghetti with Marinara Sauce**
   Ingredients: Spaghetti noodles, marinara sauce, side salad (lettuce, tomato, cucumber)

2. **Tuesday: Chicken Stir-Fry**
   Ingredients: Chicken breast, mixed vegetables (fresh or frozen), soy sauce, served over rice

3. **Wednesday: Black Bean Quesadillas**
   Ingredients: Flour tortillas, canned black beans, shredded cheese, salsa

4. **Thursday: Baked Pork Chops with Roasted Vegetables**
   Ingredients: Pork chops, assorted vegetables (e.g., carrots, potatoes, broccoli), olive oil, seasonings

5. **Friday: Tuna Salad Sandwiches with Soup**

   Ingredients: Canned tuna, mayonnaise, bread, choice of soup
   (e.g., tomato or vegetable)

Shopping List

Proteins:

Chicken breast (1 lb)

Pork chops (2 pieces)

Canned tuna (2 cans)

Canned black beans (1 can)

Grains:

Spaghetti noodles (1 package)

Rice (1 lb bag)

Flour tortillas (1 package)

Bread (1 loaf)

Dairy:

Shredded cheese (8 oz)

Optional: Sour cream or guacamole

Vegetables:

Mixed vegetables for stir-fry (1 bag, fresh or frozen)

Assorted vegetables for roasting (e.g., carrots, potatoes, broccoli)

Lettuce (1 head or bag)

Tomato (1–2)

Cucumber (1)

Pantry Items:

Marinara sauce (1 jar)

Soy sauce (small bottle)

Mayonnaise (small jar)

Soup (canned or boxed, 2 servings)

Olive oil or cooking oil

Seasonings (salt, pepper, preferred spices)

As mentioned in the recipe planning chapter, you'll base your meals and ingredients on the recipes you choose for each night's dinner.

The grocery list for the five-day dinner menu is organized by food type—proteins, grains, dairy, vegetables, pantry items, etc.—so that when you're in a specific section of the store, you can grab everything you need from that area all at once. No more getting all the way to the other side of the store and realizing you have to double back just for a carton of milk! This setup makes your shopping trip faster, easier, and way less frustrating.

Grocery Store Secrets: They Didn't Teach You in School

If you're new to meal planning and grocery shopping, I recommend starting with a simple menu like the one above. As you get more comfortable, you can expand and enjoy the creative freedom that comes with planning meals. Just remember to stay within your food budget—this is an area where it's easy to overspend. Planning your meals and making a shopping list before heading to the store puts you way ahead of the game.

One important tip: never plan meals or grocery shop while hungry. You'll be tempted to buy whatever looks good in the moment, which usually isn't the best decision. But every now and then, if you have a little extra room in your budget, go ahead and treat yourself to something special. It's a great way to reward your progress and discipline.

Also, plan to eat leftovers when you can—they're budget-friendly and reduce waste. Keep an eye on expiration dates and try to use up anything that's about to go bad. Throwing away food is like throwing away money. Good habits here will pay off over time, both financially and practically.

I don't know about you, but some grocery stores feel huge—and have you noticed that staples like bread and milk are often on opposite ends of the store? That's no accident. Stores are designed that way to guide you past more products, hoping you'll toss a few extras in your cart. I don't blame them—they're in business to make money. And truthfully, grocery stores don't have massive profit margins. I've heard the average profit is only 1% to 3% on most items.

One thing to watch out for is that the more expensive items are often the pre-made or highly processed ones. These usually bring in a little more profit for the store, too. Think microwave meals, pre-chopped veggies, or ready-to-eat snacks. When possible, try to buy whole ingredients and make things from scratch. It might take a little more effort, but it's healthier and usually saves you money in the long run.

I don't know about you, but I'm not a big fan of all the walking it takes just to grab a few groceries. It can feel like a trek just to get from the car to the store—and once you're inside, it's like a mini marathon just to find the couple of things you came for. But hey, sometimes that's just part of the process.

Thankfully, some stores now offer pickup services, which became more common during COVID. It usually doesn't cost extra, and all you have to do is place and pay for your order online, choose a pickup window, then show up at that time. They'll even load the groceries into your car. It can save time and even money, since you're not wandering past tempting things you didn't plan to buy.

Another great option is shipping. Many stores will ship pantry items or non-perishables to your door, and if you're part of a membership or "plus" plan, you can often get free shipping with a minimum purchase—usually around $50. These days, it's pretty easy to hit that in one order.

One option I'd suggest using only when necessary is delivery through a third-party service. While convenient, it often includes extra fees, delivery charges, and a tip—sometimes adding 20–30% to your total. I understand many of those workers rely on tips, and I respect that—but unless you're homebound or have a special situation, it's not the most budget-friendly choice.

Another wise choice, when you can fit it into your budget, is buying non-perishable items in bulk. If you're working with a $50 weekly grocery budget, this can still make a big difference. With an average savings of 27%, you could reduce your spending to about $36.50 per week, saving $13.50 weekly. Over the course of a year, that adds up to around $700 in savings. Stocking up on staples like rice, pasta, canned goods, baking essentials, and household supplies can stretch your budget—just be sure you have the storage space, use the items regularly, and can afford the upfront cost.

One of the biggest enemies of grocery and meal planning is being in a rush—or simply not doing it at all. At first, it may take a little extra time to learn the process, but once you get the hang of it, you'll become faster and more efficient. The payoff is worth it: better meals, better health, and a budget that stays on track.

In the end, think wisely and choose what works best for your schedule, budget, and lifestyle. You'll find a rhythm that works for you. That's part of the fun in all this—learning, trying, and growing wiser in the process.

Be informed about what you're buying and make wise choices. You'll feel better about it—and your wallet will thank you later!

Renting Your First Apartment

R enting your first apartment is a major milestone in life—it's your first real taste of living on your own, making your own decisions, and creating a space that's truly yours. It can feel exciting and freeing, but also a little intimidating if you've never navigated leases, bills, or maintenance issues before. This step into independence comes with both new responsibilities and valuable life lessons. From learning how to budget and manage your time to discovering what kind of environment helps you thrive, your first apartment is more than just a place to live—it's a powerful opportunity to grow.

Here are some pros and cons to keep in mind as you think through the process of finding and renting your first apartment.

Pros of Renting an Apartment for the First Time

- Gives you the chance to experience independence and personal responsibility in a manageable way

- Offers flexibility to explore different neighborhoods, cities, or career opportunities

- Helps you understand the true cost of living and develop budgeting and planning skills

- No responsibility for major home maintenance or property taxes

- Teaches practical life skills like managing utilities, understanding lease agreements, and building routines

- Helps you discover your lifestyle preferences and how you function on your own

Cons of Renting an Apartment for the First Time

- Can be overwhelming due to unfamiliar legal terms and tenant responsibilities

- Requires upfront costs like security deposits, application fees, and possibly multiple months' rent

- High monthly rent can strain your budget if not managed carefully

- Restrictions on personalizing or modifying the space

- Possible delays or issues with landlords handling repairs and maintenance

- Noise and privacy concerns due to close proximity to neighbors

- Risk of rent increases or being asked to move out when the lease ends

- Hidden issues like pests, poor insulation, or plumbing problems may not be obvious until after move-in

Your First Steps Toward Renting Your Own Place

Determine why you're needing to get an apartment on your own. Write down your reasons so you can stay focused and make decisions that align with your goals.

Think carefully about the location. Where do you travel most often—work, school, or maybe both? It's usually a good idea to look for places close to those spots for convenience, time savings, and even gas money.

Once you've narrowed down a general area, check local police crime maps to see how safe the neighborhood is. You don't want to end up in a high-crime area, even if the rent seems like a good deal.

You can research online or call any prospective apartment complex to get the important details ahead of time. Ask about how much the security deposit will be, what their application process looks like, and whether they currently have any units available. Getting this information early can save you time, help you plan your budget, and ensure you're not caught off guard when you're ready to apply.

Compare apartment prices in your chosen area with those in other neighborhoods. This will help you determine whether the pricing fits your budget and if you're getting a fair deal.

A common rule of thumb is to spend no more than 30% of your income on rent. Going over that can make it tough to afford other essentials like food, gas, insurance, and emergencies. Most landlords and rental companies use this same 30% standard when reviewing rental applications.

Your credit rating may also be considered when applying for an apartment. A higher credit score increases your chances of getting approved and may even affect the deposit amount.

Also, make sure you have some money saved in the bank before your move. Unexpected expenses always come up—especially during your first month. Whether it's buying basic household items, paying for extra deposits, covering utility setup fees, or replacing something you didn't know you'd need, having a financial cushion will help you handle those surprises without stress. Planning ahead gives you margin and peace of mind.

Be prepared to pay a deposit when you rent. Sometimes this includes the first and last month's rent up front, plus the first month's rent again when you move in. It can add up quickly, so plan ahead.

The deposit is usually held by the rental company until you move out. Read the lease closely to understand how they handle deposits and what might be deducted. Most landlords will charge for damage, repainting, carpet stains, broken blinds, and final cleaning. For example, if you put down a $2,000 deposit and they deduct for all these things, you might get little to nothing back—or even owe more.

Important Things to Know About Leases

One thing to take seriously when renting an apartment is the lease agreement. A lease is a legal contract between you and the landlord, and breaking it—meaning moving out before the end of the lease term—can have long-term consequences. Not only can it cost you money in penalties or lost deposits, but it can also damage your credit and rental history. Many future landlords or property managers check your rental background before approving you, and a broken lease can make it harder to get approved for another place in the future. If you're not sure you can commit to the full lease term, consider looking for a month-to-month option or shorter lease, if available.

You might also consider getting a roommate to help with costs. Rent, utilities, and groceries can add up quickly, and sharing those expenses can make things much more manageable. If you do get a roommate—or even two—they'll need to go through the application process as well. They'll be added to the lease and be equally responsible for the rent, the deposit, and the condition of the apartment.

That's why it's so important to choose roommates carefully. You want to live with people who are responsible, respectful, and able to communicate well. A good roommate can make life easier, but a careless one can create stress or even leave you stuck paying their part of the rent if things go sideways. So choose wisely, and make sure everyone understands their responsibilities from the start.

In fact, if you can do your apartment on your own and don't *need* additional roommates just to afford the rent, it's usually best not to include others in your lease. More times than not, having roommates turns out to be more challenging than expected. While it can work in some situations, it often brings added tension, disagreements, and complications. You'll already be learning a lot of new things—managing bills, caring for your space, planning meals, and handling adult responsibilities—and doing that on your own at first can help you grow in confidence and independence without the extra stress of managing shared living dynamics.

So, one helpful rule my wife and I have always lived by is this: treat the apartment like you own it, and leave it cleaner than you found it. As followers of Christ, we believe that how we care for what's entrusted to us reflects our heart and our witness. Stewardship isn't just about money—it's about how we honor God in the everyday spaces we live in.

Once you've signed the lease and have a move-in date, you're officially stepping into a new chapter—get ready to make the most of it!

The Big Day: Tips for a Smooth and Stress-Free Move

Have you ever heard the phrase "fly by night?"

It usually refers to something or someone unreliable, untrustworthy, or done without proper planning—often hastily or secretly. It can describe a sketchy business, a rushed decision, or someone who disappears without warning.

When it comes to moving in or out of an apartment, you definitely *don't* want to do it the "fly by night" way. Rushing last-minute, skipping the planning, or leaving things behind in a mess can create a lot of stress, damage relationships, and even cost you money—especially if it affects your deposit. Taking time to plan ahead, pack thoughtfully, communicate clearly, and leave things in good shape makes the whole process smoother for you, your roommates (if any), your landlord, and even your future self. A little effort on the front end saves a ton of chaos on the back end.

Here's a sample checklist to help you start preparing for your move. It's not an all-inclusive list, but it covers many of the basics. Feel free to add your own items to customize it for your situation and help make your move as smooth and stress-free as possible.

Create a Moving Checklist

Write down everything you need to do before, during, and after the move—things like packing up each room, changing your mailing address with the post office, setting up utilities (electric, water, internet), scheduling the move, and notifying your employer or school. Creating a detailed checklist not only helps you stay organized, but it also gives you a clear sense of progress as you check things off. It's easy to forget small but important tasks in the middle of a busy move, and having a plan in writing will help prevent last-minute surprises, missed deadlines, or unnecessary stress. Think of it as your roadmap for the move—keeping you on track from start to finish.

Set Up Utilities in Advance

Make sure your electricity, water, internet, and gas (if needed) are all scheduled to be turned on and active by your move-in date. It's no fun arriving at your new apartment only to realize the lights don't work or there's no running water. Some utility companies require a few days' notice to get things set up, and many will ask for a deposit—especially if you're a first-time customer or don't have an established credit history. Call ahead or set things up online in advance so everything is ready to go when you arrive. This simple step can save you a lot of frustration on moving day.

Pack Early and Smart

Start packing at least a couple of weeks before your move to avoid the last-minute rush and chaos. Begin with items you don't use daily—like seasonal clothes, extra linens, books, or décor—and work your way toward the everyday essentials. Clearly label each box with both the room it belongs in and what's inside; this will make unpacking much easier and help you find what you need quickly. Be sure to pack a "first night" box with essentials such as toiletries, bedding, a change of clothes, your phone charger, snacks, basic cleaning supplies, and anything else you might need in the first 24 hours. That one box can make your first night in your new home much more comfortable and stress-free.

Measure Everything

If you can, take time beforehand to learn the dimensions of your new apartment and your furniture. Measure the major pieces—like your couch, bed frame, and dresser—and compare those to the doorways, hallways, stairwells, and even elevators in your new place. It's much better to find out in advance if something won't fit rather than discovering it in the middle of moving day. Trust me—trying to shove a couch through a doorway that's too small is a frustrating experience you don't want to have. A little measuring now can save you a big headache later.

Clean Your New Apartment

Before you move all your things in—even if the apartment *looks* clean—it's a smart idea to wipe everything down and disinfect key surfaces. Clean the kitchen counters, inside the cabinets, bathroom surfaces, light switches, door handles, and floors. You never really know how thorough the last cleaning was, and it's much easier to do a deep clean while the space is still empty. Taking this step sets the tone for your new home and helps you start fresh in a space that feels truly yours.

Check the Lease and Take Photos

Before you start unpacking, take clear, dated photos of the condition of the apartment—especially any damage, wear, or areas that aren't in perfect shape. This step is important because if there's ever a dispute when you move out—such as management claiming you caused damage that was already there—you'll have solid proof of what the apartment looked like when you moved in. It becomes your word versus theirs, and having dated photos gives you credibility and protection.

Most apartment leases also include a move-in inspection form that lists every room and the condition of things like floors, walls, appliances, fixtures, and more. Take the time to fill this form out thoroughly, even for small things like scuffs, scratches, or loose hardware. This is your opportunity to officially document anything that isn't brand new or in excellent condition. Be sure to take photos that match what you write on the form, and always make a copy of the completed paperwork before turning it in to the manager. If you notice anything that's broken, unsafe, or just not up to standard, notify the leasing office immediately and request that it be fixed before—or as soon as—you move in.

Apartment complexes aren't trying to rip you off, but if these things aren't documented, then when they do the final inspection after you move out, any damage they find that wasn't previously noted will likely come out of your deposit. And if the cost of repairs is more than your deposit, you could end up with a bill. So don't skip this process. Be diligent. It's not just a wise move—it's good stewardship, and it protects you from having to pay for something you're not actually responsible for.

Recruit Help (or Hire Movers)

Ask friends or family to help you move, and try to coordinate with their availability as early as possible—especially if your move falls on a weekend or during a busy season. Offering snacks, drinks, or even pizza as a thank-you goes a long way. If you're planning to hire professional movers instead, get quotes from multiple companies ahead of time, read reviews, and make sure to book early to secure your preferred date. Planning in advance helps reduce stress and ensures you have the support you need when moving day arrives.

Hiring a moving company can vary widely in cost depending on the distance, the number of items, and the level of service you choose—and as with most things, you often get what you pay for. Sometimes, though, you can find creative alternatives that still get the job done well. I once had a friend refer me to a relative who was looking for some extra work and had the strength and experience to handle heavy lifting. I hired them to help with the big stuff, and it turned out to be a great experience. I was able to bless them with some cash and, of course, a few boxes of pizza during the move. Whether you go the professional route or find help through friends and connections, the key is to plan ahead and be thoughtful in how you approach the day.

Change Your Address

Update your address with the post office so your mail gets forwarded to your new place, but don't stop there. Be sure to notify your bank, employer, insurance companies, and any subscriptions or services you use—like Amazon, meal kits, or streaming platforms. Missing bills, tax forms, or other important mail can lead to bigger problems down the road. Taking the time to update your address with everyone who needs it will help you avoid confusion and make your transition smoother.

In some cases, you might want to rent a USPS PO Box—especially if you're in between places or want extra mail security. They're usually rented for 3, 6, or 12 months at a time. Prices vary depending on size and location, but a small box might cost around $13–$44 for 3 months, and larger ones can be $50 or more. It's not the cheapest option, but it can be super helpful. Check with your local post office for exact rates.

Some apartment complexes don't allow packages to be left outside your door, and they may not accept deliveries at the front office either. To solve this, many now use automated package locker systems. When a delivery arrives—whether it's from Amazon, UPS, FedEx, or another service—it gets logged into the system, and you'll receive a text or email with a code or barcode. You use that code to unlock the secure locker and pick up your package safely. It's a great setup that helps prevent package theft and keeps things organized. However, most complexes charge a small monthly fee for access to the locker system, so be sure to ask about it and factor that cost into your monthly budget.

Buy the Basics Before Move-In

You'll need more than just furniture to settle into your new apartment—think about the everyday essentials like toilet paper, a shower curtain, trash cans, dish soap, light bulbs, and maybe even a basic tool kit. These little things are easy to overlook but make a big difference. Stock up ahead of time so you're not scrambling on your first night trying to find a store or borrow something you really need.

Renters Insurance

Renting an apartment may also require you to carry renter's insurance. This is a separate policy you take out to cover your personal belongings—things like your furniture, clothes, electronics, and other valuables. It's important to understand that the apartment complex's insurance only covers the building itself, not your stuff. If there's a fire, flood, theft, or other damage, their policy won't replace your things—only yours will. Renter's insurance is usually affordable and offers peace of mind in case the unexpected happens. Some landlords even require proof of coverage before you can move in.

Pray and Invite God Into Your New Space

Most importantly, my wife and I make it a point to pray over every place we move into. It may seem like a small thing, but dedicating your apartment to God and inviting His presence into your new home sets a powerful tone. It creates an atmosphere of peace, protection, and purpose as you step into this new season. It's a way of saying, "Lord, this space is Yours—lead us, guide us, and let Your presence fill every room."

I Don't Have Much: Starting Small and Making It Work

So you don't have much furniture for your new apartment—that's totally okay. Everyone starts somewhere, and you don't need to have it all figured out on day one. The first step is to determine which items are most important for daily living and make a list of those essentials. Think about what you'll need to sleep, sit, eat, and store your belongings. Prioritize function over style for now—you can always upgrade or decorate as you go. Starting small is actually a gift; it helps you focus on what truly matters and gives you the chance to build your space slowly and intentionally.

When my wife and I moved to Vermont years ago to do some ministry work, we gave away everything we owned. We packed only what we could fit into our small Corolla—mostly just my computer, printer, and design gear so I could continue doing graphics and website work. That was it. No furniture, no extra comforts—just the basics we needed to function and serve.

Over the years we lived in Vermont, we went from having nothing to living in three different apartments, each one a little bigger than the last. Eventually, we moved into a townhouse, which was such a blessing because we hosted small group meetings in our living room several times a week. The extra space made that possible, and it served the people God brought into our lives.

When it was time to move back to Texas years later—when my mother-in-law's health was declining and we needed to be closer—we repeated the process. We gave away almost everything again and made the trip back with just the essentials. We moved into the apartment complex where Sherri's mom lived, and when I say we had nothing, I mean it. We sat on the floor on a small cushion. No bed. No table. No TV. No chairs.

The very next day, Sherri's aunt stopped by to say hello. She looked around and said, "Where's your furniture?" We told her, "This is it. We don't have any yet." She kind of laughed and said, "Well that's interesting—I just bought all new furniture. Would you like some of my old stuff?" Within one day, God had filled our apartment with everything we needed. It was completely furnished. We praise God for His incredible faithfulness and provision! We're also deeply thankful for Sherri's Aunt Adiene and her generous heart.

At that point in our lives, we were walking in a deep season of trusting God for our daily provision. And honestly, I wouldn't trade that time for anything. We experienced God's faithfulness up close and personal in ways that shaped us forever.

Paul wrote in the book of Philippians:

> "I know how to live on almost nothing or with everything. I have learned the secret of living in every situation…whether it is with a full stomach or empty, with plenty or little."
>
> —Philippians 4:12

That verse was real to us then—and it still is now.

We should always live by faith—whether we have a lot or very little. Our trust isn't in how much money we have in the bank, the furniture in our home, or even the roof over our heads. Our true security is found in God alone. He is our provider, our sustainer, and our ever-present help in every season of life.

I share this story not to highlight anything we did, but to point to everything God did.

> "Taste and see that the Lord is good. Oh, the joys of those who take refuge in him!"
>
> —Psalm 34:8 NLT

We have truly tasted His goodness firsthand.

So if you're stepping into your first apartment with very little—or maybe even nothing at all—know that I've been there. I understand how that feels. And I can tell you with confidence: you can make it work. More importantly, *God* can make it work. He is faithful, whether you have a fully furnished home or just a cushion on the floor.

Renting a House: What to Know Before You Sign

Renting a house is a little different than renting an apartment—it often comes with more space, more responsibility, and sometimes more freedom. Whether you're moving into a small house, a duplex, or a single-family home, there are a few key things to consider before signing a lease.

First, make sure you understand who is responsible for what. In a home rental, you may be expected to take care of yard work, minor maintenance, or even appliance repairs, depending on the lease. Unlike apartment complexes that often have on-site maintenance teams, landlords of rental homes might not respond as quickly—or may expect you to handle more yourself.

You'll also want to clarify what utilities are included, how trash is handled, and if there are any HOA rules or neighborhood restrictions. Renting a house can feel more private and spacious, but it also means you're part of a residential community with its own expectations.

Take time to walk through the home carefully before moving in. Check for any existing damage, take photos, and document everything on a move-in checklist. Homes can have issues you don't see at first glance—like roof leaks, old plumbing, or pest problems—so don't be afraid to ask questions.

Lastly, just like with an apartment, read the lease thoroughly, pray over the decision, and make sure it fits your budget. Renting a home can be a great step forward—it gives you room to grow and can prepare you for future responsibilities, especially if you're thinking about owning a home one day.

Apartment or House? Choosing What Fits Your Season

Ultimately, you get to decide what's the best fit for you. Take time to think through your current needs, your lifestyle, your budget, and the season of life you're in. There's no one-size-fits-all answer—what works great for one person might be overwhelming for another. Whether you choose a home or an apartment, the key is to be wise, prayerful, and intentional with the decision. It's your space, your next step, and your opportunity to steward well whatever God places in your hands.

Here are some things to consider as you make your choice.

Renting a House

Renting a house typically means more space, privacy, and a more residential feel. It often includes a yard, a garage, and multiple bedrooms—making it a great option for families, couples, or anyone needing extra room.

Pros of Renting a House:
You'll enjoy more privacy, since you're not sharing walls with neighbors. The extra space is great for hosting guests, having home offices, or simply spreading out. It often feels more personal and long-term, giving a sense of "home" that some apartments don't.

Cons of Renting a House:
You may be responsible for yard work and basic maintenance, depending on your lease. Private landlords might take longer to handle repairs

compared to apartment maintenance teams. Rent and utilities can also be higher, and you likely won't have access to community amenities like a gym or pool.

Renting an Apartment

Renting an apartment usually offers simplicity, convenience, and lower upfront costs. It's a popular choice for first-time renters, college students, or young professionals.

Pros of Renting an Apartment:

Apartments typically come with on-site maintenance, so repairs are handled quickly. Many complexes offer shared amenities like fitness centers, pools, and laundry rooms. It's usually more affordable and involves less responsibility for upkeep.

Cons of Renting an Apartment:

You'll have less privacy, as you'll be sharing walls, floors, or ceilings with neighbors. Living space is often smaller, which can limit storage and hosting opportunities. Package delivery, parking, and noise can also be ongoing challenges.

Which One Should You Choose?

It really depends on your current season of life, your budget, and your priorities. If you value space and privacy and are okay with a little more responsibility, a rental home might be right for you. If you want convenience, affordability, and less to manage, an apartment may be the better fit.

Buying a Home

Buying your first house is one of those big life moments that feels both exciting and slightly surreal. Suddenly, all those late-night scrolls through home listings turn into actual showings, real decisions, and a set of keys that are *yours*. It's more than just picking a place to live—it's about finding a space where your story will unfold, where late-night snacks, lazy Saturdays, and "oops, I burned the toast" mornings start to happen on your own turf.

There's definitely a learning curve—like figuring out what a mortgage pre-approval even means or realizing that "charming fixer-upper" might involve more duct tape than expected. But it's also a process full of discovery, growth, and a sense of freedom. You're not just buying a house; you're building a foundation for your next chapter. And even if it comes with a few unexpected surprises (hello, mystery light switch), it's a journey worth every step.

Buying a house is usually the faster option—you can move in quickly, settle into an established neighborhood, and start decorating right away. It's great if you don't want to wait and are okay with a few compromises on style or layout. But be prepared for hidden issues and a competitive market that might require some patience and flexibility.

Building a house means everything is brand new and built exactly the way you want it, from the kitchen layout to the bathroom tile. It's perfect if you love customizing and want something totally yours. Just keep in mind that it takes time, involves a ton of decisions, and can stretch your budget if you're not careful.

Most people will end up buying a home that's already built or choosing one that's being built by a builder—and honestly, both are solid options. A lot of the big decisions like layout, finishes, and permits are already handled, which makes the process way less stressful and a whole lot quicker. You get the excitement of a new home without the overload of managing every little detail.

On the other hand, fully custom-building a home from the ground up—where you hire a head contractor, work with architects, and juggle subcontractors—is a much more involved journey. It can be rewarding, but it takes significantly longer and comes with a steep learning curve. There are countless decisions, unexpected hiccups, and a level of complexity that most people don't realize at the start. For those who love total control and have the patience (and budget) for it, it can be worth it—but for many, sticking with a move-in-ready or semi-custom build is the sweet spot.

Don't Get the Cart Before the House—I Mean, Horse!

Before diving into house tours and picking out paint colors, there are some key steps and things to consider when buying a home.

Here's a simple breakdown to help you move forward with confidence.

Figure Out Your Budget

Knowing how much you can afford is the first step. Look at your income, debt, monthly expenses, and how much you can put toward a down payment. This will help you narrow your search and avoid falling in love with homes that stretch your finances too thin. A good rule of thumb: your monthly mortgage shouldn't take over your whole life.

Get Pre-approved for a Mortgage

A pre-approval shows sellers you're serious and gives you a clearer idea of what loan amount you qualify for. It's different from pre-qualification—this one actually involves a lender reviewing your financials. It also helps you act quickly when you find the right home. Plus, it sets realistic expectations and keeps surprises to a minimum.

Make sure to read the more detailed information toward the end of this chapter for a deeper dive into loan and finance options as well as information on payments. We'll break down each loan type, how credit scores really affect your rates and terms, and tips for choosing the best mortgage for your situation. Understanding your financing choices now will help you make smarter decisions later—and maybe even save you thousands in the long run. So don't skip it!

Make a List of Needs and Wants

Think about what you *have to* have—like number of bedrooms, location, or yard space—and what you *would love* to have, like a walk-in closet or a big porch. Prioritize the non-negotiables first. This list helps your real estate agent narrow down the best options. It also keeps you focused when emotions start clouding your judgment mid-tour.

Choose a Great Real Estate Agent

A good agent is like a home-buying GPS—they'll guide you through the process, spot red flags, negotiate like a pro, and help with paperwork. Look for someone who knows the local market and listens to what you want. You don't have to go it alone, and having the right guide makes a huge difference. This person is your teammate, not just a door-opener.

Best of all, in most cases, the seller pays the real estate agent fees—typically around 5% to 6% of the home's selling price, which is then split between the seller's agent and the buyer's agent. So as the buyer, you usually get expert help without having to pay that fee yourself!

Start Touring Homes

This is the fun part—but it can also be overwhelming. Take notes and pictures, because after the third or fourth house, they all start to blur together. Don't rush, but don't overthink every detail either; no house is perfect, but the right one will feel like a good fit. Pay attention to both the home and the neighborhood.

Make an Offer

Once you find *the one*, it's time to make an offer based on market conditions and your agent's advice. The seller might accept, reject, or counter—be prepared for all three. If your offer is accepted, congratulations! Now things really start moving.

Earnest Money

Earnest money is a deposit you make after your offer on a home is accepted—it's kind of like putting a ring on it to show you're serious. This money tells the seller, "Hey, I'm committed and not just window shopping." It's usually paid within a few days of reaching an agreement and is held in an escrow account until closing.

You would pay earnest money *after* your offer is accepted but *before* the official closing process begins. If all goes well and you close on the house, the earnest money goes toward your down payment or closing costs. But if you back out for a reason not covered in your contract, you could lose it—so be sure to read those contingencies closely!

Schedule an Inspection

An inspection gives you an honest look at what's happening behind the walls, under the floors, and on the roof. It's not about making the house perfect—it's about making sure you know what you're getting into. If big issues pop up, you can renegotiate or walk away. It's one of the most important steps in protecting your investment.

Secure Your Financing

Even if you're pre-approved, now is when your lender locks in the final loan terms. You'll provide updated documents, confirm details, and work closely with the lender to make sure everything checks out. This is also when you'll lock in your interest rate. Stay responsive and don't open any new form of credit or credit cards during this stage!

Do a Final Walkthrough

Before closing, you'll walk through the house one last time to make sure everything is in the condition you agreed on. This isn't the time to dream about furniture placement—this is your chance to confirm repairs were made and nothing has changed since your offer. If something's wrong, your agent will help you address it quickly. It's a quick but crucial step.

Close the Deal

At closing, you'll sign a *lot* of paperwork, hand over the rest of the money, and officially become the owner of your new home. Once everything is signed and recorded, you get the keys. It's a big moment—celebrate it! Welcome home.

Loan Types 101

When buying a home, there are several types of financing available, and the down payment requirements can vary based on your credit score, loan type, and lender. Here's a breakdown of common loan types and what kind of down payment you might need depending on your credit rating:

Conventional Loan

This is the most common type of mortgage, not backed by the government.

- *Excellent credit (740+)*: You might qualify for as little as 3–5% down.

- *Good credit (680–739)*: Expect 5–10% down, depending on the lender.

- *Fair credit (620–679)*: You may still qualify, but lenders often want 10–20% down and may charge higher interest rates.

FHA Loan (Federal Housing Administration)

Great for first-time buyers and those with lower credit scores.

- *Excellent to Good credit*: Typically requires just 3.5% down.

- *Fair credit (as low as 580)*: Still eligible for 3.5% down.

- *Credit below 580*: You may still qualify, but you'll likely need 10% down.

VA Loan (Veterans Affairs)

Available to eligible veterans, active-duty service members, and some surviving spouses.

- No down payment required regardless of credit score, although better credit will help with getting a good rate.

- No private mortgage insurance (PMI), which can save money long-term.

USDA Loan (U.S. Department of Agriculture)

For rural and some suburban homes, with income limits.

- No down payment required.

- Credit score should be 640 or higher for easier approval, but lower scores might still qualify with additional documentation.

The better your credit, the more flexible your options—and the less money you'll typically need up front. But even with fair credit, there are still paths to homeownership if you're prepared and willing to work with a lender on the right fit.

Interest Rates: The Price of Borrowing

When you get an approval for a loan which is a mortgage to buy a home, you're borrowing money from a lender and agreeing to pay it back—with interest—over time. The interest rate is the cost of borrowing, shown as a percentage. Lower rates mean lower monthly payments and less paid in total over the life of the loan. Most homebuyers choose either a 15-year or 30-year loan, with the 30-year being more common because it offers lower monthly payments, even though you end up paying more interest in the long run.

Each monthly mortgage payment includes principal (the actual loan amount) and interest (the lender's fee). At first, most of your payment goes toward interest and just a little to the principal. Over time, this flips—more of your payment goes toward reducing your loan balance. This shift is called amortization, and it continues until the loan is completely paid off.

One smart strategy is to make extra principal payments whenever you can. Even small additional amounts each month can reduce your total interest and help you pay off the loan years earlier. It's a great way to build equity faster and save money over time.

The Monthly Payment – Principal, Interest, Insurance, and Taxes

When people think about a house payment, they often just picture the mortgage—but there's more to it than just paying back the loan. Your monthly payment is usually made up of four main parts: principal, interest, insurance, and taxes. Understanding how each one works—and how they add up—can help you plan better, avoid surprises, and make smarter decisions about what you can truly afford.

Here's an example of a $300,000 home loan, showing how your monthly payment changes based on your credit score. With good credit and a 3% interest rate, your payment will look very different compared to fair credit and a 7% rate.

Keep in mind, the amounts below reflect only the principal and interest—the portion paid directly to the loan company. We'll add in estimated property taxes (which vary by location) and homeowners insurance afterward to give you a full picture of your monthly cost.

Let's break it down.

Principal & Interest Only

At 8% Interest (30-year loan): (Fair Credit Rating)
Your monthly principal and interest payment would be approximately **$2,201.29**.

At 3% Interest (30-year loan): (Excellent Credit Rating)
Your monthly principal and interest payment would be approximately **$1,264.81**.

Now let's add in a sample of what you might pay for homeowners insurance and property and school taxes. These amounts will vary depending on where you live, but this gives you a general idea of what to expect. Once you add these extra costs to your principal and interest, you'll get a clearer picture of your total monthly house payment. Let's see how it all adds up.

Added Costs: Insurance and Taxes

In addition to your mortgage payment, most homeowners also pay for homeowners insurance and property + school taxes, which are often included in your monthly payment through an escrow account.

- Annual Homeowners Insurance: $2,500

- Annual Property + School Taxes: $9,000

- Combined Annual Total: $11,500

- Monthly Cost (Insurance + Taxes): $958.33

Total Monthly Payments (Including Insurance + Taxes)

At 8% Interest: (Fair Credit Rating)
$2,201.29 (mortgage) + $958.33 (insurance + taxes) = **$3,159.62 total per month**

At 3% Interest: (Excellent Credit Rating)
$1,264.81 (mortgage) + $958.33 (insurance + taxes) = **$2,223.14 total per month**

Did you notice that adding in homeowners insurance and property taxes added over $900 to the monthly payment? It's a big jump—and it's why looking beyond just the mortgage is so important when budgeting for a home.

Also, take a look at the difference your credit rating can make. The monthly payment for someone with fair credit and a 7% interest rate is $936 more per month than someone with excellent credit at a 3% rate.

That's not just a small bump—it adds up to over $11,000 a year. Keeping your credit score strong can literally save you thousands.

You can see how the interest rate significantly changes your base mortgage payment—and how fixed costs like insurance and taxes stack on top no matter what rate you get.

Your credit rating plays a major role in the interest rate you'll be offered when applying for a home loan. The better your credit, the lower your rate—and that can mean big savings over the life of your mortgage. To keep your score in top shape, use credit responsibly: pay on time, avoid late payments, and aim to pay off your balances in full each month when possible. One key tip—try to keep your credit usage below 10% of your total available credit. Using more than that can cause your score to drop significantly, even if you're paying on time.

The HOA: Friend, Foe, or Fee?

Another little surprise waiting for some homeowners? Three letters: HOA. That stands for Homeowners Association, and it's basically the neighborhood's rulebook and maintenance crew rolled into one. They take care of things like mowing common areas, maintaining the pool, and making sure your neighbor doesn't paint their house neon green.

Their fees can feel like a mystery subscription—most run about $100 or more per month, but in fancy neighborhoods with lots of perks, they can be much higher. So before you fall in love with the house, make sure to check if there's an HOA... and what kind of strings (or swimming pools) come with it.

They are more than just a group that manages the pool and mows the common grass—it usually has authority to hold homeowners accountable to a set of community standards established when the subdivision was developed. That means they can (and will) send reminders, warnings, or even formal notices if your property isn't meeting those guidelines.

This might look like a letter telling you to cut your grass because it's too tall, fix or replace a worn-out fence, repaint fading trim, replace rotting roof wood, or even reshape or replant overgrown trees and shrubs. It's not always fun—and no one enjoys getting those letters—but it's part of the deal when you move into an HOA neighborhood.

Their goal is to keep the entire community looking well-maintained and consistent, which in turn helps protect property values and avoid a "run-down" feel. So yes, it can feel personal when you get a notice—but it's also what you've agreed to when you buy the home. Their fees are billed monthly or quarterly and vary based on your location and what services are included. Whether you love it or tolerate it, the HOA is part of the package—and there's no opting out.

Keys in Hand, Let's Go!

Before moving into your new home, it's a good idea to be prepared so moving day doesn't feel like total chaos. Here are 8 things to get ready before the big move:

Here's just a sampling of some of the things to take care of before moving in—because once the keys are in your hand, you'll want things to go as smoothly as possible. A little planning ahead can save you a lot of stress on move-in day and help you settle in faster.

This list isn't all-inclusive—you'll definitely have other tasks to handle that aren't mentioned here—but it's a solid place to start and get the ball rolling.

1. **Set Up Utilities** – Make sure electricity, water, gas, internet, and trash service are scheduled to be turned on before you move in.

2. **Change Your Address** – Update your address with the post office, banks, subscriptions, and anywhere else that regularly mails you stuff.

3. **Measure Rooms & Doorways** – Know what furniture fits where—and what might *not* fit through the front door.

4. **Schedule a Deep Clean** – Whether you do it yourself or hire someone, a clean slate before the boxes arrive is a major win.

5. **Make a First Night Box** – Pack essentials like toilet paper, chargers, snacks, tools, and pajamas—so you're not digging through boxes at midnight.

6. **Label Boxes Clearly** – Trust us, future you will thank you. Label by room and note if anything is fragile.

7. **Check HOA or Neighborhood Rules** – Some places have rules about when moving trucks can be there or where they can park.

8. **Plan for Pets or Kids** – Moving is stressful for little ones (two-legged or four-legged). Have a plan to keep them safe and cared for during the move.

9. **Line Up Moving Help** – Whether you're hiring professional movers or recruiting a few strong friends, make sure you have help lined up well in advance.

10. **Gather Packing Supplies** – Boxes, tape, bubble wrap, markers—you'll need more than you think, so stock up early to stay ahead.

11. **Pray Over Your Home** – Before the furniture goes in and the routines begin, take time to pray. Dedicate your home to the Lord, invite His peace and presence to fill every room, and ask for His protection, provision, and purpose in the season ahead.

Buying a home is more than just a financial decision—it's a step of faith, stewardship, and preparation for the next chapter God is leading you into. It can be exciting, overwhelming, and full of choices, but through it all, you can trust that He is guiding your steps. As you walk through budgets, paperwork, and moving boxes, remember that you're not just purchasing a place to live—you're creating a space where life, love, and purpose will grow.

When done prayerfully and wisely, buying a home becomes a beautiful opportunity to honor God with what He's entrusted to you.

JESUS HAD A JOB TOO!

God Doesn't Do Random

The Resumé Heaven Was Writing

I'm sharing my journey with you in hopes that it will expand your vision and raise your expectations for what your own path might look like—especially when it comes to work and calling. As you read, I invite you to open your heart, your mind, and your spiritual eyes.

My prayer is that you'll begin to see how God can use every step, every job, and every season for something far greater than you imagined.

The Unexpected Path to Purpose

Let me take you back to where it all began—my very first steps into the wild world of earning a paycheck.

My first job was at age 15, bussing tables in the cafeteria at our local ski area in Vermont. While my classmates were out skiing, goofing off, and enjoying hot chocolate breaks, I was behind the scenes—wiping tables, stacking trays, and cleaning up the chaos they left behind. Not exactly living the dream! But honestly, it was good for me. I learned how to work hard, show up on time, and answer to a boss who was kind but definitely didn't let anything slide. It wasn't glamorous, but it was my first real taste of responsibility—and a humbling start to my working life.

After my parents retired and moved to Texas, I took a summer job at a golf course. It involved 105-degree of July heat, hours of pushing a lawnmower, and yanking weeds under the blazing sun—it was intense. By the end of the first week, I was getting lightheaded every day and nearly passed out. I didn't want to quit, but I had no choice. My body made the call, I hadn't yet adapted to living in Texas after moving from Vermont. Walking away after just a week was tough—it felt like I had let my boss down. It was a humbling experience, and not the kind of lesson I expected to learn so soon.

Thank God! Then came the butcher shop. I worked there part time while in high school and college. Much cooler—literally. The average temp was 68°F, and the cooler? A refreshing 40°F. I never overheated again!

That job gave me my first steady paycheck and a taste of financial independence. Too bad I didn't know how to budget. My parents were great at it, but I never learned how they did it.

When I started college, I was majoring in music education. I loved music and being in band, so it felt like the right choice. But after a couple of years, something shifted. I realized I wasn't excited about the idea of teaching third graders how to play a flutophone—and hoping to someday move up to junior high band director just didn't feel like the dream anymore.

At the same time, I had kept taking computer programming classes on the side and really enjoyed learning different languages. I've always loved figuring out how things work—physics was one of my favorite subjects in high school and college. The more I leaned into those interests, the more they felt like *me*.

That season of life—after college, standing on the edge of adulthood—is something every young person goes through. I can still picture myself standing in the doorway of my parents' house, looking out into the world. Part of me was excited about the possibilities. But another part felt lost, unsure, and maybe a little scared. My friends seemed to be stepping confidently into jobs and careers, and I couldn't help but wonder, "Why don't I feel ready too?"

I was also pretty new in my faith—only about two years into my walk with God. I was growing, but I didn't yet have a solid foundation in God's Word. My parents loved Jesus and were faithful to church, but we didn't have that kind of home where Scripture and prayer were part of everyday life. So I was figuring it out as I went.

To help me move forward to getting a job, I started looking back—thinking about what I enjoyed growing up. That led me straight to computers and electronics. Back in junior high and high school, a good friend, Roger Oakey, introduced me to computers. And this was way before it was normal—early 1970s, long before the first IBM PC came out.

Our high school had a teletype terminal connected to a mainframe computer at the University of Vermont. You had to call on a rotary phone, then put the handset into these rubber cups on the teletype to connect (yes, really!). It would print out responses on paper, and we'd type commands back. That's how I learned BASIC programming—and I absolutely loved it.

I also got into amateur (HAM) radio around age 15. I learned a ton about electronics, and even helped build a TV from a kit. Between radios and computers, I was completely drawn in.

So when I started job hunting, I looked for something in that world. A neighbor who worked at Texas Instruments suggested I apply there, and I found an opening in a department that built custom proprietary robotic equipment used to manufacture computer chips.

It was the perfect blend of electronics and computer programming—my sweet spot. I didn't have a formal degree in it, but I had just enough experience and a real eagerness to learn. They hired me!

That was my first real full-time job—with benefits (which I didn't even fully understand yet!). But more than that, I genuinely loved the work. It brought together the very things I was passionate about.

You know the old saying: *"If you love your work, you'll never work a day in your life."* For the first time, that actually felt possible. I worked for TI for about 10 years and loved everything that I got to do.

A Journey Through the Skies, Screens, and Scripture

Somewhere along the way, I caught the flying bug. I got my pilot's license and absolutely loved it. Around that time, I met a friend who was an Air Traffic Controller—and suddenly, I saw the perfect mix: electronics, programming, and aviation all rolled into one! That really sparked something in me.

I took the ATC test, passed, and got hired by the FAA (Federal Aviation Administration). I trained to become an air traffic controller and ended up working at the ARTCC—Air Route Traffic Control Center—in the Dallas-Fort Worth area. I worked east departures and northeast arrivals, controlling commercial, military, and general aviation aircraft. I even had the chance to work with Air Force One several times and the space shuttle when it was riding piggyback on a 747!

It was one of the toughest jobs to train for—but also one of the most rewarding. Our center handled over 2.1 million aircraft per year. I eventually got to train others and work on projects with the training department, which I really enjoyed. I spent about ten years with the FAA, and it was an incredible season.

The Detour That Wasn't a Detour

But while that job was fulfilling, God was stirring something deeper in my heart—something for the people of Vermont. God was doing something deep in me—changing my heart in a way that's hard to fully explain. The only way I can describe it is this: I was falling deeper in love with Him, it was Him that was drawing me deeper.

I still had family and friends there who had walked away from God and Jesus. My wife and I began to pray, and over time, we felt led to leave the FAA and move to Vermont to do life with people there and share the love of Jesus. It was a deeply meaningful time, full of stories that could fill books. And through it all, I saw God's provision in ways I'll never forget.

During that season, I leaned into my programming background and began working in creative web development and design. It allowed me to use years of experience to provide for our family—and God blessed it.

The Toolbox Was Bigger Than I Thought

About eight years later, my wife's mom became ill, and we made the decision to return to Texas to be closer to family. It wasn't on our radar, but we knew it was the right thing to do.

Back in Texas, I continued doing website work while my wife stepped into education. We joined a large church in the area and started volunteering. I still remember walking out of the newcomers' class, holding a paper listing all the volunteer opportunities. My wife jumped right into children's ministry—her sweet spot. She also jokingly reminded me that one reason she married me was because I can act like a 4-year-old at any moment. (I take that as a compliment.)

She looked at me and asked, "What about you? Where do you want to serve?" I shrugged. She said, "You love tech stuff—why not try Tech Arts?"

I wasn't even sure what that meant, but I gave it a shot. It turned out to be audio, video, and lighting for services. I had some background—back in high school in the 70s, I worked in our school's closed-circuit TV studio. That gave me a foundation, even though I didn't know it would become such a big part of my life later on.

I started learning every video position I could at the church. It was exciting and fulfilling—using tech to serve people and help create moments where lives could be changed. Eventually, I was trained in live video directing and loved it. When a full-time position opened up, I applied—and was hired.

Over time, I began to see how God had been weaving my story together all along. From radios and programming to mentoring and ministry, each season had a purpose. I loved leading people, helping them grow, training and building leaders. One of my very close friends, Brandon Marx, and I worked closely together during that time. We both loved training others, so we developed video team training for our multi-campus church.

Eventually, a Tech Arts training school was launched, and we got to teach there. Then The King's University created a media degree and asked us to write and teach the course content. We did that for 6–7 years.

The Best Chapters Are Still Being Written

A couple of years ago, I officially retired from the 9-to-5 world. Looking back, I realize I worked for 50 years! That's a lot of coffee and calendars. But now I can clearly see how God has been using every experience—every win, every challenge, every lesson—to prepare me for something new: writing.

No, I don't have all the answers (not even close!), but I've picked up a few nuggets of wisdom along the way—things God has taught me, often the hard way. And now I feel called to pass those lessons on to anyone willing to listen (or read!).

In this new chapter of life, I've written and published several books, and I've got a couple more stirring in my heart just waiting to get out. My hope is that something in these pages helps you—maybe saves you from a few unnecessary detours, and most of all, cheers you on as you run full speed toward everything God has called and created you to do!

In the book of Proverbs God says:

> "You can make many plans, but the Lord's purpose will
> prevail."
>
> —Proverbs 19:21 NLT

In other words: We might sketch out all kinds of plans for our lives, but
it's God's purpose that wins in the end—and that's a really good thing.
His plans are always better than ours.

Looking back, I can see how God connected all the dots—things He
planted in my heart as a kid became tools He used in every season of my
life. Too often, people think their "calling" is a job title or career path. But
I've learned that your calling isn't always the job—it's the *why* behind
where God places you.

If you keep the priorities straight—God first, family next, then
work—God will be part of everything you do. Life's not about climbing
a single career ladder. For me, it's been more like a journey through a
forest—each step intentional, even when I didn't see the big picture.

God's View of the Gazebo Is Better Than Mine

I once had a mentor who explained our life journey this way: Imagine
standing in a huge field. God, looking from above, points to a gazebo far
in the distance and says, "Run to it!" All you see is thick forest. Then
God says, "See that pine tree to your left? Go there." So you run. After a
while, He says, "Now see that oak tree to the right? Head there."

God, like the most loving Father, leads us step by step, tree by tree, through the forest—guiding us with care, even when the path feels unclear. And in time, we come out the other side and find ourselves standing right where He always intended: at the gazebo.

Sometimes people don't understand when you shift directions. They say, "Wait, I thought you were called to the pine tree!" But if God tells you to move, it's not about abandoning a calling—it's about continuing the journey.

In high school, I never could've guessed that programming BASIC, messing with HAM radios, and working in a TV studio would lead to the places God would take me. But He used it all—for His Kingdom and for the people I got to walk with.

One of my life verses is found in the book of Psalms:

> "The Lord says, 'I will guide you along the best pathway for your life. I will advise you and watch over you.'"
> —Psalm 32:8 NLT

Not just any path—*the best* one. And I've learned, the best path is always the one He leads you on. I've taken a few detours trying to do things my way. Those paths? Not so fun. Trust me—you don't want to be somewhere God hasn't called you.

But when you follow His leading? You'll be amazed at where you end up.

God Doesn't Waste a Single Step

Before we dive into the next chapter, I wanted to pause and give you a bigger picture of my work journey—not just to walk you through a résumé, but to show you something far more meaningful: how God was working in *every single step*, even when I didn't realize it.

Looking back now, I can see how each job, each skill, each experience was part of something God was building—not just in my career, but in my heart. Even the odd jobs, the hard seasons, and the moments of doubt were woven into a bigger story. His story. And the same is true for you.

God doesn't waste anything. Before you ever took your first breath, He already had good things planned for your life—things only *you* can do.

We are told in Ephesians:

> "For we are God's masterpiece. He has created us anew in Christ Jesus, so we can do the good things he planned for us long ago."
>
> —Ephesians 2:10 NLT

He created you with purpose, and He's been writing your story from the very beginning. Sometimes we can't see the pattern until we look back, but I promise you—He's been there the whole time, guiding every detail.

And the most incredible part? Through all of it, we get to know Him more. Not just know *about* Him, but really *know* Him—up close and personal. The Bible uses the word *yada* for that kind of knowing. It means deep, intimate connection. That's what God wants with you.

Not just when life is going great, but in the hard days, the confusing moments, and the times when you're not sure what's next.

He's faithful through it all. Our job is to keep our eyes on Him and let Him lead us—like He says:

> "Think about the things of heaven, not the things of earth."
> —Colossians 3:2 NLT

So let's keep going. In the next chapter, we'll talk about some practical things to think about as you begin stepping into the world of work and planning for your future. But don't worry—you're not doing it alone.

God's already ahead of you, and He knows exactly where He's leading.

Equipped for a Purpose

F inding the right job or career field is more than just chasing a paycheck—it's about discovering the unique purpose God has placed inside you. As Christians, we believe that our work is a form of worship and a way to serve others. By seeking God's guidance, understanding our God-given gifts, and paying attention to what brings us joy and meaning, we can step into a career that not only provides for our needs but also brings glory to Him. Trust that He is leading you, even through uncertainty, toward a path that fits both your heart and His plan.

Once you have some clarity on the type of work you're drawn to, the next step is figuring out the best path to get there. That might mean going to college, enrolling in trade school, or jumping straight into the workforce to learn on the job. Each route has value—it all depends on your goals, the field you're entering, and how you learn best. Some careers require a degree, while others are best learned through hands-on experience or a specialized trade program. Pray for wisdom, seek advice from people in the field, and be open to starting small. God can use every step—even the detours—to prepare you for the work He has planned for you.

Count the Cost

Before you dive in, there are some important things you can do to help make a wise decision about how to reach your career goals. God encourages us to seek wisdom from others:

> "Plans succeed through good counsel; don't go to war without wise advice."
>
> —Proverbs 20:18, NLT

One of the best ways to gain insight is by talking with people who are already doing the kind of work you're interested in. Ask them thoughtful questions, like:

- Why did they choose this field?

- How long did it take to get where they are now?

- What path or training did they follow?

- How much does it pay, and is there room for growth?

- What do they enjoy most about their work?

- What challenges do they face?

- Did they ever consider a different career?

- What are their future plans—do they see themselves retiring from this field, or do they plan to transition into something else, and when?

- What would you tell someone like me who is considering this field of work?

These conversations can help you get a real-world perspective and give you the clarity you need. Be prayerful, take notes, and stay open—you might be surprised by what you learn!

Try to talk with as many people as you can who are working in the field you're interested in. The more perspectives you hear, the better! One person might absolutely love the job, while another might have had a totally different experience. Learning from a variety of people helps you get a more balanced and honest view of what the work is really like.

It's also a great idea to connect with someone who's been in the field a long time or holds a leadership role. Ask them things like:

- What do you look for in a great employee?

- What's the best way to get started in this field?

- Are there any common mistakes people make when they're new?

- What helps someone succeed and grow in this career?

You might even ask if they offer any internship opportunities. Interning is a great way to learn and see things up close while gaining valuable experience. If they don't have an internship program, they might be open to letting you "shadow" someone for a day or two. Shadowing lets you follow an employee around and get a first-hand look at what the job is really like.

Be curious, be kind, and don't be afraid to ask questions—most people are happy to share their journey and help someone who's just starting out!

When you're meeting with people in the field you're interested in—whether for an interview, a shadowing opportunity, or just to ask questions—make sure to dress nicely and wear clothes that fit the type of job you're exploring. Be clean, well-groomed, and put-together. A fresh haircut helps you look your best, and if you're a guy, make sure any facial hair is trimmed and tidy.

First impressions in the business world really matter. Sometimes, how you present yourself can open doors—or quietly close them.

Don't be afraid to speak up or ask questions. Good communication not only helps you learn more, but also gives people a chance to get to know you. Be relaxed and confident—nerves are totally normal, especially when you're stepping into something new. Remember, the people you're talking to were once in your shoes too. They know what it's like to be the new person just starting out.

While you're there, pay attention to the environment. Are the employees friendly and smiling, or do they seem stressed and quiet with their heads down? Observing the atmosphere can teach you a lot about what it's like to work there.

And don't worry if people's reactions are mixed or even discouraging. That doesn't necessarily mean the career field is wrong for you—it might just mean that particular company or team isn't the right fit. Every experience helps you learn and make a more informed choice about where you belong.

In the next few chapters, we're going to dig into the different paths you can take to get into the career field you feel drawn to. Just like I shared earlier in my own work story, you might not stick with the same job or field forever—and that's totally okay! Life is full of twists and turns, and sometimes God surprises us with new directions we never saw coming. You don't have to have it all figured out right now—seriously, don't stress. God's got you!

And if you follow what He says in Colossians—you're already on the right track.

> "Think about the things of heaven, not the things of earth."
>
> —Colossians 3:2 NLT

The big idea? Be open to the adventure. God has so much in store for you, and this journey is about more than just landing a job—it's about discovering all the good things He's created you to do.

Like it says in Ephesians:

> "For we are God's masterpiece. He has created us anew in Christ Jesus, so we can do the good things he planned for us long ago."
>
> —Ephesians 2:10 NLT

So get ready, stay curious, and let's see where this path leads.

You've got this—and even more importantly, God's got you!

You Are Unique!

B efore you jump into the next step of discovering your direction in life, let's pause and look at all of this from *God's* perspective. After all, *He* created you.

Just stop and wrap your mind around that for a moment—really let it settle in. The God of the universe *thought about you*, intentionally formed you, and has a purpose for your life ahead.

You are not a mistake.
You are not random.
You *do* matter.
You are *valuable* to God.

> "Thank you for making me so wonderfully complex! Your workmanship is marvelous—how well I know it."
> —Psalm 139:14 NLT

He fearfully and wonderfully made you. And when *He* says that, it carries a depth and weight that we can't even fully grasp on this side of eternity. It means your design is *deliberate, beautiful,* and *full of meaning*.

So take a moment—right now. Talk to Him about it. Let your heart connect with the reality of His intentionality in creating *you*.

He really does love and care about you. And He has amazing things ahead—things He's inviting you into for His kingdom, for His glory... and even for your own joy and fulfillment.

Now, Here Are Some Tools...

The following resources are just that—tools. They aren't labels or boxes to squeeze yourself into. They're simply ways to uncover some of the gifts and wiring God has placed inside of you.

There's no "right" or "wrong" with any of these. You are exactly who God created you to be. Period.

Let these tools help you discover more of what's already true. Let them broaden your vision. Use them to open your eyes to more of the plan God is revealing—one step at a time.

Tools That Help You Discover More About Yourself

There are some incredibly useful tools that have helped millions of people gain clarity about their God-given design. Here are a few worth exploring:

StrengthsFinder (now CliftonStrengths)

In 1948, Dr. Donald Clifton asked a bold question: *"What would happen if we studied what was right with people instead of what's wrong with them?"* That question launched decades of research and ultimately led to the development of the StrengthsFinder assessment.

This tool helps you identify your Top 5 natural talents—the things you do instinctively well. What's powerful is that when you *invest* in these talents, they become *strengths*.

Gallup studied over 2 million people and found something fascinating: individuals who focused on developing their strengths were many times more productive, fulfilled, and successful than those who tried to shore up their weaknesses. The effect wasn't linear; it was *exponential*. You get significantly more return by leaning into what you do best.

Here's an excerpt from the original *StrengthsFinder 2.0* book:[1]

> "Far too many people spend their lives being average at a lot of things instead of becoming excellent at the few things they are naturally wired to do well. When you focus on your top strengths, everything changes—your confidence, your energy, your effectiveness."
>
> Dr. Donald Clifton

Some common themes you might see in your Top 5 include: Strategic, Achiever, Empathy, Input, Communication, and more. Each strength brings a different contribution to the world—and to the Body of Christ.

My wife and I took the StrengthsFinder assessment many years ago, and it was a powerful tool for understanding more of what drives us—especially the deeper, heart-level motivations behind our choices. At first,

I purchased the version that shows your Top 5 out of the 34 strengths. Later on, I upgraded to see the full list of all 34. It gave me a much broader picture of how I'm wired—and confirmed a lot of things I had sensed about myself but hadn't been able to articulate.

One of the first things I noticed—and something many people do—is that we tend to skip right past our top strengths and go straight to the bottom of the list. Even though the tool calls *all 34 themes* "strengths," we still look at the ones at the bottom as weaknesses.

That's how we've been trained—starting from our early school years and reinforced by the culture around us. We're constantly asked, *"Where can you improve?" "What are your weaknesses?"* And of course, job interviews nearly always include some version of, *"Tell me your strengths... and your weaknesses."*

But the whole idea behind StrengthsFinder is that all 34 traits are *strengths*. Some are just more dominant in your life than others.

What I've learned—both from the research and from my own experience—is that one of the biggest mistakes people make is focusing all their time and energy on what's at the bottom of the list. They pour effort, money, and attention into trying to "fix" what they think is broken. And sure, you might see some improvement. But the real power comes when you do the opposite—when you invest in your Top 5 or Top 10 strengths. That's where the exponential growth happens.

Why? Because those top themes are the clearest reflection of how God uniquely designed you. They're not just random personality traits—they're clues to your calling.

There's a story from the early days of StrengthsFinder that really stuck with me. The first large-scale test of the concept was done with a group of college freshmen. Researchers assessed how fast they could read and how well they comprehended what they read. Then, they gave all the students the same speed-reading training and retested them afterward.

Most students improved—but not equally. The students who were originally *below average* improved from reading about 150 words per minute to 200. A little increase. But the students who were already *strong* in reading? They went from around 250 words per minute to over 700.

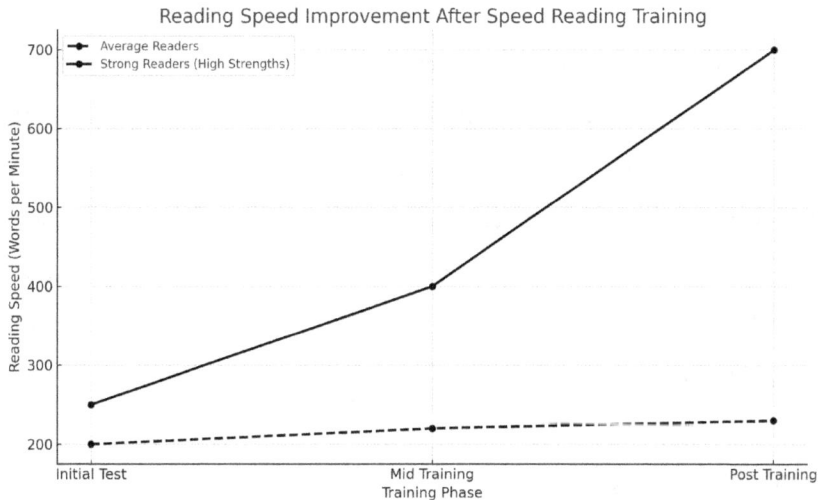

That's alot more than just a slight improvement. That's exponential!

I've found the StrengthsFinder assessment to be incredibly valuable in a work or team environment. One of the best ways to apply it is to have each team member take the test, and then intentionally invest time teaching and unpacking what each strength means. When people really understand the strengths—not just their own, but also their teammates'—it opens the door to empathy, appreciation, and better collaboration.

But it doesn't stop there. The real transformation happens when a team learns not only what their individual strengths are, but also how those strengths interact with others. Team dynamics shift when people recognize that their differences are not conflicts—they're design. God created each person with intentional wiring, and when we operate with that understanding, the whole team becomes stronger.

Let me explain a little deeper.

I've watched teams work on projects where all sorts of attitudes start to show. Some people walk in confident, ready to share. Others sit quietly, unsure why they're even on the team. Some feel like imposters, thinking they don't have enough experience or insight to contribute. And occasionally, there's someone who seems to shoot down every idea, frustrated or skeptical of the process. That kind of environment can quickly shut people down.

Take this example:

Tom brings up an idea. Immediately, Sam shoots holes in it—makes Tom feel like it was a dumb idea in the first place. But Tom's the only one even trying, tossing out more suggestions, and Sam keeps cutting them down. Eventually, no one wants to speak up. The energy is gone. Creativity dries up. The project flounders.

Now imagine the same scenario—with the same team, same project, but one big change.

Everyone on the team has taken StrengthsFinder and has been through teaching sessions that explain both the individual strengths and how they play out in team dynamics. Now, things look different.

Tom has discovered that one of his top strengths is Ideation—he naturally comes up with creative ideas and alternatives. It's how he's wired. He's not trying to dominate; he's trying to contribute.

Sam has learned that one of his top strengths is Analytical—he sees all the gaps, risks, and data behind every idea almost instantly. He's not trying to be critical—he's trying to protect the team from wasted effort and make sure the best ideas rise to the top.

With this shared understanding, Tom doesn't take offense when Sam raises concerns. And Sam doesn't dismiss Tom's creativity. Instead, the team sees the dynamic as a gift. Tom keeps tossing out ideas, and even if Sam questions 98% of them, the other 2%—the cream of the crop—rise up. Those few ideas may end up saving time, money, and energy. The team gets to the best solution faster, and even better, they become a more unified, respectful group in the process.

That's the power of using this tool well. When you create space for people to thrive in their God-given strengths, you don't just get better project results—you build stronger relationships, healthier work environments, and a culture of honor and trust.

That's worth the investment. Every time.

And that's the heart of the strengths-based approach: Don't spend your life trying to be someone you're not. Instead, lean into who God already made you to be, and you'll grow further and faster than you ever imagined.

Myers-Briggs (MBTI)

The Myers-Briggs Type Indicator (MBTI) is a well-known personality tool that helps you understand how you're naturally wired. It assigns you a four-letter type—like INFJ or ESTP—based on your preferences in four key areas: how you gain energy (Introvert or Extravert), how you take in information (Sensing or Intuition), how you make decisions (Thinking or Feeling), and how you prefer to live your outer life (Judging or Perceiving).

My wife and I took this test years ago, and it was surprisingly helpful—especially in understanding how differently we each process things in life. I'm more of an external processor, meaning I often talk things out to gain clarity. My wife, on the other hand, is an internal processor. She needs quiet, space, and time to think things through before she's ready to talk. Neither approach is right or wrong—it's simply how God made each of us. Realizing this has brought a lot of peace and grace into our marriage. When we walk through something challenging or important, I've learned to give her space to process privately, knowing that we'll come back together to talk through it and find unity.

This kind of understanding isn't just valuable in relationships—it's also incredibly helpful in the workplace. Knowing how your coworkers process information, make decisions, and communicate can help build stronger teams, reduce frustration, and create an environment where everyone feels seen and valued.

DISC Profile

The DISC personality model is a simple but powerful tool that breaks down behavior into four main styles: Dominance, Influence, Steadiness, and Conscientiousness. It's kind of like discovering the "operating system" behind how people interact, make decisions, and handle tasks. Once you understand which style you tend to lean toward, things start to click—both in how you work and how you relate to others.

What makes DISC especially helpful is how easy it is to apply in real-life situations—especially in teams. Ever wondered why someone is super direct and always pushing for results, while someone else wants to make sure *everyone* feels heard and valued? That's DISC at play. It gives language and insight to those personality differences that can otherwise lead to frustration or miscommunication.

The best part? It helps you see that these differences aren't problems—they're strengths. Every team needs a mix: the go-getters, the encouragers, the peacemakers, and the detail-masters. When you learn to recognize and respect each style, you stop trying to change people and start celebrating how God wired them. That kind of understanding can transform the way a team works together.

Enneagram

The Enneagram is like having a cheat code for understanding yourself—and everyone around you. Instead of just describing *what* you do, it goes deeper and helps you explore *why* you do it. It's all about motivation, fear, and what your heart is really after.

There are nine core types in the Enneagram. Each one sees the world through a different lens and has a unique inner drive. No type is better or worse—they're just different. And honestly? Once you start learning about them, you'll start seeing them everywhere. ("Ohhh... *that's* why Uncle Bob double-checks every light switch before leaving the house!")

Here's a quick breakdown of the nine types:

- **Type 1 – The Reformer**: Motivated by a need to be good, right, and ethical. Big on integrity. Also big on lists.

- **Type 2 – The Helper**: Driven by a desire to be loved and needed. They'll bring you soup before you even realize you're sick.

- **Type 3 – The Achiever**: Wants to be successful and admired. Often wins "Most Likely to Succeed" and already has a plan for it.

- **Type 4 – The Individualist**: Desires to be unique and authentic. Deep feelers, often artistic, and a little allergic to anything fake.

- **Type 5 – The Investigator**: Craves knowledge and self-sufficiency. Basically human encyclopedias with strong "do not disturb" energy.

- **Type 6 – The Loyalist**: Motivated by security and support. Super loyal, cautious, and always thinking two steps ahead.

- **Type 7 – The Enthusiast**: Wants to be happy and free. Bursting with energy, new ideas, and "Hey, what if we bought a food truck?" energy.

- **Type 8 – The Challenger**: Desires control and independence. Bold, confident, and not afraid to say what everyone else is thinking.

- **Type 9 – The Peacemaker**: Wants inner and outer peace. Chill, agreeable, and fluent in keeping the vibe calm.

Now, let's see how this plays out in real life...

Without Enneagram knowledge:
Sarah (a Type 1) is planning a big event with Jake (a Type 7). She shows up with spreadsheets, timelines, and color-coded post-its. Jake waltzes in with a latte and a wild idea involving fire dancers, bubble machines, and possibly alpacas. Sarah is mortified. Jake is confused why she's so tense. Sarah thinks Jake is irresponsible. Jake thinks Sarah needs to breathe into a paper bag. The project limps along in awkward tension.

With Enneagram knowledge:
Sarah now *knows* she's a perfectionist who values order and excellence. She also knows that her rigidity can be tough on others. Jake realizes his love for fun and freedom can sometimes derail real progress. Instead of clashing, they get curious about each other. Sarah lets the creative ideas fly before sorting them. Jake respects the plan and chooses the best of his ideas to fit within it. No more power struggle. Just teamwork, laughter—and yes, they compromise on bubble machines *without* the alpacas.

The Secret Sauce to Team Harmony

In a team setting, the Enneagram is like having secret glasses that let you see everyone's *why*. Why someone hesitates. Why someone dominates the meeting. Why someone always finds the risk—or the joke. When team members understand their own types and the types of others, the room shifts from tension to teamwork.

Let's say your team has a Type 3 (Achiever), a Type 6 (Loyalist), and a Type 9 (Peacemaker). The 3 is charging ahead with a plan, laser-focused on getting results. The 6 is throwing out all the "what ifs" and spotting the risks. The 9 is just trying to keep everyone happy and the vibe chill. Without awareness, the 3 gets annoyed, the 6 feels ignored, and the 9 checks out. But *with* Enneagram knowledge? The 3 slows down to hear concerns, the 6 feels valued for their insight, and the 9 helps everyone stay connected. Boom—power team.

Now picture a Type 4 (Individualist) and a Type 8 (Challenger) brainstorming. The 4 tosses out a creative idea from the heart. The 8 immediately challenges it with "That won't work—here's why." Without Enneagram insight? Ouch. Feelings hurt. Walls up. With Enneagram insight? The 4 knows not to take it personally, and the 8 learns to challenge ideas gently. Result? A stronger idea and no hard feelings.

And in project planning, say you've got a Type 5 (Investigator) and a Type 2 (Helper). The 5 wants data, spreadsheets, and quiet time to think. The 2 wants to make sure everyone is okay and the team feels supported. With Enneagram awareness, they stop frustrating each other and start collaborating. The 5 provides solid strategy, the 2 brings heart and people-care, and together they make something that actually works *and* feels good.

When people understand the Enneagram, they stop seeing differences as annoyances and start seeing them as superpowers. The result? Better projects, better meetings, and way better vibes in the workplace. Trust grows. Communication gets clearer. And the team becomes more than a group of people doing a task—they become a team that actually *wants* to work together again.

That's the strength of the Enneagram. It won't fix all your problems, but it gives you the language and grace to grow—and to love the people around you better, quirks and all.

You Were Made for This

These tools are helpful, but remember—they're not your identity. Your identity is found in Christ. These just help reveal the beautiful handiwork He already placed inside you.

You're not starting from scratch—you're uncovering the masterpiece He's been crafting since the moment you were born.

> "You made all the delicate, inner parts of my body and knit me together in my mother's womb."
> —Psalm 139:13 NLT

So lean in to the process. Learn. Grow. And above all—trust the One who made you.

It's Not Just About You (But Starts With You)

The more you discover about how God wired you, the easier it becomes to spot where you fit—and *why*. You'll start seeing purpose in places that used to feel random. You'll recognize roles, environments, and rhythms where you thrive. And you'll also start noticing how others shine in their own unique way.

That old saying is true: "If you love what you do, you'll never work a day in your life." When you understand your design and step into work that aligns with it, it doesn't feel like a grind. It feels like partnership—with purpose, passion, and peace.

Better yet, you'll stop feeling intimidated by people who are different from you. Instead of avoiding that coworker who "just doesn't get you," you'll start understanding them—and maybe even appreciating them. That's the beauty of knowing both your wiring *and* theirs.

Give Them Space—God's Still Working

But here's something important to remember: not everyone is operating from their God-given wiring all the time. Some people react out of pain, past trauma, or emotional strongholds. As believers, we can recognize that. Instead of judging them, we pray. We ask the Holy Spirit how to love them well—right where they are—and whether He wants us to say something, help in some way, or simply *wait*.

I remember a time when a friend of mine was going through intense financial stress. I wanted so badly to help. When an opportunity came up to hire him to build a fence, I jumped on it. It seemed like the perfect way to bless him and his family. But I had this subtle check in my spirit—just a whisper that maybe I shouldn't.

In my excitement, I ignored it. I thought, *This will solve everything!* But as soon as I hired him, I heard the Lord speak clearly:

"You just extended the work I was doing in his life by six more months."

That hit hard. God had a plan, and in trying to fix it myself, I accidentally slowed it down.

Sure enough, about six months later, that friend and I had a heart-to-heart. He and his wife had come out of that season right around the time God had spoken to me. It was humbling—but also a reminder. Sometimes the "good thing" we want to do *isn't* the *God thing*. That's why it's so important to listen, to ask, and to stay sensitive to the Spirit. Because God is always at work—not just in us, but in *everyone around us*.

And in the end, that's what all this self-awareness is about—not just knowing your wiring, but tuning into His voice.

> "For, 'Who can know the Lord's thoughts? Who knows enough to teach him?' But we understand these things, for we have the mind of Christ."
> —1 Corinthians 2:16 NLT

So as you learn more about how God made you—your strengths, your personality, your gifts—keep bringing it back to Him. Ask Him what He's doing in you and through you. Ask Him how to love your team, your coworkers, and even the tough ones. And above all, ask Him to lead your steps so that your "good things" are really God things.

Because when your work, your wiring, and your walk with God all come together—that's the sweet spot – when the adventure really begins.

Resources

1. CliftonStrengths (StrengthsFinder)

www.gallup.com/cliftonstrengths

Take the online assessment to discover your Top 5 strengths. You'll need to purchase a code (usually included with the *StrengthsFinder 2.0* book or available directly from the website).

2. Myers-Briggs (MBTI)

www.16personalities.com

This free version of the Myers-Briggs test offers a great introduction to your personality type with easy-to-understand results and descriptions.

3. DISC Personality Profile

www.truity.com/test/disc-personality-test

A simple, free version of the DISC test that gives you insights into your communication and work style.

4. Enneagram Personality Test

https://iancron.ieq9.com/Discover your type and better understand your strengths, challenges, and personal growth path.

5. *StrengthsFinder 2.0* by Tom Rath

This bestselling book introduces the strengths-based approach and includes an access code for the assessment. Great for deeper understanding of each strength theme.

6. *The Road Back to You* by Ian Morgan Cron and Suzanne Stabile

An accessible and popular introduction to the Enneagram from a Christian perspective.

7. *Discover Your God-Given Gifts* by Don and Katie Fortune

A biblical approach to spiritual gifts that helps you identify how God may have uniquely equipped you for ministry and service.

College: Caffeine, Classes & Calling

Why Even Consider College?

So, should you go to college? It's a big question—and not just because everyone's asking. Maybe you're excited about dorm life, picking a major, or diving into a dream career. Or maybe you're thinking, *"Do I really need this to figure out my life?"* The truth is, college can be way more than textbooks and finals. It's a chance to grow, meet lifelong friends, explore new ideas, and start becoming the person you're meant to be. It's a place where you get to try things, fail safely, and find out what lights you up.

Here's the awesome part—there's more than one way to build a great future! College can open a lot of doors, offering a strong foundation and amazing experiences. At the same time, many tech companies are just as excited to see real-world skills backed by professional certifications. Whether you earn a degree, stack up some certs, or even do both, what really matters is that you're learning, growing, and getting ready to make an impact!

This chapter isn't here to sell you a one-size-fits-all dream. Instead, let's look at what college *can* offer, how to figure out if it fits *your* goals, and how to get the most out of it if you go. Whether you end up loving campus life or taking a different route, the goal is the same: grow wiser, take responsibility, and step into your life with purpose and confidence.

College isn't just about the degree at the end—it's about the journey in between. You'll learn how to manage your time (or at least how *not* to procrastinate), juggle priorities, and solve real-life problems. You'll meet people from different backgrounds, be exposed to new perspectives, and have conversations that stretch your thinking. Whether you're sitting in a lecture hall, grabbing late-night food with your roommates, or figuring out how to budget your meal plan money, you're gaining skills that go way beyond the classroom. These everyday moments shape your character, your habits, and how you approach the world.

And let's not forget: this is also a time when your faith can grow in new ways. For the first time, you will be making spiritual choices on your own—choosing to go to church (or not), finding Christian community, or wrestling with big questions. That's not something to be scared of; it's an opportunity. College can be a season where God shows up in unexpected ways—in the quiet moments, the hard conversations, and even in the chaos of finals week. So whether you're sure about your future or still figuring it out, college can be a space where God shapes your story one step at a time.

No matter where you're starting from—whether you graduated high school with honors and scholarships in hand, or did just okay and are looking for a fresh start, or never finished high school but still dream of going to college—there's a path forward. College isn't just for one "type" of student. What really matters is being honest about where you are and where you want to go. Everyone's journey looks different, and that's okay! The key is to look at your options with clear eyes and an open heart.

Here are a few things to consider:

- **Why do you want to go?** Are you aiming for a specific career? Hoping to grow personally? Looking for community or a fresh start? Knowing *your why* will help guide your decisions.

- **What kind of environment fits you best?** Big university or small college? Online or in-person? Close to home or a new city?

- **What's realistic financially?** Explore scholarships, grants, work-study options, and affordable schools. Don't rule out community colleges—they can be a smart, budget-friendly launch point.

- **Do you need to take care of anything first?** If you didn't finish high school, consider getting your GED or looking into colleges with flexible admissions paths.

- **Are you ready for the responsibility?** College takes motivation, time management, and maturity. But don't worry—you'll grow in all of those as you go!

No matter your background, if you're willing to work, stay open, and trust God with each step, college can absolutely be part of your story.

The Making of a President

If you've ever thought, *"There's no way someone like me could ever do something big,"* then let's talk about Abraham Lincoln—because his story proves that where you start doesn't have to be where you finish.

Lincoln was born in a tiny log cabin in Kentucky in 1809, and let's just say—he didn't have much going for him on paper. His family was dirt poor. His mother died when he was just nine. He barely had any formal schooling—maybe a year total—and spent most of his childhood doing hard labor to help his family survive. No special connections, no fancy tutors, no silver spoon. Just a quiet, hardworking kid with a curious mind and a whole lot of grit.

But instead of giving up or staying stuck, Lincoln decided to grow. He read whatever books he could borrow, taught himself new skills, and learned from every failure along the way. He ran for office—*and lost*—multiple times before eventually being elected president. And not just any president—he led the country through one of its darkest seasons and helped bring an end to slavery. His leadership literally changed history.

So if you're feeling like you are stuck or that your background disqualifies you, or your circumstances are just too hard to break out of—hold up. Look at Lincoln. He came from nothing, faced setback after setback, and still rose to become a world-changer. That kind of hope isn't just for history books—it's for *you*, right now.

You don't have to have it all figured out today. Just take the next step. Keep growing. Keep showing up. Because your story isn't over—and it might just be more powerful than you ever imagined.

Associate to PhD: What's Up with All These Degrees?

Colleges offer several types of degrees, and don't worry—you don't have to do them all at once! Some people finish a 2-year or 4-year degree, jump into the workforce, and then come back later—sometimes part-time—to earn a master's or even a PhD while working.

In fact, many companies offer tuition assistance programs to help pay for those advanced degrees. Just know that these programs often come with a catch: you may need to stay with the company for a certain number of years afterward, or you could be asked to pay the money back if you leave early. It's a great option if you're looking to grow your skills without footing the full bill!

Here are some of the degree options you'll find at many colleges—each one is a different step on the path, depending on how far you want to go and what you want to do!

Associate Degree (2 years)

This is your first step into college-level learning. Usually takes about two years at a community college or technical school. Great for jumping into a career sooner or as a stepping stone toward a bachelor's degree.

Bachelor's Degree (4 years total)

This is the classic "college degree" most people think of. It usually takes four years and is offered by universities and colleges. You'll dive deeper into your field of study and also take general education classes to round things out.

Master's Degree (2 more years)

Ready to level up? A master's degree typically takes an additional two years after your bachelor's. It lets you specialize in something specific and can open doors to higher-level jobs or leadership roles.

Doctoral Degree / PhD (2–4 more years)

This is the big league. A PhD (or other doctoral degree) is all about original research, deep expertise, and academic contribution. It can take anywhere from 2 to 4 more years—or even longer depending on the field. Definitely a marathon, but worth it if you're passionate about research, teaching, or becoming a top expert in your area.

Think of it like climbing a mountain—each level gets you closer to your goals, but you don't have to climb the whole thing unless it fits your calling!

So You Found Your College... Now What?

So, you've narrowed it down to one or more colleges you're interested in—awesome! But here's your friendly reminder: don't wait until the last minute to apply. The college application process can take longer than you think, especially when you factor in gathering documents, writing essays, and waiting on things like transcripts and recommendation letters. Most colleges have their steps clearly laid out on their websites, so do your research. And if something isn't clear or you have specific questions, don't be shy about contacting the school directly—they're used to helping students like you.

Many students apply to more than one school, and for good reason. Each college has its own acceptance criteria, enrollment limits, and sometimes unpredictable admissions decisions. So don't bank everything on just one place. Imagine going through months of effort for one school, only to find out you didn't get in—and now it's too late to apply anywhere else. Give yourself some options and have a plan B just in case.

Here's something a lot of people don't realize: colleges, as exciting and inspiring as they may seem, are still businesses. Their product is education—knowledge, experiences, and opportunities—and you're the customer. You're the one paying the cost, whether through time, money, effort, or all of the above. So approach your decision wisely, like any big investment.

Also, it's important to know that getting a degree doesn't automatically guarantee a job. One common mistake is choosing a super-specific degree that sounds exciting but only applies to a tiny corner of the job market—maybe even in a location you'd never want to live. When picking a major, think long-term. Choose something that's not only interesting to you but also *marketable*—something that companies are actually hiring for in the career field you're aiming toward.

And here's a real-world example: when I started working at Texas Instruments programming robotic machines that built computer chips, most of the people doing that kind of work weren't computer science majors—because back then, that degree wasn't common yet. TI hired electrical engineers and trained them to be software developers. That's still how it works in a lot of places. A degree gives you a solid *foundation*—but most companies will build on that and train you to do the specific job they hired you for.

So think of your college education as the launchpad, not the finish line. It's the beginning of something great, and with a thoughtful, open-minded approach, you'll be ready for wherever it takes you.

Alright, let's talk real life for a sec. Below is a list of things that are totally worth thinking about as you step into the college application world. Some of these might fit your situation perfectly, some maybe not—but that's okay! Everyone's journey is different. The goal here is to give you a bigger-picture look at what goes into applying to college so you're not caught off guard. Think of it like a "starter pack" to help boost your chances of hearing that sweet word: *accepted!*

Dream a little

Start by letting your imagination run a bit. What do you love learning about? What kind of people energize you? Do you picture yourself in a big university with tons of activity or a small college with cozy class sizes and personal connections? You don't have to have everything figured out yet—this is just about starting to notice what lights you up and what kind of environment might help you grow. It's totally okay if you change your mind later. The goal here is to begin dreaming.

Do some exploring

Now that you're dreaming, it's time to get curious. Start researching colleges online—check out their websites, social media, and YouTube channels. See what kinds of majors they offer, what campus life is like, and if they have clubs or programs you're into. Talk to friends, older students, mentors, or even teachers who've been through it. If you can, visit a few campuses in person—it makes a huge difference. This is like window shopping for your future—enjoy the process!

Take the tests (if needed)

Some colleges still ask for SAT or ACT scores, so find out which schools on your list require them. Not all do, and many are test-optional now—but if you need to take a test, go ahead and schedule it early.

There are free resources online to help you prep, and you don't have to be perfect—just do your best. Think of it as one small step in a much bigger journey, not the whole story of your potential.

Get your transcripts

Your transcript is basically your report card from high school, and colleges want to see it. Most schools have a pretty easy process for sending it to colleges—just ask your counselor or school office. Make sure it gets sent to every college you apply to. You don't need to stress about having perfect grades, either—colleges are looking at the whole picture, not just numbers.

Write your story

Your college essay is your chance to share who *you* are—not just as a student, but as a person. What have you been through? What matters to you? What have you learned along the way? Be honest, be real, and don't try to sound like someone else. This is your moment to tell your story in your voice. A well-written, heartfelt essay can leave a big impression.

Ask for references

Colleges often want to hear from people who know you well—like a teacher, coach, youth leader, or boss. Ask them early, be polite, and maybe even share what you're excited about. They'll write recommendation letters that give colleges a glimpse of your character, work ethic, and the kind of person you are when no one's looking. It's like having a few cheerleaders in your corner.

Fill out the applications

Most college applications are online and ask for basic stuff: your contact info, high school history, extracurriculars, and your essay. Take your time, be accurate, and double-check everything before hitting submit. It might feel like a lot of forms, but remember—each one is a step closer to a new adventure. You've got this.

Send it off

Once everything's filled out, reviewed, and you've hit that glorious submit button, it's time to celebrate! Seriously—do a happy dance, eat your favorite snack, or text a friend. You've just completed a major milestone, and that's a big deal. Now the waiting begins, but in the meantime, know you've already done something brave.

Apply for financial aid

College isn't cheap—but don't let that scare you. There's help out there! Start by filling out the FAFSA (Free Application for Federal Student Aid), which tells you what financial aid you're eligible for.

Then check with each college for scholarships, grants, and work-study options. It's kind of like treasure hunting—there are resources out there, you just have to dig a little to find them.

Watch your inbox

After applying, colleges will start sending updates, decisions, and next steps—so keep an eye on your email (and your spam folder just in case). You might get requests for extra info or (fingers crossed) an acceptance letter! This part can feel like a rollercoaster of emotions, but trust that what's meant for you won't miss you.

Make your choice

Once the decisions are in, it's time to prayerfully consider your options. Which school feels right? Where do you sense peace, purpose, and possibility? Talk it over with trusted people—parents, mentors, friends—and ask God for wisdom. Remember, it's not about picking the "perfect" school; it's about choosing a place where you'll grow into who you're becoming.

Get ready for the adventure

After you've said yes to your school, there'll be a whole new to-do list—like registering for classes, choosing housing, and maybe even shopping for dorm stuff. Orientation will give you a head start, and soon enough, it'll be move-in day. A new chapter is waiting, and you're walking into it with courage, purpose, and excitement. Let the adventure begin!

Skilled and Ready: The Trade & Tech Advantage

C ollege is a great choice for many, but it's not the only way to build a successful and fulfilling career. Trade and tech schools offer a different kind of opportunity—one that's hands-on, practical, and focused on teaching the exact skills you need to jump into the workforce. Whether you're into building, fixing, creating, or solving problems, these programs are designed to get you trained and hired without spending years in a lecture hall.

What's exciting is how many career fields today are wide open to people who take this path. These are not "backup plan" jobs—they're strong, reliable careers in industries that keep the world running. From healthcare and IT to construction and automotive work, trade and tech programs lead to real-world roles that are in high demand, pay well, and give you room to grow. This chapter will help you see what's possible and why this path might be a perfect fit for your future.

So, what exactly *is* the difference between a trade school and a tech school?

They sound similar, and honestly, sometimes people use the terms interchangeably. But there are some key differences worth knowing—especially if you're trying to figure out which path might be right for you.

Trade school focuses on hands-on careers—think working with tools, fixing things, building structures, or providing services that keep everyday life running. If you've ever watched someone install a new AC system, repair a car, wire a house, or cut hair with skill and precision, you've seen a trade professional in action. These schools train you in practical skills, often in under two years, and lead to certifications or licenses that get you straight into the workforce. They're direct, focused, and often include real-world apprenticeships.

Tech schools, on the other hand, center around careers that are more technology- or science-driven. The hands-on part is still there, but you might find yourself in a lab instead of on a job site, or working behind a screen instead of behind a toolbox. Tech schools train students for careers in fields like IT, cybersecurity, medical imaging, web development, or even robotics and automation. Some programs lead to certifications, while others offer associate degrees, depending on the job and the school.

The beautiful thing is, both trade and tech schools share the same heartbeat: teaching you real-world skills that matter. They skip the fluff and get right to the stuff that helps you land a job, start earning, and build something solid for your future. Whether you see yourself wearing steel-toed boots or sitting behind a screen solving tech puzzles, there's a place for you in this world of skilled, in-demand work.

Hard Hats, Lab Coats, and Laptops

There are so many different directions you can go with a trade or tech school education. While this list doesn't include *every* possible option, it does give you a good look at some of the most common and high-demand areas of training available in each path. Whether you're drawn to fixing, building, healing, or solving—there's likely a program designed to help you get there.

Trade School Careers

These roles are typically hands-on, often involve working with tools or machinery, and may require state certifications or licensing:

Electrician

Plumber

Welder

HVAC technician (heating, ventilation, and air conditioning)

Carpenter

Automotive technician or mechanic

Diesel mechanic

Masonry or concrete worker

Heavy equipment operator

Elevator installer and repair technician

Cosmetologist or barber

Commercial truck driver (CDL training)

Lineworker (utility/power company)

Firefighter or EMT (in some programs)

Tech School Careers

These roles lean more into technology, healthcare, and lab-based or computer-driven work, often involving certifications or associate degrees:

IT support specialist

Network technician or administrator

Cybersecurity technician

Web developer

Computer programmer or coder

Medical laboratory technician

Radiologic technologist (X-ray tech)

Ultrasound or sonography technician

Dental hygienist

Pharmacy technician

Surgical technologist

CAD (computer-aided design) technician

Electronics or robotics technician

Mechatronics specialist

These programs are built to prepare you for real jobs in the real world—many of them with strong starting salaries, career growth, and long-term stability. So whether your interests are in tools or tech, helping people or solving systems, this kind of training is a powerful first step.

Punch In with Purpose: Building While You Work

One route you might take after high school is to jump straight into the workforce without going to college or a trade school right away. If you're unsure about what career path you want to follow, getting a job can be a great way to start figuring things out. You could begin with an entry-level position in retail, food service, or at a local business—something that lets you earn money, learn how to manage your time, and build real-world skills. As you work, you'll gain valuable experience, meet all kinds of people, and start to get a better sense of what kind of work you enjoy and what environments help you thrive.

This season of life is also a powerful opportunity to grow personally and spiritually. While you're working, you can seek God for direction, trusting that He'll guide you as you go. Every job, no matter how small it seems, can teach you something meaningful about responsibility, teamwork, and perseverance. You might try different roles, pick up side gigs, or volunteer—using this time to stretch your skills and discover your passions. It's okay not to have it all figured out right now.

As God reminds us:

> "Trust in the Lord with all your heart; do not depend on your own understanding. Seek his will in all you do, and he will show you which path to take."
>
> —Proverbs 3:5-6 NLT

Be wise in this season and don't settle into a job just because it's comfortable or familiar. Many people before you have started working just to get by, and years later, they found themselves stuck in a job that didn't lead anywhere. Don't let that be your story be intentional. While it's good to take that first step and start working, always keep your eyes open for growth opportunities. Ask yourself if this job is building skills that could transfer into a long-term career or open doors for the future. If not, use it as a stepping stone, not a destination.

Also, be thoughtful about your finances. Consider the pay you're receiving and whether it's truly enough to support the life you're trying to build. Don't avoid hard questions like rent, transportation, food, or savings. Learning to budget wisely in this early season can protect you from unnecessary stress and debt down the road.

God reminds us:

> "But don't begin until you count the cost. For who would begin construction of a building without first calculating the cost to see if there is enough money to finish it?"
>
> —Luke 14:28 NLT

Trust God for guidance, but also take responsibility to make wise, informed decisions while you figure out your next steps.

To keep this season of your life fruitful, it's important to be intentional with your time, energy, and focus. Start by setting some personal goals—not just big, long-term dreams, but small, measurable steps that help you grow. These could be as simple as learning a new skill, saving a certain amount of money, reading one book a month, or exploring different career paths. Goals give your days purpose and help you see progress, even in a season that may feel uncertain. Don't let the routine of a job make you stagnant—use this time to stretch yourself, challenge your comfort zone, and keep moving forward.

Most importantly, seek God in every part of this journey. Make space for Him in your daily life—through prayer, Scripture, and quiet moments of reflection. Ask Him to guide your decisions, shape your desires, and reveal His plans for you. He promises to lead those who trust Him. Jeremiah 29:13 says, *"If you look for me wholeheartedly, you will find me."* NLT. When you include God in your goals, He gives you wisdom, peace, and the clarity you need to take your next step. This season may not be permanent, but it can be deeply meaningful if you invite God into it and commit to growing through it.

The Entrepreneur's Path: Dreaming Beyond the Day Job

Some people have a deep desire to become entrepreneurs, and starting out by simply working a job can actually give them the freedom and space to dream. A steady job can provide the income and structure needed while you begin developing your business ideas on the side. Whether you have a degree or not, whether you're working full-time or part-time, this approach allows you to gain real-world experience, understand how businesses operate, and learn valuable lessons that will help you when it's time to launch your own. Working a job doesn't have to be the end goal—it can be the foundation that supports your vision.

In fact, this season can be the perfect time to test ideas, build skills, and slowly start creating something you can eventually own and lead. If you're faithful with your time, diligent with your work, and open to learning, God can use this season to prepare you for entrepreneurship in powerful ways.

We are told in Proverbs:

"Commit your actions to the Lord, and your plans will succeed."

—Proverbs 16:3 NLT

As you dream and plan, bring it all before God. Ask Him to guide your steps, connect you with the right people, and give you the courage to build something meaningful. Being an entrepreneur isn't just about making money—it's about creating value, taking responsibility, and stewarding what God puts in your heart to build.

CEO in the Making (and Slightly Freaking Out)

Entrepreneurship is full of exciting potential, but it's also a path that requires wisdom and awareness. Along the way, many aspiring business owners make some great choices—like starting small, staying teachable, and seeking God's direction.

But there are also common pitfalls that can trip people up, such as jumping in without a plan, trying to do everything alone, or chasing money over purpose. The key is to move forward with intention, learn from others, and stay rooted in truth as you build something meaningful.

Smart Moves Aspiring Entrepreneurs Make

Start Small, Dream Big

You don't need a fancy office or a huge budget to begin. Test your ideas in simple ways—sell to a few people, get feedback, and grow from there. Great things often start in humble places.

Seek Out Wisdom

Mentors, books, podcasts, YouTube channels—there's so much wisdom out there. Don't try to figure it all out on your own. Learn from others who've already walked the path.

Keep the Bills Paid

Working a job while building your business on the side is not a lack of faith—it's a wise strategy. Let your job fund your dream while you build something solid.

Set Goals, Not Just Vibes

Dreams become real when you attach action steps to them. Break your vision into small, doable goals. It keeps you focused and helps you measure progress.

Commit It to God

This is huge. Prayerfully invite God into your planning process. He gives direction, peace, and clarity when things get foggy. *"Commit your actions to the Lord, and your plans will succeed."* Proverbs 16:3 NLT

Pitfalls to Watch Out For

Jumping Without a Plan

It's exciting to take a leap of faith, but don't jump without a parachute. Starting a business with no plan, no savings, and no safety net can lead to stress and burnout.

Going Solo for Too Long

It's tempting to do everything yourself, but entrepreneurship is a team sport. Collaborate, delegate, and invite trusted voices into your journey.

Ignoring the Numbers

A great idea without a solid budget can quickly turn into a financial mess. Know your numbers, track your expenses, and don't be afraid to ask for help with the money side of things.

Perfection Paralysis

Waiting for everything to be "just right" will keep your dream stuck in neutral. Start messy. Learn as you go. Your first version doesn't have to be your final one.

Making It All About the Money

Yes, businesses need to make money—but don't let profit be your only purpose. The most fulfilling ventures are the ones that serve people, solve problems, and reflect your God-given calling.

No matter your reason for choosing to just get a job and work for a while, make sure you do it with purpose—don't let yourself get stuck. Whether you go on to start your own business, head to school later, or take another path entirely, keep walking with God and following His lead. When you do, you'll find purpose in every step of the journey.

What Really Is a Resume?

A resume is kind of like your personal highlight reel. It's not your whole life story—it's just the best parts that show a potential boss who you are, what you've done, and what you're capable of doing. Think of it as a one-page snapshot of you in action. You want it to say, "Hey, here's what I bring to the table, and here's why you should totally call me."

Try to keep your resume on one page if you can. If you've got more experience, it's okay to stretch to two—but absolutely no more than that. You want it clean, sharp, and easy to read. No one wants to dig through five pages to figure out who you are.

What Do You Put On a Resume?

Start with the basics—your name, phone number, email (make sure it's professional), and maybe your city and state. If you've got a LinkedIn profile or online portfolio, go ahead and link it.

You can include a short intro or career goal at the top if you want—it doesn't have to be fancy. Just one or two lines about what kind of role you're aiming for and what makes you a solid candidate. Something like, "Friendly, organized, and ready to grow in a creative team environment," is great.

Next up are your skills—things like customer service, time management, video editing, communication, Excel, leadership... anything that makes sense for the job you want. These can be a mix of technical know-how and personal strengths.

Then there's your education. Include your school name, what you studied, and when you graduated or expect to graduate. If you've got a great GPA or special honors, you can include that too—but only if it helps your case.

When it comes to work experience, keep it relevant to the job you're applying for. You don't need to list every job you've ever had—just the ones that show responsibility, growth, and skill. Focus especially on how you helped the company, team, or organization you worked for. Even something like, "Helped run the live stream for Sunday morning services," is a great example, because it shows leadership, teamwork, technical skill, and how you played a part in making things happen smoothly.

Under each job you list, add a couple of short bullet points explaining what you did, what you learned, and how you made a positive impact. Employers aren't just looking for a list of tasks—they want to see how you contributed and made things better.

Don't forget about volunteer work, personal projects, or internships. If you helped plan an event, built a website for a family member, ran a fundraiser, or led a youth group team—those are *great* examples of real-world experience.

What *Not* to Put On It

You don't need your full home address (city and state are plenty). Definitely don't include a photo (unless you're applying for acting or modeling). But the most important thing? Don't exaggerate. Ever. It's not worth it. Always be real and honest about your experience and skills. Employers can usually spot exaggeration, and integrity will take you further anyway.

Make It Fit the Job

Every job is a little different, so your resume should be too. If you're applying for a tech job, focus on the software, systems, or code you know. If it's a retail or customer service role, highlight your people skills and how you handle pressure. For creative roles, feel free to show some personality and include links to your work. Whatever the job is, make sure the most relevant parts of your story stand out.

Wait... Some Jobs Have Tests?!

Yep, some jobs will ask you to take a quiz or two. You might get a typing test, a basic math or logic test, or even a personality quiz. Some will give you a "what would you do?" scenario to see how you think on your feet. Don't panic. These are normal, and there are tons of free practice tests online if you want to brush up beforehand.

Starting From Scratch? No Problem.

If you're just starting out and don't have much work history—don't be discouraged. Everyone starts somewhere. Use what you *do* have. Did you volunteer at church? Babysit? Help with a family business? Take a leadership role at school? That all counts. The goal is to show that you're responsible, motivated, and willing to learn.

And again—always be honest. Your resume is just a tool. It helps tell your story, and gives a potential boss a quick snapshot of who you are. But it's not the full picture.

Any good boss will know that. They'll look past the paper and, when they meet you, they'll sense your attitude, your heart, and your potential. A resume might get your foot in the door—but it's *you* who makes the lasting impression.

"I'm Staring at a Blank Page... Now What?"

First of all—take a deep breath. You are *not* the only one who's ever sat in front of a blank screen wondering how in the world to start a resume. Everyone starts there at some point, and you're in exactly the right spot: ready to take the first step.

Now, here's the good news: You don't have to figure it all out alone. There are a few different ways you can go about building your resume:

1. Use a Template (Seriously, They Help)

You can find *tons* of free resume templates online. Some are built into word processors like Google Docs or Microsoft Word, and others are available on websites like Canva, Zety, or even job search platforms like Indeed. Templates help you see what goes where—like a guide to get you rolling.

2. Ask for Help (No Shame in That Game)

If you've got a friend, sibling, parent, teacher, or mentor who's done a few resumes before, ask them to sit with you and help. Sometimes it's easier to talk it out with someone and let them help you shape your story into words on the page.

3. Hire a Pro (If You Want Polish)

There are services out there (some free, some paid) that will help you write and polish your resume. These can be helpful if you're applying for something competitive or just want that extra boost. But remember, if you're just starting out, it's totally okay to do it yourself with a little guidance.

Keep a Copy—Always!

One super important tip: every time you send a resume to a company, save a copy of exactly what you sent. Keep it digitally and also print one out and tuck it away somewhere safe. You'll thank yourself later.

Why? Because as you move through life and apply to new jobs, you'll probably need to update your resume again and again. And when that time comes, it helps to know where you've been—what job you worked, what you did, and when you did it.

I can't tell you how many times someone I helped with a resume came back later needing a copy... and hadn't kept it. It's way easier to update something than start over from scratch every time.

A Note About Job History & Applications

Over time, those job dates, company names, and job descriptions become gold. Most applications ask for your start and end dates and a description of what you did in each role. If you write it down now while it's fresh, you won't be struggling to remember details five years from now.

Even if the job didn't feel important at the time—maybe it was just seasonal or part-time—if it taught you something, it's worth documenting.

Should You Add References?

At the bottom of your resume, you can include a note like: "References available upon request."

This is a polite way of saying, "I've got people who can vouch for me if you want to talk to them."

Some people choose to list their references right on the resume, which is totally fine too. Either way, don't skip the step of checking with your references first. You never want a potential employer to call someone who has no idea you gave out their name.

When you ask someone to be a reference, give them a heads-up about the company you're applying to and confirm they're comfortable being contacted. Ask how they'd prefer to be reached—phone or email—and make sure they're okay with you sharing that info.

Final Thoughts

If you're just getting started and don't have a long job history, don't let that discourage you. You're not trying to impress someone with a packed resume—you're just being honest about where you are and what you've done. That's all a resume really is: a snapshot. It shows who you are and what you've learned so far.

A good boss isn't only looking at the paper—they're looking at *you*. They'll hear your heart, see your potential, and imagine what you could bring to their team.

So be honest, be proud of what you *have* done, and start there. The rest will grow with time and experience.

You've got this!

You're Fired!

Wait... What Just Happened?

O kay, so this section of the book is about *getting a job*—and hopefully finding a great one where you learn, grow, make some money, and maybe even have fun along the way.

But here's the deal: you may or may not experience getting fired or let go from a job. I sincerely hope you never do! But life being what it is, sometimes it happens—and when it does, it can shake you. More often than not, it's not even your fault. You didn't blow it. You weren't lazy. You weren't a disaster employee.

Usually, it's because a company is shifting its focus. Restructuring. Downsizing. Moving in a new direction. And you—without warning—get caught in the crosshairs of that change. Suddenly, you're sitting across from a manager who says something like, *"This isn't easy, but..."*

And before you know it... you're out. Now what?

And It Might Be the Best Thing That Ever Happened

Let's talk about something that no one puts on their vision board: getting fired.

There's no way to sugarcoat it—being let go from a job stings. It's like getting dumped, but with less ice cream and more paperwork. But the truth is, for many of us, getting fired isn't just a possibility—it's part of the journey.

Let me tell you about when it happened to me. Buckle up.

The Job That Just Didn't Fit

Early in my working life, I landed a job I was determined to crush. I worked hard, brought my best, smiled wide, showed up early. I was in sales—yep, *sales*. Spoiler alert: not my lane.

I didn't know that yet, of course. I was young and trying to learn how the grown-up working world operated, and let me tell you... it was kind of rough. Buyers saw me walk in with my new haircut and eager face and basically thought, *"Aw, how adorable. A child is trying to sell us something."*

I was inexperienced. They knew it. And some of them treated me like a lion treats a slow gazelle. But to be fair, not everyone was like that. There were kind souls who saw the effort I was putting in and gave me a shot. I had a few small wins and those felt like gold medals.

Eventually, I got better. I learned the ropes. I started to feel like, *"Hey, maybe I can actually do this!"* My confidence grew, sales were happening, and I was finally hitting my stride.

Then... the plot twist.

Enter: The New Boss

Corporate made some "big picture" decisions (which is usually code for "bad news is coming"). My branch wasn't a priority anymore, and we were headed for a restructuring—though no one said it out loud.

They sent in a new manager from the home office, and almost overnight, the vibe changed. The camaraderie in our branch started fading like cheap carpet in the sun. People were nervous. Eyes darted at meetings. We all sensed it: something was up.

One day, my direct sales manager asked if I wanted to go out to lunch with him. I was like, *"Awesome! He must've noticed my progress. Maybe I'm getting promoted!"*

Yeah... no.

We sat down at lunch, small talk happened, and then—boom—he dropped the hammer.

"Tim, I'm really sorry, but we're going to have to let you go."

Cue internal collapse. It was like someone turned off the lights inside me. I wasn't just shocked—I felt like I had failed at life. My self worth didn't feel like I hit zero—it felt like it hit -100 on the scale. I walked out of that restaurant feeling rejected, confused, and totally crushed.

The Lies That Tried to Stick

In the weeks that followed, I did what a lot of people do after getting fired: I picked myself apart.

What did I do wrong? Was I not working hard enough? Was I really that bad? Am I cut out for any job?

The truth was... I had actually been doing well. But a few things were going on that had nothing to do with my performance:

1. I was in the wrong field for my gifting.

2. The company was restructuring, and I was collateral damage.

3. The branch I worked for eventually got shut down altogether. I just got to experience the guillotine first.

Looking back, I can even see that the manager who let me go did it with kindness and grace. He hated doing it, but he had no choice. I respect him for the way he handled it—(I hope he got reimbursed for the lunch). It still hurt, but he made it a little more bearable.

What I Learned (The Hard Way)

It took time, but eventually, I landed in a job that was a much better fit—and you know what? I was never fired again. Not once. Ever.

And here's what I learned from that painful chapter:

- Just because a job doesn't work out doesn't mean *you* are a failure.

- Being fired doesn't mean you're broken—it might mean God's redirecting you.

- Some jobs are seasonal and strategic, not permanent.

- There's only one place where real contentment and purpose can be found: the job God has for you.

"The Lord directs the steps of the godly. He delights in every detail of their lives."

—Psalm 37:23 NLT

When you're in the place God's called you to be, there's peace, provision, and even joy—even if the work is hard. But when you're not in the right spot, no amount of striving will make it click.

So What If You Get Fired? (Seriously... You'll Be Okay)

Laugh. Cry. Eat a pizza. Take a drive. Call your mom. Watch a dumb comedy. Do whatever helps you breathe again.

And then remember:

- You are not your job.

- You are not your performance.

- You are not your paycheck.

You are a child of God. That identity never changes—whether you're in a corner office or in the unemployment line.

Sometimes God allows something to end, not to punish you, but to position you. To protect you. To prepare you. That job might've looked like your future, but God sees a bigger picture—and He's not scrambling to fix your story.

"And we know that God causes everything to work together for the good of those who love God and are called
according to his purpose..."

—Romans 8:28 NLT

Everything. Even being let go. Even awkward goodbye lunches and cardboard boxes and "what now?" moments.

And here's the proof:

It took time, but eventually, I landed in a job that was a much better
fit—and you know what? I was never fired again. Not once. Ever.

In fact, the next job I got was working with robotic equipment, and I
loved it. It was challenging, innovative, and fit me like a glove.

But early on, during my first year or so, my manager caught wind that
the company was about to lay off a percentage of employees—and the
newest hires were going to be the first to go. Uh-oh.

This time though, things were different. My manager saw the value I was
bringing and believed in me. He called me into his office and said, "Look,
I want to keep you. Here's what we're going to do... we're sending you
offshore."

So off I went—to Plymouth, England—for three and a half months. Not
fired. Not laid off. *Relocated for preservation.* Turns out, being shipped
off can be a blessing in disguise!

That trip was wild in all the best ways. I learned so much about the
company from a totally different angle.

I learned about another culture—*and* that English food wasn't really my thing (sorry, UK). I basically lived off Italian and Chinese restaurants the whole time. BUT... the bread and cheese? Absolutely divine. I could've eaten just that every night and been completely happy. (Okay, I did eat that often.)

And then—because why not?—I ended up playing in a rugby game.

Let me just say: rugby is *not* for the faint of heart. They put me on the front line of what they called a scrum. I thought I was just standing there until—suddenly—the guy behind me reached under me, grabbed my jersey at my chest, and launched me like a battering ram into the other team. I didn't make it very far into the game, but everyone had a great laugh watching the "Yank" get his first taste of full-contact British Rugby.

That whole experience—what could have been a job loss—turned into a once-in-a-lifetime adventure. God didn't just protect me; He promoted me in a way I never expected.

So if you find yourself reeling from the loss of a job, pause and press in to God. Ask Him:

- *Lord, what are You doing in this?*

- *Is there something You want me to see?*

- *Is there anything in me You want to grow or change?*

- *What's the next step You're leading me into?*

These moments—though painful—can be powerful turning points if you lean into the lessons. God's reroutes always lead somewhere better when we walk with Him.

So take heart. Trust Him. Stay soft. Stay faithful.

And hey—save a slice of that pizza for me. Or if you're in England... grab me some of that cheese and bread. Maybe just skip the rugby and the beef and kidney pie.

The Rhythm of Rest

When I look back over the different seasons of my life, one thing stands out: I was *busy*. Not just physically busy, but mentally full. Most of the jobs I've done have required a high level of focus, problem-solving, and a mind that didn't exactly "clock out" when the workday ended.

For example, during the time I was programming robotic equipment, my mind was constantly running. These machines didn't even exist until we designed and built them from the ground up. Every detail had to be thought through—how the machine would handle jams or errors, how it would recover and keep going, how it would interact with operators, and how to collect and report performance data.

Then I'd travel—often internationally—to install the first version and train people on how to use it. Since I wrote the code, I was the only one who really *knew* the machine inside and out. That meant I had to explain, troubleshoot, and refine things on the fly—usually while navigating a foreign language, unfamiliar food, and a ticking clock. The goal was always to get the job done efficiently, maybe squeeze in a day of sightseeing, and then get back on a plane home.

Even when I wasn't actively working, my brain kept going. I'd be off the clock and suddenly the answer to a coding issue would just come to me.

It was like part of my mind kept processing things in the background, whether I wanted it to or not.

Later, I worked as an air traffic controller—and if programming was intense, this was a whole new level. The training alone was one of the hardest things I've ever done, more demanding than anything in high school or college. It was a constant stream of new information, applied immediately under pressure, often while being observed and critiqued in real-time. I remember waking up in the middle of the night, sitting straight up in bed, giving ATC instructions out loud.

Once I got certified, the pressure shifted from training to the daily grind of live traffic. At my center, we worked over 2.1 million aircraft a year, including military flights, general aviation, commercial traffic—even Air Force One. The airline hub system meant we'd get big departure waves followed by big arrival waves, all packed into tight windows of time. It was fast, demanding, and required a lot of focus—every single day.

I'm sharing all this to give you a little glimpse into what some of my work seasons have looked like—full, demanding, and mentally consuming.

You'll likely walk through seasons like this too. Maybe not with airplanes or robots, but in your own version—whether it's work, school, family, relationships, or leadership. Sometimes the load is given to us; other times, we voluntarily carry more than expected.

And that's okay—for a season.

But one of the most important things I've learned is this: You have to rest in every season. Not just when things slow down. Not just when you hit a wall. But intentionally—along the way.

In the rest of this chapter, we're going to explore what real rest looks like, how to make space for it, and why it matters more than you might think. It's not just about sleep or time off—rest is part of how we were designed to live.

So... What Is Rest, Anyway?

Most dictionaries define rest as a period of ceasing work or movement in order to relax, recover strength, or refresh oneself. It can also refer to a state of peace, calm, or freedom from disturbance—whether physically, mentally, or emotionally.

In other words, rest is your body's way of saying, "Hey, let's hit pause for a minute." It's that deep breath after a busy day, the quiet moment when your brain stops racing, and the freedom to just *be* without needing to do. Rest isn't lazy—it's how we refuel so we can keep showing up as our best selves.

God Did It First: The Rest That Started It All

Let's take a look at what God has to say about rest. He doesn't just recommend it—He actually created it, modeled it, and gave it a name: Sabbath. The concept of Sabbath wasn't man's idea—it was God's. So let's go back to the beginning and see where this rhythm of rest began.

Creation Rest

> "On the seventh day God had finished his work of creation, so he rested from all his work. And God blessed the seventh

day and declared it holy, because it was the day when he
rested from all his work of creation."

—Genesis 2:2–3 NLT

God didn't rest because He was tired—He rested to set a pattern for us,
to mark the end of the work, and to declare that rest is holy.

The Sabbath Command

"Remember to observe the Sabbath day by keeping it holy.
You have six days each week for your ordinary work, but the
seventh day is a Sabbath day of rest dedicated to the Lord
your God.

On that day no one in your household may do any work...
For in six days the Lord made the heavens, the earth, the sea,
and everything in them; but on the seventh day he rested.
That is why the Lord blessed the Sabbath day and set it
apart as holy."

—Exodus 20:8–11 NLT

God ties our rest to His rest—a direct link to creation. He even built it
into the Ten Commandments. That's how important it is.

A Sign Between God and His People

"The people of Israel must keep the Sabbath day by observing it from generation to generation. This is a covenant obligation for all time. It is a permanent sign of my covenant with the people of Israel. For in six days the Lord made heaven and earth, but on the seventh day he stopped working and was refreshed."

—Exodus 31:16–17 NLT

God didn't just rest—He was refreshed. What a picture: the Creator of everything taking a holy breath.

Sabbath Was Made for Us

Then Jesus said to them, "The Sabbath was made to meet the needs of people, and not people to meet the requirements of the Sabbath. So the Son of Man is Lord, even over the Sabbath!"

—Mark 2:27–28 NLT

Jesus wasn't canceling the Sabbath—He was reminding everyone of its original purpose. It's not about rule-following; it's about meeting a deep need for rest.

The Ultimate Invitation to Rest

> Then Jesus said, "Come to me, all of you who are weary and carry heavy burdens, and I will give you rest. Take my yoke upon you. Let me teach you, because I am humble and gentle at heart, and you will find rest for your souls. For my yoke is easy to bear, and the burden I give you is light."
>
> —Matthew 11:28–30 NLT

This is Jesus offering soul rest—a kind of rest that goes far beyond just taking a day off. It's freedom from striving, performing, and living under constant pressure. And the best part? It's something He invites us to receive daily, right in the middle of our normal, everyday lives.

I love how He says, *"I will give you rest."* That has to be the best rest ever—straight from the One who knows exactly what our souls need.

But like everything in our walk with Him, He never forces us. He teaches us, shows us the way, and then gently invites us to follow. All we have to do is accept the invitation, obey, and walk with Him in it. After all, He gives the best gifts, and everything He offers is for our good—never to harm us, always to bring us life.

God Said Rest—What's Holding You Back?

Let's be honest—God's command to observe the Sabbath hasn't expired. In fact, in the book of *Exodus* it says:

"The people of Israel must keep the Sabbath day by observing it from generation to generation. This is a covenant
obligation for all time."

—Exodus 31:16–17 NLT

That includes *you and me*. It's still for today.

So why don't we take it seriously?

Part of the reason is cultural. Most of the world doesn't recognize Sabbath anymore. It's easy to skip, forget, or explain away as "Old Testament." But God never canceled it. And for those who *do* still honor it,
the blessing is undeniable.

Look at companies like Chick-fil-A, Hobby Lobby, and Discount
Tire. They've made it a priority to close one day a week—often Sundays—when most businesses push for seven days of profit. People
thought they were crazy for turning away revenue, but the truth is,
these businesses have outpaced their competitors in growth, income, and
expansion.

Why? Because they're modeling something bigger than smart business—they're walking in obedience and trusting God to provide in six
days what others try to chase in seven.

And it's not just businesses that understand the power of resting—farm-
ers do too.

In agriculture, there's a practice called letting the land lie fallow, where
a field is intentionally left unplanted for a season every 7 years. Why? To
give the soil time to replenish nutrients, recover its strength, and become

more fruitful in the future. It's a strategic pause that leads to long-term productivity.

But it's more than just smart farming—it's a biblical principle.

> "But during the seventh year the land must have a Sabbath year of complete rest. It is the Lord's Sabbath. Do not plant your fields or prune your vineyards during that year."
>
> —Leviticus 25:4 NLT

God Himself instructed His people to give the land a Sabbath rest—not just for soil health, but as an act of trust. They had to believe that God would provide enough in six years to cover what they would need in the seventh.

Just like those businesses that choose to close one day a week, resting the land was a step of obedience and faith. It's a reminder that God's ways work, and when we honor His rhythms—even when it doesn't make "earthly sense"—He brings blessing and provision beyond what we could accomplish on our own.

It's not about legalism. It's about trust.

It's about saying, *"God, I believe You can do more with six obedient days than I could with seven on my own."*

A Shabbat Meal: Welcoming Rest with Intention

My wife Sherri and I try to plan a Shabbat meal together at least a few times each month. It's become such a meaningful and sacred rhythm in our lives—a time to slow down, seek God, and welcome His rest in a way that's tangible and heartfelt.

One of the things I've come to love most is the preparation. We don't just throw a meal together—it's a whole-day journey, and even that part feels sacred. We often take time during the day to bake fresh challah bread, a beautiful braided loaf traditionally made for the Sabbath. It's more than baking—it's a reminder of God's provision, His sweetness, and the joy that comes from creating something together as a family.

Everyone gets involved. One person sets the table, another stirs the pot or shapes the dough—each one contributing in their own way. There's this growing anticipation in the air, a shared excitement that we're getting ready for something holy. It's not just about food—it's about creating space for God to dwell among us.

As the sun begins to set, we gather around the table. There's a quiet hush as we prepare to light the Shabbat candles, marking the official start of the Sabbath. That moment always feels sacred—a turning point between the noise of the week and the peace of rest. We bless the meal, pray over one another, and speak words of gratitude, setting the tone for the next 24 hours.

And here's the beautiful part: you don't have to be married or have a full house to experience this. Whether you're doing this with a spouse, with friends, or by yourself—you are *never* alone. It's you, God, Jesus, and the Holy Spirit at the table. The invitation to Sabbath isn't dependent on your relationship status—it's based on your relationship with the One who created rest for you in the first place.

If you're just starting out or want a helpful guide, one book Sherri and I really love is called *Sabbath: A Gift of Time* by Bonnie Saul Wilks (Eternal Promise Series)[1]. It's a wonderful introduction to celebrating Sabbath from a Christian perspective. It offers simple, meaningful steps to begin hosting your own Shabbat meal and cultivating a rhythm of rest that honors God.

Over time, you'll find this practice becomes more than a tradition. It becomes a life-giving pause, a sacred space where your heart settles, your family draws near, and your soul is refreshed in the presence of your Abba Father.

It becomes more than food—it's a spiritual reset. A holy pause after six days of spinning plates, solving problems, and showing up. Sabbath isn't just about stopping—it's about remembering that God is our Provider, and that His rest is for *our good*.

So maybe the question isn't, *"Can I afford to take a Sabbath?"*

Maybe it's, *"Can I afford not to?"*

Life: Plan It or Wing It?

Aim for Something

When I was a young Christian, Gordon Jones from The Navigators who was discipling me, said something that stuck with me: "He who aims at nothing hits it every time."

And yep... that's absolutely true. I've lived it in certain seasons, and I've seen it in other people's lives too.

The idea here isn't to plan every second of your life like a drill sergeant. It's about living with a sense of intentionality. Knowing what matters and actually making space for it in your life.

I'm not naturally one of those super-organized list makers—far from it. But I've learned that if something's important, or if I need to remember it for later, I have to write it down or I'll forget. So I started using tools that help me keep things straight. Now, if I think of something I need to do, I just drop it in my phone or on my computer, and it'll even remind me at the right time. It takes the pressure off trying to juggle everything in my head.

I use an app called *Things* (it's just for Mac users), but if you're on a PC or Android, don't worry—there are tons of apps out there. The key is to find something that works for you.

Another game-changer for me has been my calendar. I started putting not just the "must-dos" but also the "really want-to-dos" on there. Something happens when I block out time for things that matter—it gives them priority. Somehow, they actually get done.

It's kind of like budgeting your money—but with your time. Think of your calendar as a focus budget. When you schedule something ahead of time, you're saying, "This matters enough to make room for it."

I once heard a story about a guy who had always wanted to get his pilot's license. For years he said it was a dream, but it never happened—until he finally scheduled flying lessons. Once it was on the calendar, he started taking steps, lesson by lesson, and eventually made it happen.

The same principle applies to anything that's important to you. Whether it's a goal, a relationship, a hobby, or quiet time with God—if you don't block out space for it, life will fill that space with something else.

I also remember hearing this little truth bomb:

"You're doing the most important thing in your life right now."

Kind of sobering, right? Whatever you're doing at this moment, you've chosen it over everything else. That statement challenged me to look at my time and ask: "Am I giving my best energy to the things that matter most?"

We all get the same 24 hours a day. No one gets extra. The only difference is what we do with it. So, will you float through your days and hope things just work out? Or will you be intentional, making room in your life for the things God has placed in your heart?

"So be careful how you live. Don't live like fools, but like those who are wise. Make the most of every opportunity in these evil days."

— Ephesians 5:15–16 NLT

Getting Things Off Your Mind (and Actually Done)

Another great resource that's helped a lot of people learn how to be more intentional and effective in planning is the book *Getting Things Done* by David Allen[1]. If you've ever felt overwhelmed by everything swirling around in your brain, this book is worth checking out. Allen teaches a simple but powerful principle: "Your mind is for having ideas, not holding them." That one line helped me realize that I don't have to keep everything in my head—goals, to-do's, things I need to remember, dreams I want to pursue. When I write things down and get them into a trusted system—whether it's an app, a planner, or my calendar—I feel more at peace, more focused, and honestly, way more productive.

Allen's method isn't about overloading your life with more lists—it's about clearing mental clutter so you can focus on what really matters. It's a practical tool for living with intentionality instead of just reacting to whatever's loudest in the moment. Whether you're a natural planner or not, learning to capture and organize your thoughts can be a game-changer.

The Jar on the Shelf

After all, the main reason we use tools and systems to manage our lives is twofold:

First, to get the thoughts out of our heads so we're not carrying them around all day (or worse, all night).

Second, to plan them out so we can actually get them done and cross them off the list.

When I was a little guy, my mom would tuck me into bed at night. Sometimes, she'd notice I had things on my mind—little worries, big thoughts, or just a full day swirling in my head. And in those moments, she'd share a story her mom, my grandmother, told her. That story stuck with me, and honestly, I still picture it even now.

She'd say, *"Whatever is on your mind and heart, picture a jar sitting on a shelf. Open the jar and gently place each thought or worry inside it. You don't have to carry them tonight. They'll still be there tomorrow, but for now, you can rest. You can sleep peacefully."*

It's a simple picture, yet packed with profound wisdom. As Christians, we're offered something even greater. God extends to us that same invitation—and beyond.

It's like a jar on the shelf where we place our burdens and worries, giving them over to God so we no longer carry them ourselves.

He tells us:

> "Don't worry about anything; instead, pray about every-
> thing. Tell God what you need, and thank him for all he
> has done. Then you will experience God's peace, which
> exceeds anything we can understand. His peace will guard
> your hearts and minds as you live in Christ Jesus."
>
> —Philippians 4:6–7 NLT

God invites us to bring everything—big or small, overwhelming or uncertain—and talk to Him about it. He wants our lists. He wants our
worries. He even wants the things we haven't figured out how to put into
words yet. And when we do that, something amazing happens: He gives
us peace. Not maybe. Not sometimes. His Word says, He will.

That's the jar on the shelf—but now, we're handing it to the One who
can actually do something about it.

And as Scripture reminds us,

> "Nothing is impossible with God."
>
> —Luke 1:37 NLT

So write it down, hand it over, and roll over in peace—because God's got
it, and His peace is better than anything we could ever create on our own.
What a gift!

The Power of Wise Counsel

There's an almost endless supply of tools and resources out there to help you get organized, plan well, and follow through on both your daily tasks and your lifetime goals. Whether it's books, apps, planners, or productivity systems, you can find something that fits your style and helps you stay on track. But don't forget to tap into one of the most valuable resources God has placed in your life—people.

Your parents, relatives, friends, mentors, pastors, and even coworkers can all offer something meaningful. There's a wealth of wisdom in the experiences of those who've walked a little farther down the road—in both their victories and their mistakes. Don't try to figure everything out alone. Learn from them. Ask questions. Walk in wisdom by seeking their counsel.

"Get all the advice and instruction you can, so you will be wise the rest of your life."

— Proverbs 19:20 NLT

There is real strength in community. God often uses the people around us to sharpen our thinking, confirm our direction, and help us avoid missteps. So yes, explore all the tools and systems—but don't overlook the wise voices He's already placed in your life.

All Work and No Play?

Pause on Purpose

In today's hustle-driven world, it's easy to forget that rest isn't option-al—it's essential. Some people never take their vacation days. They just roll them over or let them expire, thinking they're being productive or responsible. But the truth is, you can't bank time like money. Once a day passes, it's gone.

Earlier in my career, I had the opportunity to work in Europe, including a few months living in England and time spent working in Switzerland. And let me tell you, they approach rest *very differently* than we do in America.

In Europe, they take "holiday" (their word for vacation) seriously. They plan for it, they look forward to it, and they actually take it. In fact, in countries like Switzerland, the average worker takes 25–30 days off per year, and it's completely normal.

I remember working on a project in Switzerland when I was invited to dinner at the home of the software manager from the company we were partnering with. What struck me most was how down-to-earth his family was. They made me feel incredibly welcome, and the evening felt so natural, as if I were truly part of their lives. The meal itself was a reflection of their culture—simple, yet full of flavor and warmth. As we shared the meal, the conversation flowed easily, giving me a glimpse into their traditions and way of life. It was a beautiful reminder of how inviting and open people can be.

While working together, I realized that it wasn't about rushing through the work or checking off tasks—it was about doing things well and building relationships. They might take twice as long to complete a project, but the quality was excellent, and the relationships among the team felt more like family than coworkers. They truly built margin into their lives—and it showed in everything they did.

In contrast, in America, we often wear busyness like a badge of honor. I remember a time when companies actually looked down on employees who *used* all their vacation time. It was almost expected that you'd sacrifice your time off to prove your commitment.

Back in the early days of my career, when our children were born, I had to use vacation time just to be there for their birth. My wife got maybe three days off—unpaid—and then she was expected to return to work or resign. Family didn't shift the priority—work came first. Thankfully, we've come a long way. Today, many families receive up to 12 weeks of paid parental leave—and I say, *praise God for that!*

Who Rests and How Much?

Here are some average days off that people in these countries receive each year. These numbers can vary depending on the type of work and the benefits each employer offers, but they give a good general picture of how different countries approach rest and time away from work—and how that compares to what's typical here in America.

France
Workers get 36 paid days off (25 vacation + 11 holidays). With maternity/paternity and sick leave, total time off often exceeds **50 days/year.**

Sweden
Employees receive 36 paid days plus up to 480 parental leave days, 390 of which are paid. **Total time off can exceed 100 days/year for parents.**

Germany
Between 29–43 days off (vacation + holidays), plus paid parental and sick leave. Total time off can range from **40–60+ days/year.**

United Kingdom
Workers get 28 paid days, including holidays. With maternity/paternity and sick leave, many reach **40–60+ days/year.**

Switzerland
Offers 27–35 paid days off, with modest parental and sick leave. Total time off usually ranges from **30–45+ days/year.**

United States
No federal requirement for paid vacation or holidays. Average is 10 vacation days + 8 holidays, with limited paid parental leave. Total paid time off is typically **15–20 days/year,** making it among the **lowest in developed countries.**

Make Time for What Matters

You only get so much time, and the clock ticks at the same speed for all of us. So the question isn't *"Do I have time?"*—it's *"What am I prioritizing with my time?"*

Yes, start with the Sabbath each week, but also think about your year, your month, your day. Make space for the "big rocks" in your life—time with God, time with family, and time to simply breathe.

That could look like taking a vacation, picking up a hobby, spending a day in the woods, or just stepping away from the daily grind to reconnect with your soul. One thing that's been life-giving for Sherri and me over the years is something really simple: we go for drives in the country.

Sacred Country Drives... and Cows

It actually started with my parents. Growing up in Vermont, we'd sometimes pile into the car after dinner and head for the mountains. My dad never drove fast—he just took his time. I'd stare out the window, soaking in the beauty of the landscape.

Now, Sherri and I do the same. No matter where we've lived, we've found a back road or two and made it our quiet space. On those drives, we talk, pray, process life, listen to podcasts—or just drive in silence. It's peaceful. It's refreshing. And yes, we still play our favorite game: the first one to spot a cow points and yells, "COW!"

That's what rest can look like. It doesn't have to be complicated—it just needs to be intentional.

Even Jesus Went Away to Rest

Jesus modeled this perfectly. He often withdrew to quiet places, away from the crowds, the noise, and even His closest followers, to pray and spend time alone with His Father. He knew the importance of stepping away from the demands of daily life to be refreshed in God's presence. These moments weren't just optional pauses—they were essential to His strength, clarity, and purpose.

> "Before daybreak the next morning, Jesus got up and went out to an isolated place to pray."
>
> —Mark 1:35 NLT

If Jesus, the Son of God, made it a priority to regularly retreat and reconnect with the Father, how much more do we need to make that space in our lives?

How Do We Draw Near? We Sit at His Feet

We draw near by reading His love letter to us—the Bible, and by praying, listening, and allowing the Holy Spirit to teach us.

> "My sheep listen to my voice; I know them, and they follow me."
>
> —John 10:27 NLT

My pastor reminds us often saying, "If you spend just 15 minutes a day reading the Bible, you'll finish it in a year."

It's true. And once you do, don't stop—read it again and again. Every time I open the Word, I get to know my Abba Father more deeply. The Holy Spirit speaks and teaches me—not just in head knowledge, but in heart transformation.

On average, people spend about 8 hours a day on screens—phones, computers, and TV streaming—scrolling social media, watching videos, browsing the internet, or chatting. That adds up to around 56 hours a week, 240 hours a month, and over 2,900 hours a year—more than 120 full days just staring at a screen. WOW can you believe it?

So taking just 15 minutes a day—which is only about 1% of your day—to read God's love letter to you, the Bible, is a small commitment with a big impact. And here's the beautiful thing: the more you read it, the more you'll come to know God, and He'll begin to reveal Himself to you in personal and powerful ways. It's one of the best ways you can spend your time, and it will absolutely change your life—for the better!

I love listening to the Bible, and one of my favorite ways to do that is with the YouVersion Bible App.[1] It has a really helpful audio feature that reads the verses out loud while the text scrolls on the screen—great for following along. There are plenty of Bible apps out there, but YouVersion is the one I always come back to. It's free, easy to use, and you can check it out at youversion.com/the-bible-app.

You can also read the Bible right from your browser at bible.com if that's easier for you.

Sometimes I just read, but often I'll turn on the audio too—it really helps me when I read and hear it at the same time. Try both ways! I think you'll find that it will take you deeper into God's Word.

> "But when the Father sends the Advocate as my representative—that is, the Holy Spirit—he will teach you everything and will remind you of everything I have told you."
>
> —John 14:26 NLT

There are no shortcuts to this. No spiritual cliff notes. This is the slow, daily rhythm of sitting at His feet, like Mary did.

> "But the Lord said to her, 'My dear Martha, you are worried and upset over all these details! There is only one thing worth being concerned about. Mary has discovered it, and it will not be taken away from her.'"
>
> —Luke 10:41–42 NLT

Final Thought: Make It a Daily Priority

This kind of intentional, daily time with God isn't just a "nice idea"—it's the most important habit you can build into your life. It's where you learn to truly *"yada"*—that's the Hebrew word for deep, intimate knowing God. Not just head knowledge, but the kind of knowing that lives in your heart and shapes who you are.

This is where God speaks, leads, corrects, comforts, and fills you back up when you feel empty. It's how He shapes your character, sustains your soul, and walks with you through every high, low, twist, and turn. Life's a journey, and daily time with Him? That's your lifeline, compass, and fuel stop all rolled into one.

Live Big. Love Well. Trust God.

Well look at you—flipping the final page like a champ! Making it to the end of this book is no small thing. It means you cared enough about your life, your future, and maybe even your fridge (finally stocked with more than just energy drinks) to grow up with wisdom and purpose. That's worth celebrating—preferably with tacos, your favorite playlist, and maybe a sunset drive where you yell "COW!" just because you can.

We've covered a lot together.

You learned how to *buy a car*—not just any car, but one that won't leave you stranded on the side of the road with a dented bumper and a broken heart. You learned how to *budget your money* like an adult (and that yes, YNAB is your friend), how to *stay out of debt*, and how to live with *freedom instead of financial stress*.

We dug into *food*—because life isn't just about feeding your stomach, it's about feeding your soul. Cooking isn't just survival; it's creativity, hospitality, and sometimes just laughing when the pancakes look like abstract art.

You got real about *responsibility*: how to show up, follow through, clean up your messes (literally and relationally), and be someone other people can count on. We talked about *communication*—how to say what you mean, listen when it matters, and work as a team, especially when tensions are high and everything is happening live (shoutout to my video production crew folks!).

You heard some stories from my life—career shifts, big decisions, parenting wins (and fails), and moments where God showed up in ways I didn't expect. Hopefully they reminded you that growing up isn't about a perfect path, it's about walking forward, learning as you go, and letting grace carry you when you trip.

We talked about *rest*—how your brain and heart weren't designed to be "on" 24/7, and how drives in the country, quiet dinners, or even just breathing deep can help you reset and reconnect with God.

You also learned how to *make decisions*, how to *balance your time*, how to *embrace seasons of change*, and how to ask good questions—because curiosity is the fuel of growth. And through it all, I hope you've seen how *faith* isn't something you carry in your back pocket for emergencies—it's the thread that runs through every area of life, holding it all together when things get real.

And Now—You Get to Live It

You won't do it perfectly. You'll burn the rice sometimes. You'll overdraw your bank account once or twice. You might even call your dad or mentor and say, "Soooo... help?" But that's part of it. You're not expected to nail it all right away. You're expected to *grow*.

So take what you've learned, give yourself grace, and keep becoming the kind of person you'd be proud to know. Be honest. Be kind. Be a light. Be someone who loves well, works hard, and laughs loud. This is your moment. And you're ready.

As I said at the beginning of the book—I don't have all the answers. I sure have had my share of mistakes along the way. But I've learned... and I'm still learning. My only hope is that this book will help *you* along the way, as I've shared the wisdom and knowledge that God has given me over the years.

I know this for sure: if you follow Him, seek Him, and learn from Him, you'll have an awesome journey through life. A real one. A meaningful one. And through it all, know this—He loves you so much.

I want to leave you with three sections of Scripture that have meant the world to me. I call them my *life verses*:

"Taste and see that the Lord is good. Oh, the joys of those who take refuge in him!" — Psalm 34:8 NLT

"This is what the Lord says: 'Don't let the wise boast in their wisdom, or the powerful boast in their power, or the rich boast in their riches. But those who wish to boast should boast in this alone: that they truly know me and understand that I am the Lord who demonstrates unfailing love and who brings justice and righteousness to the earth, and that I delight in these things. I, the Lord, have spoken!'" — Jeremiah 9:23–24 NLT

"The Lord says, 'I will guide you along the best pathway for your life. I will advise you and watch over you.'" — Psalm 32:8 NLT

Blessings on your journey!
May you truly taste of the goodness of God!

With Love and Blessings!

Tim

About the Author

Tim Sawtelle

Tim Sawtelle's life has been a journey of creativity and leadership, driven by a passion for helping others grow into their full potential—whether in technology, aviation, ministry, live video production, or education.

As a software engineer, Tim designed and programmed robotic equipment, diving deep into problem-solving and innovation. Later, he became an air traffic controller at a major Air Route Traffic Control Center (ARTCC), helping control and support the safe operations of over 2.1 million aircraft each year—including military, commercial, and general aviation flights (and even working Air Force One a few times).

Tim eventually moved into full-time ministry, serving as a video director at a large multi-campus church, where he built volunteer teams and created training resources to equip others. He also taught live production courses as an adjunct professor at The King's University, sharing his experience with worship and media students. A teacher at heart, Tim has a genuine love for encouraging others to grow in their gifts.

Now retired, he enjoys peaceful writing days and has published several books—with more still on the way. He lives in Arkansas with his wife, Sherri, where they look forward to their country drives, sweet family time, and the joy of grandparent life.

Learn more at timsawtelle.com[1]

Also by Tim Sawtelle

Life Unveiled is the second book in the Unveiled Series, following *Hope Unveiled*. *Jesus Unveiled* is the next to release, with *Holy Spirit Unveiled* in progress. Tim has also co-authored *Stewarding the Atmosphere* with Brandon D. Marx, a book on live video production. And keep an eye out—another fun project titled *2.5*!

Want to stay in the loop on his latest releases? Follow Tim on Amazon and other places that books are sold to get notified as soon as new titles drop. Just head over to amazon.com, search for "Tim Sawtelle," and hit that follow button.

For more info about Tim's writing, speaking, and creative work, check out his personal site: timsawtelle.com

Make sure to check out the ministry website that he and his wife, Sherri work together telling others about Jesus—packed with resources, stories, and inspiration—you can find it at greenmountainjourney.com[1]

Hope Unveiled
By Tim Sawtelle

Embark on a remarkable journey alongside Tim Sawtelle as he shares events from his life in *"Hope Unveiled: Stories of God's Unwavering Faithfulness."* This captivating book chronicles Tim's life, a amazing testament to God's steadfast presence through every twist and turn, through moments of triumph and adversity.

Discover a narrative woven with the threads of Tim's experiences, where the journey of faith meets the embrace of the most faithful Father. Through these compelling stories, witness the profound ways God revealed Himself, transforming Tim's life and illuminating the path with hope even in the darkest hours.

Join Tim on his quest for meaning, purpose, and truth, as he unveils the intimate relationship he experienced with the greatest Father of all—God. *"Hope Unveiled"* invites you into the heartwarming journey of one man's life, a testament to the enduring faithfulness and the unending love of a Father who never lets go.

Available on Amazon https://a.co/d/hjIagVI[2]

Stewarding the Atmosphere
By Brandon D. Marx and Tim Sawtelle

Unlock the full potential of your ministry by investing in your most valuable asset: your people. Equipping them with advanced video and lighting techniques and a healthy team dynamic will have a profound impact on your ministry.

Stewarding The Atmosphere is crafted for pastors, worship leaders, college students, technicians, and volunteers, offering innovative strategies to elevate your visual experience and cultivate an atmosphere that truly connects people with God.

Available on Amazon https://a.co/d/hjIagVI[3]

Endnotes

Dating

1. More on this series by Pastor Craig at:
   https://www.life.church/media/save-the-date/?utm_source=life_church&utm_medium=header&utm_campaign=navigation

2. YouVersion Reading plan:
   https://www.bible.com/reading-plans/33729-wisdom-for-dating

Marriage

1. Jimmy and Karen Evans XO Marriage Ministry for every marriage:
   https://www.xomarriage.com

You Are Unique!

1. The Gallup Store
   https://store.gallup.com/h/en-us

The Rhythm of Rest

1. *Sabbath: A Gift of Time* by Bonnie Saul Wilks (Eternal Promise Series)

Life: Plan It or Wing It?

1. *Getting Things Done* by David Allen available on Amazon

All Work and No Play?

1. YouVersion Bible app, https://www.youversion.com/the-bible-app/and read it on a browser at https://www.bible.com/

About the Author

1. Check out Tim's website at:
   https://www.timsawtelle.com

Also by Tim Sawtelle

1. Our Ministry Website:

2. *Hope Unveiled* available at Amazon

3. *Stewarding the Atmosphere* available at Amazon

www.ingramcontent.com/pod-product-compliance
Lightning Source LLC
Chambersburg PA
CBHW061547120626
46550CB00004B/1395